Ponzinomics

The Untold Story of Multi-Level Marketing

By Robert L. FitzPatrick

FitzPatrick Management Inc., Charlotte, North Carolina

ISBN: 978-0-578-44351-5

Library of Congress Control Number: 2020921740

info@ponzinomics.com

About Ponzinomics...

Hannah Martin – *UK-based Consumer Activist and Educator, Co-Founder of Talented Ladies Club*

Ponzinomics is essential reading for anyone who wants to truly understand the MLM industry – where it originated, why it's not treated as illegal, and how it works (or rather, why it doesn't work for over 99% of participants). This is a thorough, well-researched and wonderfully written account of the MLM industry, from arguably the world's top expert on the subject, and even after four years of investigating MLMs I learned an enormous amount from it.

Douglas M. Brooks – *Attorney, MLM Expert*

As an attorney with almost 30 years of experience representing victims of multilevel marketing scams, I can say that *Ponzinomics* is a book that had to be written and that Robert Fitzpatrick is the only person on the planet who could have written it. Mr. Fitzpatrick carefully and methodically weaves together the threads that led to the modern MLM industry, including direct selling, snake oil products, positive psychology, the human potential movement, evangelical Christianity, the prosperity gospel, Ponzi schemes, the American dream of self-reliant entrepreneurial success, and the corrupting influence of big money politics. The result is a devastating portrait of a uniquely American scam that continues to deceive millions of victims throughout the world, causing not only hundreds of billions in financial losses but also the destruction of countless relationships between families and friends. *Ponzinomics* should be a case study in every business school, and should be read by anyone interested in economics, psychology, sociology, political science, law or finance. Moreover, *Ponzinomics* is essential reading for anyone who wants to understand Donald Trump, who among his many other business ventures was a failed MLM promoter and has placed MLM advocates at the highest levels of his administration.

Christine Richard – *Author, Financial Researcher*

Before working as a researcher, I was a financial markets reporter and wrote a book called *Confidence Game: How Hedge Fund Manager Bill Ackman Called Wall Street's Bluff.* It's the story of a sophisticated financial fraud (and a successful short), in which companies sold insurance policies on risky bonds, turning them into triple-A-rated securities. Robert and I once discussed how Herbalife was the Main Street version of this too-good-to-be-true Wall Street business model. But, he stressed there was a difference that made the Herbalife and MLM fraud so much more insidious: "Herbalife has become part of the fabric of Main Street," he told me. "It has tampered with the souls of millions of people."

How are normal everyday people duped into ceding their financial futures and their souls to such obvious frauds? Why has the government largely stood by and allowed this business not only to flourish in America but to be exported around the world? Until someone unearths the history of these rackets and uncovers their roots, we will not understand how MLM has managed to plant itself so deeply in the American psyche and to shield itself from the scrutiny of regulators. No one is better prepared to undertake the telling of this epic history than Robert Fitzpatrick. He has an ability to bring clarity to a world that shrouds its true nature in every type of obfuscation.

Dr. Máire O'Sullivan – *Consumer Culture Theory Researcher, Ireland*

Ponzinomics is a phenomenal resource for those interested in pyramid schemes and multi-level marketing. This incredibly comprehensive book covers everything from the initial birth of a multi-billion dollar industry to the modern day, and is full of both interesting anecdotes and academically rigorous investigation. I can't recommend this book highly enough.

Bruce Craig – *Asst. Attorney General (Retired) Wisconsin*

Mr. Fitzpatrick's new book, *Ponzinomics*, chronicles the development of pyramid schemes over the years up to and including their current status. This status involves a lack of meaningful governmental oversight, the participation of 118 million victims in 170 countries, annual revenues in excess of $190 billion and failure rates around 99%. The collective revenue data over the past 30 years, in today's dollars, must exceed a trillion dollars. Our government has made only minimal attempts to publicize the substantive problems.

Mr. Fitzpatrick recites the factors which have resulted in this phenomenon - cult manipulation, religious persuasion, false depiction of ultimate success, misrepresentation of the factual realities facing these victims, lack of meaningful governmental participation, and governmental involvement via revolving door policies. Victims and potential victims have chosen to ignore these factors in the hope that they will achieve the greatness they have always desired via the alternative facts presented to them. Of course there is a chilling resemblance of this problem to the current political situation. I strongly recommend a full reading of this book in order to understand the manipulative and destructive elements involved and how it will continue in the absence of substantive academic, journalistic and enforcement efforts.

Dr. Elizabeth Villagomez – *Policy Advisor, International Consultant-Researcher, Victoria BC, Canada*

Robert's Fitzpatrick's *Ponzinomics* is the most compelling and researched work I have read on the realities of what Multi-Level Marketing is and does: a fraudulent pyramidal practice that preys on the most vulnerable and that has powerful lobbyists protecting it in almost every continent. Seeing how in my own family and circle of friends these companies present themselves as business opportunities, only gives a longer lease of life to these companies that even dare to organize events and support for women's issues such as breast cancer and women's economic empowerment to name just two. The pyramidal scheme covered up by a product does not make less of a pyramidal scheme, and has only made it more difficult to unmask the real nature of these schemes. Fitzpatrick's careful dissection of these characteristics should serve any regulators, chambers of commerce and consumer protection entities around the world to put a stop to these companies.

Dr. D. Anthony Miles – *Author, Startup and Marketing Expert*

In my years of research and expertise on multilevel marketing-based businesses, I continue to be captivated by the multitude of people that fall prey to MLMs. Robert Fitzpatrick's newest book, *Ponzinomics,* delivers the whole truth on MLM. It should be required reading in university MBA and business programs. It is a wake-up call to emerging entrepreneurs. The chapter, "The Plan: The Blueprint of a Pyramid Scheme," gives a robust research on the MLM pyramid structure and why it is flawed, doomed by design. One of the best features of *Ponzinomics* is its historical content on MLM and its foundation. This is a history that everyone who considers this type of business should read. Robert Fitzpatrick and I have collaborated on research on MLM for many years. *Ponzinomics* is a must-read book of our times.

Acknowledgments

Investigative work that leads to disruptive and iconoclastic conclusions is among the lonelier and less recognized of endeavors. It provokes those whose power rests on lies and disturbs those who take comfort in those lies, while often being ignored or undefended by those that may benefit from its revelations.

On this long and lonely road, I have been greatly aided and inspired by attorney Douglas Brooks and former state regulator, Bruce Craig. Their own work in law, ethics and civic engagement has been indispensable to my perseverance. Susanna Perkins has steadfastly supported me in truth-telling with her technical expertise in web development and her moral support.

For ongoing inspiration in seeking the deepest truths about "multi-level marketing" I am especially grateful to UK writer, David Brear, author of the blog, "MLM, the American Dream Made Nightmare." His deconstruction of "MLM" as a "rigged market swindle" and a "ritual belief system," elevate his work in recognizing the deeper threat multi-level marketing poses to democracy and personal freedom.

My appreciation is extended to my New York City-based editor, Rebecca Shoenthal, for structural and line-editing recommendations to connect the many tentacles of MLM deception and convert them into one coherent narrative of truth-telling. Also grateful to Charlotte NC-based editor, Leslie Rupracht for further refinements to the text.

My deepest and greatest acknowledgment is to my wife and life partner, Terry Thirion. Her commitment to the truest expression of herself as a fine artist has upheld my own quest. Her personal support and continued encouragement have been unwavering, even when we were faced with the prospect of losing home and life savings from one of MLM's meritless but vicious SLAPP lawsuits directed at truth-tellers.

The current predominance of the Big Lie of MLM, and the failure of the news media, publishing industry, academia and institutions of government to confront it, is not an absolute or a permanent circumstance. The truth is still being told, often in unexpected and unconventional ways, including satire, comedy, civil lawsuits, drama, blogs and podcasting. It is my intention that this book add to those citizen-based resources, in the face of official disinformation, dereliction and denial.

Contents

Definition and Disclaimer

Ponzinomics: noun / pän-zē-'nä-miks / a pseudo-economic, all-encompassing, delusional belief system that promotes the swindle of a Ponzi or pyramid scheme as a valid economic model that promises believers a fulfilling and financially rewarding way of life, complete with mission, values, leadership and worldview. The societal spread of *Ponzinomics* is necessarily accompanied by governmental collusion.[i]

Disclaimer: *Ponzinomics* was independently researched and written solely by the author. It is an exercise in free speech with an intention of public education. The conclusions and declarations are the opinion of the author. Nothing in the book constitutes a claim that any referenced company is a criminal or illegal enterprise within the framework of current law and law enforcement.

While the book owes much to the insights, work, and interest of many other people, the writing of the book was not requested by any other party or as part of any consultation agreement. Robert FitzPatrick does not currently own, to his knowledge has never owned, and has no plan ever to own an equity position in any multi-level marketing company. He has not received or ever received any compensation from any party contingent on future stock performance of any multi-level marketing company. This report does not constitute and is not intended as advice or recommendation regarding investment decisions or strategies. It is not intended to cause any actions by individual consumers,

---

[i] Without government collusion, unsustainable and harmful systems collapse quickly, are exposed as frauds, thefts or injustice, or they are driven out by civic action. When backed by the power and authority of government and involve public figures who use the system for political and financial benefit, unsustainable and harmful systems can persist and become normalized.

other than to consider the information provided. The information contained in this report has been obtained from sources that are publicly available and which the author believes to be reliable. Some data cited in the report are estimates based on relevant available information.

Foreword: Read at Your Own Risk

After a baffling involvement in a national mania called the "Airplane Game" that spread across America in the late 1980s, I began obsessively researching pyramid schemes and multi-level marketing (MLM). I *had* to understand the mysterious force of attraction that had lured me — and so many thousands of others — into a delusional dream world and financial folly. This eventually led to my writing and publishing *False Profits* in 1997, the first book on the market to critically examine the exploding phenomenon of multi-level marketing, its relationship to illegal pyramid schemes, and the mirror it holds up to America's darker and less explored values and aspirations.

My book prompted an almost immediate and totally unexpected request to appear on *CBS 60 Minutes* in a segment about a popular multi-level marketing company that had defrauded more than 150,000 people. My role was to explain what MLM is and how it operates. This request from one of the country's most authoritative news sources reflected that pyramid schemes disguised as sales companies were sweeping the country, and though they operated in plain sight, the public could not recognize this new type of fraud. They did not understand how they worked, even as millions poured money and hope into the schemes. Even more amazing, there was general unawareness in the news media as to why Americans were flocking to MLM.

This national exposure was soon followed by a request to serve as an expert in a federal court case against the oldest and largest MLM, Amway. The lawsuit was brought by the Recording Industry Association of America for Amway's unauthorized use of famous and copyrighted music at its massive recruiting events. The attorneys for the music artists fully understood copyright law violations. Reflecting the wider confusion and unawareness about MLM, they called on me to explain how Amway *used* the rousing and inspirational music as part of its money scheme. I explained its *economic* value and purpose for Amway in inducing millions of people to invest — without due diligence — and in maintaining a grip on the minds of followers even as they lost money. My testimony and consultation about Amway's recruiting, control, and redirection methods helped the recording artists recover $9 million from Amway in a settlement.

My knowledge and interest in MLM evolved and expanded into a distinct intellectual discipline shared only with a handful of others around the world. This MLM topic intersects business law, criminology, politics, business economics, psychology, accounting, marketing (of course), and even includes inquiries into the origins of authoritarianism and methods of cult persuasion. More on that later.

By 2001, I co-founded *Pyramid Scheme Alert*, a non-profit consumer education and advocacy group. I have continuously managed its website, one of the most comprehensive and accessed resources on "MLM."[1] Since the Amway court case, I personally combatted the MLM phenomenon in more than 30 other cases as an expert witness, consultant, friend of the court, and even once as defendant. I've also provided professional consultations to dozens of Wall Street analysts, investors, and researchers seeking an understanding of the MLM "business model." I have been featured in film and radio investigations of MLM, on NPR's *This American Life* and Netflix's *Betting on Zero*. I appeared in and worked closely with the producer of John Oliver's hilarious 2016 exposé of MLM on HBO and viewed on YouTube more than 25 million times, as well as Penn & Teller's 2010 take on MLM on Showtime. In 2018, I was extensively interviewed on the popular 11-segment podcast, *The Dream*, distributed by Stitcher, on the history and realities of MLM. I also assisted and appeared in a news documentary on MLM deception produced for Channel One, Russian television.[2]

The majority of my time and effort is expended as an unpaid educator and advocate in thousands of face-to-face, online, and email inquiries from MLM victims, families of victims, and those trying to understand or seek a way out of MLM's hall of mirrors. I have listened to stories of bankruptcy, divorce, alienation from friends and family, and suicides tied to experiences in multi-level marketing. I never argue with someone committed to promoting MLM. I don't try to persuade. There is not time enough on earth for that.

None of these efforts has measurably affected the epic spread of MLM. I have watched "MLM" — operating under hundreds of company names — spread like a forest fire, from blue collar sectors, among evangelical Christians, and in small towns, up the social and economic ladder through suburban management ranks to professionals, doctors and dentists, buying vitamins and supplements promoted as miraculous cures by Mormon-run MLMs from Utah where the "supplement" industry is concentrated. I have seen it invade and conquer Facebook communities of stay-at-home mothers on the Upper West Side of New York City with cosmetic- and clothing-based MLMs, and then, without changing its structure or basic message, also pour down upon undocumented immigrants, struggling military spouses, impressionable high-schoolers, and debt-burdened college students.

Globally, MLM's most aggressive invasion has been among the 1.4 billion people of China, whose Communist Party-controlled government fully opened the country to MLM only in 2005. Tens of millions have been led to believe MLM embodies the true spirit of capitalism and offers deliverance from deadening jobs assembling iPhones, plastic junk, and appliances.

My work and words have also not awakened interest among regulators or legislators. To the contrary, U.S. regulators have weakened consumer protections against pyramid schemes, even exempting MLMs from disclosure rules when making financial solicitations. The "MLM" movement is now syndicated into an "industry" with its own lobbying and PR organization on K Street in Washington, D.C., and has assembled a protective caucus of lawmakers in the

U. S. House of Representatives. Donald Trump is MLM's most famous and highest paid spokesman, endorsing and promoting it for more than 10 years, leading up to his presidential candidacy in 2015. MLM's leading and largest enterprise is the Amway Corporation. Its most controversial representative is Herbalife, which you may recognize as the subject of a five-year battle between billionaire investors Bill Ackman and Carl Icahn. Hundreds of other MLMs will be explored further in the coming pages.

Multi-level marketing, sometimes also called "network marketing," is now fully global, with a claim of more than 100 million households paying into it every year. In America alone, where it all began in 1945, official MLM representatives claim that in excess of 18 million households — one in six — are under contract to MLM companies *each year*. More than half of that figure joins yearly, replacing those who quit. Every year, the recruited participants expend $20–$30 billion in fees and purchases, though that estimate does not come close to actual total expenditures when related expenses and opportunity costs are included.

My efforts have not even made a significant difference, that I could tell, among my own friends and family, some of whom have sheepishly admitted to joining and losing their money in MLMs without telling me. They explained they had been taught that a positive attitude and unflinching belief were the most important factors for success in MLM. Negative voices from non-believers and cautious calls for "due diligence" are to be shunned and avoided. In the ideology of the MLM movement, I am fiendish dream-stealer, malevolent negative-thinker, Pathetic Loser.[i]

---

[i] "Pathetic Loser" is a term of special meaning and usage in the MLM world, apparently coined and promoted in Amway training sessions to demonize critics or skeptics. I have a small file of emails and letters received from MLM believers who, in scripted messages, express their abhorrence at my views and activities. Some begin, "Dear Pathetic Loser."

In the face of all this — the unrelenting spread of MLM, the massive consumer losses in its wake, its enchanting attraction, the resistance to facts or exposure, and seeming immunity from fraud prosecution — I am often asked to explain the larger meaning of the MLM phenomenon that would keep me engaged. I warn questioners, and now readers of this book, that deeper inquiries into the areas of cultural habit and belief that give rise and support to MLM may cause the ground beneath them never to feel stable again.

To separate MLM from its benign and uplifting disguises of "direct selling" and "income opportunity" requires an unflinching inquiry into the words and practices of sales, marketing and advertising — the drivers of our consumer economy — where sociologist Jules Henry wrote that "pecuniary truth" rules, not factual reality.[3]

To see how MLM's money transfer scheme remains safe from regulation, one must re-examine other areas of the economy that are based on manipulated transfers, such as in the stock market, investment banking, unpayable government debt, housing, and commodity bubbles, or the prevalence of state lotteries replacing sustainable taxation for current public services.[4]

To understand how MLM's leaders are revered, even by followers who lost money, the inquiry must also venture into matters of religion and faith where financial "prosperity" is theologically defined as a *divine* blessing and poverty a pre-ordained or self-inflicted punishment.

To grasp how MLM seemingly shuts down critical thinking, leading to financial self-destruction, requires that the term "cult persuasion" also be considered in modern advertising, marketing, economic beliefs and political propaganda.

And to make sense of MLM's historical immunity from fraud prosecution, one must delve into the world of K Street lobbyists, revolving doors between the Federal Trade Commission and MLM, and the selling of the public trust by some of our most famous leaders, naming these individuals from the mid-1970s up to Donald Trump himself.

To get to the core reality that can explain MLM's phenomenal spread, one must also re-examine the state of opportunity in America today, the decline of the middle class, and popular views of wealth as measures of "success," happiness, and human worth.

These are the hallowed grounds of American society, guarded by firmly held but seldom examined beliefs. They are areas of reality and truth generally outside the bounds of news media coverage. To date, not a single book has been published in America that examines the MLM phenomenon, its roots and how it operates. Similarly, MLM is not a focus of independent research by government or any university.

Those who pursue the untold story of multi-level marketing risk being cast as heretics or accused of cynicism, socialism, negativity, or blasphemy. Those who follow this inquiry into the depths of "MLM" do so at their own risk.

LOSERS

Legions of Losers

There is a well-known saying that history is written by the victors. I hope to prove the exception. *Ponzinomics* chronicles the untold story of what is currently called "multi-level marketing," aka MLM. Those who encounter enterprises such as Amway, Nu Skin, Mary Kay, Avon, Usana, and hundreds of others, have a universal experience: loss. The failure of millions each year is its calculated product on which MLM gains its returns and, therefore, the true story of MLM must be a tale told by losers.

If you haven't yet experienced loss from MLM, you likely will or someone close to you surely will. Measured by the sheer numbers of people who join, quit, and rejoin every year, the billions of dollars invested that produce no profit, and the intensity of hope and commitment it evokes from adherents, if only briefly, "multi-level marketing" must be recognized as one of the most powerful forces shaping social and economic behavior today on Main Street USA. MLM has become the most prominent standard bearer of the American Dream today. As the late pioneer MLM promoter (and pyramid scheme felon), Glenn W. Turner, claimed in his famous allegory, MLM is "the village where everything is possible."[5]

MLM signals important changes in social relationships, aspirations and values on Main Street, yet it remains unstudied. MLM is legally exempted and protected from any disclosure regulations. It operates on Main Street as mysteriously and unnoticed as shifts that develop in everyday language. In *The Mind of the South*, W. J. Cash took notice of the massive change in Deep South states as they were violently uprooted from the pre-Civil War rural and farming values and took up opportunistic moneymaking in sales, manufacturing, and trading. "Made any money today?" Cash observed men casually asking each other, who previously would have chatted about family, crops, church, health, or the weather. Now, in Cash's 1930s era, it was as if "making" money and being "on the make" were the primary common bonds. It was all in that phrase.[6]

Today, the term "I want to share an exciting opportunity," signals a similar societal change driven by MLM, yet one that cannot be defined merely as economic. This hallmark phrase signals a redefinition and new purpose of personal relationships. Friends and colleagues are now recruiters and prospects. Trust, affection, and shared experience are casually appropriated for opportunistic commercial purpose. Deceiving and misleading friends and family about the true nature of these solicitations is now considered normal. The ancient boundaries between the private and pecuniary are obliterated along with the parameters of work life and social life. In MLM, work is perpetual, 24/7, and encompasses all relationships. All assume the new identity of "contractor," and are expected to adopt the values and behavior of a branded corporation, maximizing "returns" — on each other.

In myth and legend MLM is, famously, for winners, a pathway to *total* success and *unlimited* wealth. Indeed, it is said to be the last remaining pathway to wealth in an era of consolidation, unaffordable housing, declining wages, wealth disparity, and even lowered life expectancy. MLM's amazing proclamation that it is a "safe haven," and the *last best hope* is made in every MLM website, recruiting video, and mass spectacle.

Nevertheless, it is an easily documented fact that virtually everyone, 99.99%[i], who has ever participated in an MLM — and we are speaking of hundreds of millions of people worldwide over seven decades — failed, lost, or quit with zero financial gain. And that only begins the count of losers.

Beyond those millions are the millions more who tried to warn them. These include whistle-blowing bloggers who testified to MLM's income deceptions; market researchers who documented the absence of "customers;" consumer advocates who calculated the scale of losses and quitting rates; economists who traced the pathway of money flowing from "last ones in" directly to the recruiters at the "top;" class action attorneys who gathered evidence of fraud and racketeering; cult experts who exposed mind control methods; and concerned people the world over who tried to awaken their own friends or family with common sense — they are also among the legions of losers. Their sparse and occasional successes are maddeningly outweighed by frustration, disregard, and rejection.

---

[i] The 99% loss rate is based on examinations of MLM-published "income disclosures," data from the MLMs themselves. I produced a study of 11 representative MLMs in 2008 that documented this rate of loss (https://pyramidschemealert.org/PSAMain/news/MythofIncomeReport.html). It has also been revealed in state and federal prosecutions in the USA and the UK and in class action cases. Other researchers have produced the same numbers. Yet, even the figure of 99% does not capture the financially lethal reality. MLM disclosures are for one-year time frames, a mere snapshot of an ongoing scam. Fifty to eighty percent (50–80%) of MLM adherents quit and are replaced each year. The "winners" tend to be the same individuals positioned at the top year after year. The losers comprise a constantly churning base of new "failures" yearly. When the cumulative losers are included, the number of actual individuals who ever earned a profit — as a percent of all who were ever enrolled — drops to a tiny percent of one percent, a virtual zero. An excellent library of MLM "income disclosures" has been assembled and published by forensic accountant and fraud investigator, Tracy Coenen on "Fraud Files Blog" at https://www.sequenceinc.com/fraudfiles/2019/11/mlm-income-disclosure-statements/

As whistle-blower, researcher into consumer losses, exposer of MLM deceptions, consumer advocate, and talking-head critic in innumerable news stories and articles, I am prominent among those losers. Few have experienced loss over a longer period of time but many others have lost far more.

Biggest Loser

The biggest loser in MLM history — financially and famously — is Wall Street "titan" and hedge fund manager, William "Bill" Ackman. He is allegedly endowed with rare powers to grasp hidden advantages or flaws in large enterprises, unseen by their own management. He holds the record for losing the most money in history in multi-level marketing.

In 2002, Bill Ackman displayed the rare insight that earned him a reputation as stock market guru. He invested millions in a "short" position — earning profit only if the company's fortunes turned down significantly — against the financial firm MBIA, the nation's largest insurer of state and municipal bonds at the time. These bonds were considered extremely safe and MBIA's insurance of them gained the highest rating for investor safety. Ackman challenged not only the security of the mortgage-backed assets behind the bonds MBIA was insuring, but also the validity of the sacrosanct rating MBIA enjoyed and on which shareholders relied for its equity value.

During his six-year campaign of market research and publicity to support his MBIA stock position, Ackman endured vicious ridicule, threats, government investigations, and possible criminal prosecution for stock manipulation. All the while, MBIA's stock only continued to rise, devaluing his investment. The crash of the housing market in 2008, six years after Ackman launched his short-investment, exposed the fatal weakness in MBIA's business model that Ackman sought to expose. At the beginning of 2007, MBIA stock had traded at about $70 per share. By June 2008, it fell to about $6 and has never recovered. Ackman's thesis was validated — though it required a catastrophic collapse of the *entire* securities market — transferring as much as a billion dollars in profit to Ackman and his investors from all those who had remained "long."[7]

In 2012, Ackman purchased a dossier of research from a small consulting firm about multi-level marketing company, Herbalife, one of the oldest and largest companies of this type and among about a dozen publicly traded on Wall Street.[8]

At the end of 2012, with great fanfare, Ackman presented a 300-slide, multi-media show to the investor community, billed as the Herbalife "fraud thesis." He announced that his firm, Pershing Capital, had taken a one-billion-dollar short position against Herbalife and was launching an information campaign to compel the Federal Trade Commission (FTC) to close it down as an illegal pyramid scheme. Over the following five years, 2013–2018, Ackman reportedly spent more than $50 million on further research, lobbying, and PR to support his case, even sending investigators to China to document Herbalife's violations of China's anti-pyramid scheme law[i], and to Latin America to expose Herbalife's storefront recruiting centers disguised as "nutrition clubs."

Using his celebrity status and guru reputation, Ackman also waged a publicity campaign, including producing a short documentary film with interviews of victims who had each lost thousands in Herbalife[ii], all to support his fund's massive short position in Herbalife's stock. His profit would be achieved, he confidently told the skeptical business media, when government regulators dutifully closed down the business, sending the stock to zero value.

---

[i] On Sept. 27, 2019, more than five years after Ackman made his charge that Herbalife was violating China's anti-pyramid law, the U.S. Securities and Exchange Commission (SEC) announced that Herbalife agreed to pay $20 million for making false and misleading statements about its China business model in numerous regulatory filings over a six-year period. (https://www.sec.gov/news/press-release/2019-195)

[ii] I served as volunteer (no fee) moderator of the victim panel discussion at this event in New York on May 2, 2014. Just days before the scheduled event, Bill Ackman's attorney, David Klafter, asked me to take this role after the planned moderator, former CBS news anchor, Connie Chung, abruptly withdrew. (https://nypost.com/2014/04/27/ackman-documentary-stars-alleged-herbalife-victims/)

It never happened. The Herbalife stock, in fact, rose to new heights. The extensive research and media attention Bill Ackman generated were largely overshadowed by coverage of Wall Street intrigues to engineer a "short-squeeze," in which other large investors acquired Herbalife shares and boosted the stock price, forcing Ackman to cover his position and drive the stock price even higher. In tandem with the "long" position, taken by rival hedge fund manager, Carl Icahn, and others, Herbalife launched a smear campaign to redirect attention to Ackman personally. *Fortune, The Wall Street Journal,* and *The New York Times* depicted Ackman as an arrogant, publicity-seeking opportunist and "stock manipulator." His claims of a massive fraud perpetrated by a 30-year-old company were displaced by personality pieces about his growing rivalry with Icahn. His lobbying efforts, miniscule against the entrenched K Street forces of the Direct Selling Association and Herbalife itself, were characterized as unfair influence on government.[9]

It took four years from Ackman's first presentation, but in 2016, the FTC brought action against Herbalife, the first against a large MLM regarding its business model in 35 years. The FTC complaint cited most of the practices that Ackman had identified as deceptive and illegal. The FTC spent two years on its own study of Herbalife and found, just as Ackman and previous lawsuits had documented, that "retail selling" was largely non-existent, making Herbalife's "direct selling" identity false. The "nutrition clubs" Herbalife promoted to low income Latinos were shown to be financial traps, as a *Forbes* article reported four years earlier. In reality, the clubs were pyramid-recruiting centers, as Ackman's researcher, Christine Richard, had documented back in 2012.[iii]

[iii] Herbalife's nutrition clubs represented a new and even more insidious element of the MLM scam, designed specifically for people with low income and no credit cards, by inducing frequent low dollar expenditures. See https://factsaboutherbalife.com/the-facts/nutrition-clubs/

The FTC investigation revealed that most of Herbalife's revenue ultimately came from *purchases by the salespeople themselves*. These purchases were induced by promises of rewards for recruiting. Ultimately, Herbalife was falsely promising millions of consumers that it would pay them — later — *if* they made purchases now, an extreme form of advanced-fee fraud. The FTC found that virtually no one who enrolled in Herbalife's plan and made the purchases ever received the promised rewards. The FTC concluded that all promises and claims about "income opportunity" were deceptive.

The FTC's formal complaint against Herbalife announced on July 15, 2016, on which Bill Ackman had based his billion-dollar short, eloquently described the methods of a disguised pyramid scheme. But the FTC did not charge the company with operating a pyramid scheme, which would have closed it down. Instead, the FTC collected a $200 million restitution, minimal against the scale of Herbalife's global operation, and signed a settlement with Herbalife under largely unenforceable terms and applicable only in the U.S. The settlement gave the company months to enact changes from current illegality, and no Herbalife executives were charged personally. The $200 million was refunded to 350,000 victims, a tiny fraction of the actual number harmed.

On the day the complaint and settlement were simultaneously announced, it was also revealed that a lead negotiator working for Herbalife, Jon Leibowitz, was the immediate past chairman of the FTC, appointed by President Barack Obama. Since leaving his public FTC post, Leibowitz had been "advising Herbalife in connection with its $200 million settlement with the FTC relating to allegations that it engaged in unfair and deceptive acts and practices."[10] Herbalife triumphantly announced its settlement agreement with the FTC and named Leibowitz "Senior Advisor to the Herbalife Board responsible for advising on implementation and compliance matters."[11]

Ackman claimed a pyrrhic victory, a moral vindication on the facts, the booby prize on Wall Street. The business media seized on what the FTC did *not* do: charge Herbalife with running a pyramid scheme. Herbalife's stock continued to go up and up. The total losses Ackman and his investors ultimately suffered extended to the hundreds of millions when he finally closed his position in February 2018. As predicted, this boosted Herbalife's stock to the highest price point in its history.[12] Ackman's image as diviner of markets and his reputation for steadfastness blackened. He promised to pursue Herbalife "to the ends of the earth" and never back down; instead, he folded and fell silent.

American Pie

To the small number of people who understood the truth about MLM and Herbalife, the complete failure and rout of William Ackman's campaign was seen as a moral, civic, and criminal travesty. Yet, historically, the outcome was entirely consistent with all previous attempts in America to expose the realities about MLM.

In his 1906 masterpiece, *Sin and Society* — to explain the apparent immunity of white-collar criminality that was exploding in America — Edward A. Ross, founder of the American Sociological Association, turned to a Norse myth. In a land of giants, he wrote, Thor was challenged to lift a "certain gray cat." Applying his mighty strength, the hero could only raise one paw off the base and was ashamed and confused at his failure. He was later told the feat was virtually impossible since the "cat" *girds and keeps up the created world.*

Applying the myth to the prevailing conditions of his day, in which perpetrators of social crimes — adulterating food, chartering self-dealing banks, exploiting children in factories — escaped punishment, Ross explained that when law enforcement sought to curb these crimes, they discovered they were contending not with the criminal underworld but with the respected establishment in local finance and politics.[13]

When Bill Ackman sought to expose Herbalife, he learned, as Ross explained a hundred years earlier, "he had unwittingly laid hold on a pillar of society and was therefore pitting himself against the reigning organization in (American) finance and politics."

What Ackman seemingly did not realize is a key to understanding the deeper truth of multi-level marketing and the rise of the predatory pyramid scheme — *Ponzinomics* — as a politically protected business model. The absurd claims and deceptive promises of Herbalife and all MLMs are now enshrined in American culture and even political ideology. Ackman believed he could lift Herbalife into the light of true facts, revealing inherent and pervasive fraudulence, while leaving the established order on Main Street, Wall Street, and Capitol Hill undisturbed. This was impossible. Herbalife's structure and practices are identical to hundreds of other MLMs. For the FTC to declare it a pyramid scheme, the entire MLM house of cards would be threatened. Herbalife, and all other MLMs, are defended by millions in campaign contributions made to Congress members who also oversee the FTC's annual budget. Ackman's wager, large as a single transaction, was dwarfed by the billions Wall Street stood to lose if the foundation of publicly traded MLMs was eroded. Herbalife, like Amway and other large MLMs, are influential members and officers of the U.S. Chamber of Commerce. Their recruiting schemes are advocated by the U.S. Department of Commerce in nations around the world.

To understand how embedded Herbalife's deceptive scheme is in the fabric of the economy, Ackman would have been better served to set aside SEC filings and take up a study of Eric Hoffer's classic treatise on mass movements, *True Believers*. Hoffer's seminal text helps explain the enormous social forces favoring Herbalife as it absurdly poses as the standard-bearer of the American Dream. Hoffer wrote:

A rising mass movement ... cures the poignantly frustrated not by ... remedying the difficulties and abuses which made their lives miserable, but by ... enfolding and absorbing them into a closely knit and exultant corporate whole.[14]

Ackman would have been wise to also study the remarkable growth and social impact of the faith-healing, positive-thinking "Christian Science" religious movement, founded by Mary Baker Eddy, which spread across America in the late 1800s and early 1900s. "Christian Science," a nonsensical term invented by the founder (similar to the term "multi-level marketing"), was skeptically chronicled by Mark Twain. His turn-of-the-century book on the subject acknowledged the movement's almost irresistible appeal and its alignment with financial and social currents of the day, and speculated whether it might become America's dominant religion. Even as the American frontier was closing and massive Trusts were consuming entire industries, the Christian Science movement assured followers they still held *ultimate power* over their personal fortunes and physical health by reforming and aligning their thoughts as prescribed by Mrs. Eddy.[15] Mark Twain captured Christian Science's redemptive appeal, which could later be applied to MLM's utopian promises:

She has delivered to them a religion which has revolutionized their lives, banished the glooms that shadowed them, and filled them and flooded them with sunshine and gladness and peace ... a religion whose heaven is not put off to another time, with a break and a gulf between, but begins here and now, and melts into eternity as fancies of the waking day melt into the dreams of sleep.

From the Puritans, to Mary Baker Eddy's successors and apostates alike, all would successively claim a mystical chord connecting the angels of financial success with unflinching belief in their positive-thinking dogmas. It was only MLM, however, that made a global business out of selling feathers from the angels' wings. Others promised great wealth or perfect health from believing and paying the teacher. MLM made a business of selling the teaching rights.

The MLM phenomenon may be recent, beginning about 1950 when other distinctly American institutions exploded in popularity, such as franchising, fast food, Las Vegas, and Disneyland, but its roots are as old as America itself. We invented MLM, as we invented consumerism, Mormonism, Christian Science, and Prosperity Gospel preached by Oral Roberts, Pat Robertson, Jimmy Bakker, and Joel Osteen. Wrapped in American beliefs and dogma, the fraudulence of a financial pyramid scheme is barely noticed.

How and why William Ackman's truth-telling campaign against Herbalife was doomed will be made very clear in the coming chapters. The unraveling of MLM deception, diversion and corruption begins, as it must, with the very first deception about how MLM all got started.

LEGENDS

The Legend of Carl Rehnborg

The true story of MLM, *told by the losers,* begins not with revelation but by removal of myth, starting with the "once upon a time" account of MLM's genesis. All fairy tales include a myth of nativity and MLM's is no different. According to MLM lore, Carl Rehnborg, founder of California Vitamin Company (later renamed Nutrilite), not only invented today's MLM phenomenon, but is also the father of today's vitamin and supplement business.

There is no *Wikipedia* entry for Carl Rehnborg. He is not referenced as a significant figure in any history of nutrition, except in articles related to or promoted by Amway. Details of Rehnborg's life and work have changed over time and rely almost entirely on his biography, *The Nutrilite Story, Past, Present and Future,* written by his son, Sam Rehnborg, and published by Amway.[i]

Rehnborg's biography is widely believed to be the official text for a historical account of MLM's formation; the MLM movement's Book of Mormon. The publisher's description on Amazon states that Rehnborg's supplement pills "spawned the dietary supplement industry" and that he was "instrumental in creating a new method of distribution known as multilevel marketing."

Rehnborg's Nutrilite was a tiny, localized, and virtually unknown enterprise. From its inception, it was inconsequential and barely solvent until a chance encounter between Rehnborg and the *actual* inventors of MLM's pyramid recruiting plan, Lee Mytinger and Wil-

---

[i] A 2005 article in South China Morning Post, with Rehnborg's son as the main source, conflicts with accounts in the biography. It erroneously states that Rehnborg was "a chemist and biologist by training." He had no such training of any kind. It describes his U.S.-based vitamin company as if it were introducing a new concept to America when, in fact, the vitamin industry was already booming. The true inventors of multi-level marketing who had complete control over Rehnborg's sales and marketing, Lee Mytinger and William Casselberry, are not referenced at all. "Tale of an Intrepid American in China" by Tom Mitchell, South China Morning Post Oct. 17, 2005

liam Casselberry. Details of *their* biographies are strangely missing in the MLM fairy tale. Neither has a *Wikipedia* entry and they are referenced in the Nutrilite entry only as "national distributors" for Rehnborg. Casselberry and Mytinger were also the direct managers and precursors for the two founders of Amway, Richard DeVos and Jay Van Andel.

Nutrilite's actual historic notoriety today has nothing to do with inventions and business models. It is infamous for being prosecuted by the federal government for outrageous and dangerously false medical claims about its non-pharmaceutical pills and potions, viewed by the FDA as snake oil and by medical professionals as quackery. The prosecution began shortly after Nutrilite was reconfigured as the first "MLM" and during the time Van Andel and DeVos were among its top recruiters.

The Nutrilite Story documents the legendary narrative previously retold as oral history. It is the official transcript of MLM's founding by virtue of its copyright owner and publisher, the Amway Corporation. As the oldest and largest of current multi-level marketing enterprises, Amway plays the role of MLM's priestly authority and primary source in matters of MLM invented history. To promote the legend, Amway not only underwrote the "biography," but, in 2014, commissioned the casting of a life-size bronze statue of Rehnborg at the "Nutrilite Center" in California, where "visitors are invited to sit by (the) bronze portrait likeness of Carl for a unique photo opportunity."[16] Carl Rehnborg died in 1973, a year after Amway acquired his company.

There are obvious problems with *The Nutrilite Story* as with any sect's narrative. Yet, in plumbing the origins of new American creeds and movements, researchers including me must examine and quote from official texts, scrolls, tablets, and scriptures. Only from a re-examination of Rehnborg's life and times can we learn the true drivers and threads of American culture that gave birth to MLM. When the actual characters and historical events are uncovered, MLM's true character behind its current disguises will become evident.

The Legend of "Christian" MLM

In reverent voices, millions will declare that — while Carl Rehnborg is the father of the vitamin and supplement business — Amway's famed founders, Richard DeVos and Jay Van Andel, are the true inventors of today's "MLM industry." They are the leaders responsible for MLM's mission as a vanguard of Christian principles. With these godly credentials, criticisms or questions of MLM's legitimacy are viewed as not only erroneous, but blasphemous.

The "MLM" model was already well established and beginning to proliferate when DeVos and Van Andel formed Amway. The two Amway owners worked at the original MLM, Nutrilite, for more than a decade. There they learned the MLM "business model" and gained their training. Then, in a pattern that has produced perhaps more than a thousand other MLM companies, DeVos and Van Andel defected from Nutrilite, took thousands of Nutrilite salespeople with them, and set up Amway as a virtually identical and directly competitive enterprise.

DeVos and Van Andel did not originate or invent anything related to the MLM model. They did, however, graft a theme of religious righteousness onto Mytinger and Casselberry's established pyramid model, spawning the "Christian" legend. Assuming a self-anointed moral authority, they escalated MLM's deceptive promises to a dogmatic belief system. One noted sociologist, reflecting the mythology in academic papers, called Amway a "quasi-religious corporation."[17]

Acting and speaking like prophets, DeVos and Van Andel portrayed their pyramid-recruiting scheme as a moral crusade, promising wealth as a salvation and proclaiming failure a sin. On the cover of DeVos's 1975, book, *Believe*, it says, "Discover how you can attain success and personal fulfillment through belief in free enterprise, human dignity, God and His Church,

17

the American Way." The moral tone and the Christian rhetoric, blended inexplicably with patriotism and capitalism, were adopted by many MLMs that followed. Christian churches became hotbeds of MLM recruiting with clergy in the uplines.[18]

DeVos's and Van Andel's religious pretenses for their pyramid money scheme were rooted in the authoritarian and evangelistic training of the extremist Dutch Protestantism of their childhoods in Grand Rapids, Michigan. They attended the same insular religious high school and conservative religious college, and never deviated in their entire lives from the fundamentalist doctrines and rigid political views of their upbringing.

The Christian Reformed Church in Grand Rapids, a secessionist sect of the larger Dutch Reformed Church, spread with Dutch immigration. In South Africa, the church became a major force in support of the apartheid system. In the United States, the Christian Reformed Church split from the larger group over matters of ritual in 1857. The parents of both Van Andel and DeVos were members of the secessionist group. The newly formed Christian Reformed Church continued strict adherence to fundamentalist views and basic tenets of Calvinism, including predestination, the association of wealth with righteousness, strict patriarchy, and conservative views on sexuality. Richard DeVos and Jay Van Andel are among the group's "prominent" members.[19] Reflecting the fundamentalist character of his religious views, Van Andel gave $500,000 and his own name to a "research institute," the Van Andel Creation Research Center, in northern Arizona, to study and promote creationism and (biblical) flood geology.[20]

The indoctrination shaped their brand of the "MLM" movement. MLM leaders claim entitlement to advise and pass judgment on MLM recruits in matters of marital roles, sexual practices, church attendance, child rearing, and political affiliations. As MLM developed into a large political lobby to protect against fraud investigations, its moneymaking scheme, portrayed in religious and moral terms, blended with other extremist religious and conservative movements, and culminated in Richard De-Vos's daughter-in-law, Betsy DeVos, serving in Donald Trump's Cabinet.

With this assumed moral authority and righteousness of purpose, MLM leaders could impose a stigma of shame and humiliation upon adherents who lost money and quit or criticized the program. They were stigmatized as "losers and quitters" or "negative thinkers." Shrouded in the silence and shame of the disgraced and discredited "losers," the massive program of proselytizing and soliciting funds for a non-existent "income opportunity" proceeded without public outcry, leaving millions with losses in its wake.

DeVos's and Van Andel's religious imprint on a pyramid recruiting scheme has endured as protective coloring and adopted by many other MLMs, with variations for conservative Mormonism and socially liberal "prosperity gospel" creeds.

Van Andel died of Parkinson's disease in 2004. Richard De-Vos died at age 92 in 2018.

Stripped of its pseudo-religious camouflage and the fabricated legend of a visionary "inventor," the untold story of MLM proceeds in this next section to examine MLM's true origins revealed in the life and times of Carl Rehnborg. It will disclose how some of America's most infamous scams and fads, financial delusions, and unsavory aspects of door-to-door selling, became ingredients of the MLM "model." Rehnborg's almost comical follies took him to New York, Alaska, Mexico, China, and the dreams-come-true world of 1930s California. Discovering these banal and absurd beginnings, it becomes possible to grasp today's colossus of deception called "multi-level marketing."

DREAMS AND SCHEMES:
JOURNEY TO MLM

Dreams of Gold

In 1913, at 26, a rather mature age for a young man in that era, Carl Rehnborg left his parents and the family business in South Carolina to travel by train to Seattle, Washington. His final destination: Alaska, where deep veins of gold were said to be awaiting intrepid and determined prospectors. Rehnborg's hope-filled journey was part of what historians have called one of the largest *voluntary* migrations in history at that time. News spread widely about discoveries in Alaska, which became a U.S. territory in 1867. More than 100,000 wealth-seekers flocked to Alaska and Klondike in Canada's Yukon. Fewer than 4,000 prospectors found any gold, and even fewer actually became rich.

The famed Alaska Gold Rush was one of America's legendary get-rich chapters, in the league with an earlier California gold discovery, and followed by booms in Florida real estate and the ballooning stock market in the 1920s. Writer Jack London is the most famous adventurer who searched for Alaska gold. He did find gold, of a sort, and wrote popular novels, including *Call of the Wild*, based on his experiences. According to *The Nutrilite Story*, Carl Rehnborg was inspired by London's quest and took the same voyage 16 years later.

Upon arriving in Seattle, Rehnborg quickly learned that, while the gold in Alaska was real, the widely held belief in the opportunity for wealth — the very motivation for his trip — was false. The boom over, he was "too late." Prospectors were no longer striking it rich but, rather, were "working like slaves for mere ounces" of the metal.[21] Some, like Rehnborg, abandoned the venture quickly, while others stayed and moved from place to place as news broke of yet another strike. As is now widely known, the real money in this and other gold rushes was not in gold itself, but in selling to gold-seekers supplies, tools, transportation — anything that fed their hopes.

Rehnborg's ill-fated trip was a typical folly, yet perhaps like the ventures of many others, his journey did lead to other unexpected discoveries. Rehnborg learned of another wealth opportunity while in Seattle — not in gold, but in commerce, in the newly opened and still mysterious China. He made plans to go there after returning to the East Coast where he could gather the means.

Carl Rehnborg's decision to travel to China in search of *business opportunity*, like the plan to discover gold in Alaska, was in no way original for the time, but part of a large-scale movement. Only a little more than a decade before, the United States government had aggressively announced to the world that it intended to enforce an "open door" trade policy toward China. Europe, Japan, and Russia had all signaled intentions to seize land and control lucrative markets inside this vast country. England had forcibly opened markets during the so-called Opium Wars. The whole world was eyeing China for new wealth, and Carl Rehnborg, like many others, caught the get-rich spirit. In the U.S., as the American frontier was closing, natural resources were already exploited and trusts started taking over vast areas of commerce. The prospect of sales opportunities in China revived the spirit of ever-expanding capitalism, not unlike a later era of "open door" that began for American business in China in 1978. While Rehnborg was too late for gold in the Pacific Northwest, his timing in China was better.

Of the tens of thousands of men and women who headed west in search of the fabled gold opportunity, many were impelled strongly by frustration, personal failures, and a general sense of receding opportunities in the eastern U.S. Rehnborg was no exception. His work life began in the employ of his parents, who sold handmade souvenir jewelry and paintings to the wealthy in Gilded Age vacation sites along the east coast, such as St. Augustine, Florida, and the golfing center of Pinehurst, North Carolina. There, his biography informs, young Carl met people he viewed as America's "highest and best." He adopted them as role models, including the "DuPonts and Morgans and Mellons."

Like the iconic character Jay Gatsby in F. Scott Fitzgerald's novel, Rehnborg reportedly was inventing a "dashing personality," and writing down what he viewed as "rules" for self-improvement, addressing his own diary, as if to an alter ego, as "Old Book" when he made entries.[i] His rules, as his son noted admiringly in the biography, were aimed at impressing others, rising in status, and attracting women.

Rehnborg's job was in the sales and marketing of his parents' handmade crafts. Yet, as he stated in his journal, "Business has been so poor for two years, and I have been so little of a man, that Dad and I amicably concluded that I would reap benefit from working for someone else."

Rehnborg's first real job outside the family's business lasted only a few weeks. He was reportedly fired for being unable to motivate the factory workers he was supposed to be supervising. He went back to work for his father. In a short time, though, he was sent off to New York under parental patronage to attend a jewelry design school but, according to his biographer, he harbored a deeper interest in becoming an actor.

Rehnborg lasted less than a year in jewelry design. He did not leave to pursue an acting career, but instead launched into another profession as "inventor." His first invention, developed with an unnamed partner, and described as "a revolutionary flooring material made out of melted rubber, sawdust, and other special ingredients. It was fireproof. It was waterproof. People told him

---

[i] Jay Gatsby in *The Great Gatsby* used the term "old sport" to affect English aristocracy. Oxford students from affluent families commonly used the term. The American character in the novel had been "penniless" and "came from nothing." He changed his name, assumed a new identity and gained wealth illegally.

it was good, a surefire success." Rehnborg envisioned "covering the floors of the world." Unfortunately, as the first installation revealed, the product had a serious flaw: it cracked. The project was abandoned.

Returning home to his father, who was now a widower and living in Camden, South Carolina, the young Rehnborg enrolled at the University of South Carolina in the fall. He was now 26. By the next spring, he quit school. It was his final encounter with formal education of any kind.

It was at this point, 1913, when Rehnborg set off from South Carolina to Seattle seeking gold, which eventually led to his new plan to go to China and pursue mythic business opportunities. He was consumed, his filial biographer wrote, with a belief that his "destiny is to blaze new trails."

China Dreams

After dropping out of college, Rehnborg secured an ac-counting job at an American oil company in the burgeoning new petroleum industry. At the time, the U.S. was the world's largest oil producer and an aggressive exporter. Rehnborg's job in China involved tracking inventory of barrels of oil being sold and delivered to local Chinese distributors. Rehnborg started to learn Mandarin, and lived with other company employees in luxury, where Chinese house servants, called "boys," waited on them.

Within his first year in China, Rehnborg was fired for trying to "tell top management what they should do."[22] However, he al-ready had plans for an independent venture in China as an agent with an import/export company. Rehnborg also planned to mar-ry a woman whom he met while in jewelry design school in New York. She came from a wealthy family in Boston. In 1917, while America was entering World War I, Rehnborg's fiancée sailed to China and they married. The horror of war engulfing the globe did not touch Rehnborg directly, but its geopolitical aftermath would eventually end his China venture.

According to his biography, while working in imports/ex-ports, Rehnborg was making keen observations about the health and diet of Chinese people. Less than a year into this new role as an independent agent for the import/export company, Rehn-borg's wife became pregnant. The couple moved back to America where Rehnborg was able to arrange a stateside position with the company working on shipments out of Guadalajara, Mexico. There, he arranged exports of cow leather to China where it was made into shoes. After the first trip to Mexico, while en route back to Boston, Rehnborg turned down an offer to work in Bos-ton where his wife's affluent family resided, and he abruptly quit the company. Instead, he decided to pursue work with another company in Beaumont, Texas, in the shipping industry. Due to the war, shipping resources were in short supply, which Rehnborg believed presented a unique profit opportunity. However, he soon learned the company was unorganized and failing. Nevertheless, Rehnborg managed to persuade his wife, over strenuous objections, to move to Beaumont. As the business moved toward total collapse, Rehnborg joined in yet another large-scale and historic event of the time: along with millions of others, he contracted Spanish Influenza.

During this health crisis, Carl Rehnborg formulated a new career plan, another invention of sorts in its originality. Recalling the absence of milk in the Chinese diet, he thought he could improve China's national health by selling them canned "evaporated" milk, which required no refrigeration. It would provide the country with nutrients that he believed the Chinese did not realize they were lacking in their diets, despite thousands of years of advanced culture. The plan led to successfully persuading the Carnation Milk Company to hire him as the first agent to establish exports of Carnation milk to China. At 30 years old, Rehnborg planned to move back to China with his wife and infant.

The Carnation Milk Company developed into a large international enterprise partly from value and utility, but also from the owner's wily marketing skills. Canned evaporated milk could be stored indefinitely on store shelves, at a time when many households did not have refrigerators or even ice boxes. Its decline in popularity followed rapidly as refrigeration became more common in households. But sales and marketing were also based on a contrived brand appeal. The company's name, Carnation, for example, seemed to conjure nature, freshness and beauty in a product that was actually processed, boiled, and canned with added sugar. The health-inspiring name was taken not from nature, but from a brand of cigars. Carnation developed breeding and feeding processes for its cows that forced them to increase lactation. About a decade before Rehnborg joined the company, Carnation coined the term "milk from contented cows." Soon, Carnation's milk cans were on store shelves coast to coast and Carnation was just beginning its export business. Rehnborg's timing was excellent, but as he would soon discover after returning to China, and reminiscent of his revolutionary flooring, there was one big problem with the plan.

Rehnborg gathered his wife and baby for his new mission to introduce cow's milk into the diet of the world's most populous nation. Though China has an ancient culture, he perceived that it had never discovered the nutritional importance of cow's milk. Upon arrival in Shanghai, Rehnborg observed "a country where most people had never seen a cow. So many in real need: little children with bellies distended from starvation, women weak and pale from pregnancy, rickshaw pullers with scaly sores of pellagra...." Rehnborg believed he would deliver the relief the Chinese did not realize they needed.[23]

Despite his previous experience in China and some familiarity with Mandarin, and despite his recognition that, "Everywhere (in China), the interest in food was linked to the interest in nutrition,"[24] Rehnborg was forced to admit his plan to save China's health with canned milk had a major weakness: millions of Chinese became ill from consuming milk due to a genetic disposition to lactose intolerance. His biography reports, "He was finding that many Chinese just didn't seem to like the taste of milk. It often made them sick, and it was expensive. It was beginning to seem like there was simply no way to create a mass market for milk in China."[25] Thus ended the Carnation milk crusade and Rehnborg's income.

With a second child on the way, Rehnborg took his family back to America yet again where he sought new product lines and money for his latest planned venture. The anchor product he soon landed was toothpaste. He would offer Colgate toothpaste to China. "If he couldn't save Chinese teeth with Carnation Milk, maybe he could at least help keep them clean with Colgate toothpaste," his biography reports.[26] For the capital to start his new independent distribution company, Rehnborg had just one investor from his wife's family, who provided about $35,000 (in current dollars).

With toothpaste as its main line, Rehnborg's distribution business thrived, dubbing him a "tycoon." Yet, referring to Rehnborg's future in the health food supplement field, the biography ominously notes that, back in the U.S., the Federal Trade Commission posed a future threat and started reporting that an increased number of "Americans are annually robbed of hundreds of millions of dollars through fraudulent medical advertisements."[27]

In China, there was a far greater danger to Rehnborg's agenda: violent resentment against foreign businesses. Chinese rioters and "warlords" wiped out one of his agencies. The attitude of the Chinese people changed dramatically from the days when Rehnborg first arrived and lived in luxury with Chinese "boys" waiting on him and his family. The new mood threatened "tycoons," the export business model, and profit margins.

Turmoil in China in the late 1920s led to a civil war, drove out Japanese occupation forces, expelled western companies, and eventually led to today's unified China under a single political party. Unrecorded in history books, it also ended Carl Rehnborg's toothpaste business.

The toothpaste debacle, preceded by a misguided plan to sell canned milk in China, and an interim shipping business folly and ill-timed move to Beaumont, Texas, according to his biographer, led to the end of Rehnborg's marriage and separation from his children. But even the dissolution of his family and the encroaching chaos in China did not deter him. His wife returned to Boston with the children, but Rehnborg stayed on in China until total loss occurred, leaving him without the means even to get out. In 1927, destitute and with unpaid creditors and unaccounted inventory, Rehnborg was only able to get back to the U.S on the generosity of others who provided his fare.

California Vitamin Dreams

The next chapter of Rehnborg's odyssey remained true to course. Having lost his family as a cost of his China dream-quest, he joined the latest mania back in the U.S at the time: vitamin pills. As when he followed Jack London's path to Alaska for gold, Rehnborg gravitated to where countless other wealth-seekers were already congregating in Southern California. Meanwhile, Rehnborg formally lost custody of his children in the divorce, but never saw the custody papers when they were delivered. He was already immersed in his newest venture at another address.

Rehnborg's newfound obsession with producing and selling vitamins pills in the late 1920s to mid 1930s, especially in California, was part of an accelerating trend that attracted many believers and opportunists. Well before Rehnborg filled his first pills with processed alfalfa, a large industry with outrageously false medical claims was quickly forming. In 1912, a decade and a half before Rehnborg's exodus from China, Casimir Funk, a Polish scientist working in London, coined the term "vitamines" to describe the newly discovered elements of rice that were vital to preventing beriberi disease. Over the next few years, university and corporate researchers began to isolate and identify more of these hidden nutritional components and their relationship to disorders such as rickets and pellagra that had plagued the world wherever a severe food deficiency occurred.[28]

In short order, leveraged by the enormous power and authority of science, these minuscule food elements were hyper-commercialized by non-scientists as miracle discoveries that could now be extracted and made available in pill form — for a price. Though scientists had shown that the abnormal absence of these nutritional elements could lead to disease, the commercial promoters distorted these discoveries into claims that *adding them to a normal diet* could ward off illness and even cure diseases.

A little more than a decade after their discovery, "vitamines" were already advertised in the pages of the *Saturday Evening Post*. The bombastic health claims and public mania sparked by these discoveries reinvigorated and vastly expanded the fragmented but well-defined earlier industry of medicine show doctors, mail-order "nostrums," and other "patent medicines" that had operated robustly in America for several decades. The American Medicine Show remedies were mostly useless, if not harmful, and often based on morphine or alcohol. Many of the traveling "doctors" claimed their secret remedies were based on Native American wisdom, or some exotic, distant, or esoteric body of knowledge unknown or even nefariously suppressed by the conventional medical community.

With its supposed authority of "science," and supposed traditional wisdom recovered from the ancient past or far distant peoples, including China, the vitamin craze would grow vastly larger than its predecessor, the patent medicine field.

One of the earliest of the vitamin pill promoters was Forrest C. Shaklee, who quickly recognized the financial potential in vitamins and other herbal remedies. He sold pills containing plant materials, as early as 1915, door to door. In 1931, five years before Rehnborg registered his own company, Shaklee was manufacturing and selling pills filled with alfalfa plant matter in Oakland, California. Shaklee was well prepared for his pioneering role in selling vitamins with unproven and misleading health claims. In his youth, he traveled with a medicine show as a "strong man" performer, lifting huge weights that were actually hollow.[29]

Concurrent with "vitamania" that began to grip the country were barely-heard caveats from actual medical doctors and food scientists — warnings that vitamins in pill form were not needed by people with normal American diets.[30] Doctors and scientists also noted there was no verifiable evidence that vitamins — distilled from actual food or synthetically manufactured, then ingested as discrete, separated elements in pill form — actually improved health at all or functioned as they did in nature within actual food. Furthermore, it was not known if ingesting hyper-doses of the distilled or manufactured vitamins caused physical harm. The newly formed American Medical Association (AMA), which previously fought alcohol and other drug-laced "nostrums" hawked by wily, itinerant "doctors" and "professors," now battled the far more aggressive and widely spread pseudo-scientific claims of "vitamins," calling them a novel form of "quackery."[31]

Absence of evidence for the need for vitamins where a normal diet is available, lack of any verification of health benefits, and questionable ingredients remain the status quo of the vitamin industry to this day.[32] But none of these conditions slowed the frenzied sales of vitamins and supplements, nor resulted in any significant regulation against the onslaught of false claims, or led to any requirements even for proof of ingredients.[33]

As marketable goods, vitamins and other "food supplements" operate outside normal market forces. With unverified ingredients, each product in the vitamin and supplement field can be claimed "unique" thus preventing price comparisons and making tests of efficacy impossible. "Testimonials" from alleged users — some contrived, others merely imagined — replace evidence. Placebo effects reported by those "healed" serve as cause-and-effect proof and discredit the voices of all others who report no results. Extraordinary marketing claims by vitamin producers and sellers about restored health, prolonged youth, instant vitality, enhanced beauty, and "proven" bulwarks against diseases can command exorbitant prices charged to the truly sick, as well as the far more numerous fearful and uninformed people.

Over the next four years, while working full-time once again as an accountant for an oil company, Rehnborg returned to his earlier off-hours role as "inventor." Now he was packaging plant nutrients processed into a "supplement" that supplied elixirs of health, just as Shaklee and others were doing. He built a laboratory of sorts in his home kitchen, eventually focusing on alfalfa as his base nutrient. During this time, Rehnborg remarried. His new wife's full-time job supported his experiments and allowed him to quit his own job. In early 1936, they had a child together.

Testimony to the explosive commercial value of "vitamins" is demonstrated in Rehnborg's and other early promoters' initial experiences of finding interested investors. With virtually no revenue, no scientific proof, and no relevant academic training, Rehnborg's newly formed "California Vitamin Company" was able to attract various people willing to offer some funding for a stake in the fledgling enterprise. Rehnborg was in booming California, concocting a product with widely promoted scientific pretensions for curing and preventing age-old diseases. Even more important, when they found buyers for their pills and potions, the price Rehnborg and others were able to charge showed the emerging field held electrifying profit potential.

In the same year his third child was born, Rehnborg attracted the first of several financial backers. Their modest investments covered his basic costs, enabling him to bring to market the product he labeled "Vitasol." Like all such products, its ingredients were not fully disclosed or ever tested for any health benefits or potential harmfulness. Rehnborg had no evidence that the product provided any practical health value at all. Yet, "(Rehnborg) was wildly excited and sure it would eventually be a million-dollar business."[34] The exact price for "Vitasol" is not reported,[35] except that it was equivalent to a "half day's wages."[36] Rehnborg soon added "Vitaphyll" to the product line, converted "Vitasol" from liquid to pill form, and developed a new "skin cream." Yet, with all the growing products, sales languished and debts rose. He was forced to move his family into a small room behind his "laboratory."

Eventually, a more promising investor, R. Templeton Smith, arrived. Smith bought out the interests of Rehnborg's other small investors, who were mostly friends and sympathizers, but then withdrew in just a few months.[37] Rehnborg's bank account balance dropped to less than $10.

Then, another investor appeared — this time, a local woman described as "strong-willed and gruff, who wore slacks ... and (was) rather mannish."[38] Lela "Cal" Calcote was a widow with a "small real estate empire." The biography reports her primary interest in Rehnborg's vitamins was, "whether there was any connection between vitamin and mineral rations and sexual desire."[39]

The pair formed a separate, jointly owned company dedicated to sales and marketing. They attracted a small cadre of salespeople, and Rehnborg's new identity, along with more aggressive product claims, began to emerge. In a local newspaper story, the contents of Rehnborg's concoctions were revealed only as "fruits, and many types of green materials, such as alfalfa ... and unclassified factors such as auxins, chlorophyll and others." The process of transforming the products into remedies was a "trade secret." Rehnborg was quoted as claiming his products would alleviate "anything that isn't an infection." Rehnborg told the reporter that his laboratory, where he processed the nutrients to concentrate their curative powers, functioned "just like a 'human stomach.'"[40] Simultaneously in 1938, the U.S. Food, Drug, and Cosmetics Act passed, prohibiting false or misleading statements about products related to health and nutrition.

Then, in a seeming replay of when Rehnborg's first wife left him and took the children, his current wife of six years, who supported him financially and manually, also abruptly left with their two-year-old son.[41] Rehnborg responded like he had before by doubling down in his work.

He began delivering talks to local groups, and now portrayed his time in China — when he counted oil barrels, promoted evaporated milk, and sold toothpaste — as a period of "active research" on the "relations of vitamins and minerals to health, happiness and beauty."[42] The new claim that Rehnborg had been in China primarily to conduct nutrition "research," tapped, the biography notes, into "a growing fascination and sympathy with things Chinese in American popular culture ... (including movie characters) Dr. Fu Manchu and Charlie Chan." These fictional characters added "adventure and intrigue" to Rehnborg's somewhat fictionalized biography and presentations. Along with this newly constructed history, Rehnborg's credentials were also upgraded. In one newspaper account of a Rehnborg presentation, he was identified as a "recognized authority" (without naming who did the recognizing).[43]

Despite the embellished credentials, romanticized backstory, and pop culture interest in all things "Chinese," sales did not grow significantly. Products from Rehnborg's "laboratory," however, continued to adapt. In the shadow of new federal oversight, Rehnborg began including synthetic vitamin material into his "natural" concoctions. To broaden the customer base, he introduced children's candy, infused with synthetic vitamin materials, at $13 a jar (in today's currency). He offered products said to be valued according to "potency." They were classified as "Maintenance, Standard, Hi-B and Special," and priced respectively from about $40 to more than $200 for a month's supply in today's dollars.[44]

Meanwhile, Rehnborg searched for a sales manager. His business was still not sustainable and his production remained primitive. In 1939, the operation was described in the biography as "a shell with no contents ... no assets and no liabilities ... equipment consisted of two picnic tables with attached benches and a big milk can of about 10 or 20 gallons, a galvanized milk can, and a steel slab about a foot long or maybe a little longer, and about an inch or inch and a half deep, with 31 holes in it."

Sales management candidates came and went, without success, until one person, whom Rehnborg believed could fulfill his vision, arrived. A "merchandising consultant" personally recommended the new sales manager.

It was at this time of high hopes for sales that Rehnborg adopted the "Nutrilite" brand name, replacing the old title, California Vitamins. Along with adoption of a fresh company name and a corporate charter, the new sales manager recommended that Rehnborg undertake a makeover and secure money for a major expansion. He convinced Rehnborg's current investor, Calcote, to make an infusion of $35,000 (in today's currency). Nutrilite moved to spacious new quarters in Los Angeles, and the product line included 10 other branded goods, among them, "a laxative and two skin creams."[45]

However, the biography reports one "sour note." Rehnborg "was not quite current" on rent he owed on the former facility, and he left "on short notice." He did not even notify his one part-time local worker.

The new sales manager, whom Calcote funded with thousands of dollars, lasted less than six months. He was plotting a takeover, which emulated the enterprise's dodgy but profitable marketing potential. Constructed of "speculative" but scientific-sounding justifications, extraordinary medical claims (unfounded and later determined also to be illegal), exorbitant pricing, and a concocted history of exotic research, Rehnborg's Nutrilite operation attracted a certain type of person. Its provocative, if untrue, marketing lures overshadowed the negative factors of unproven value, primitive facilities, and meager revenue.

The ejection of the new sales manager led to reverting the newly formed Nutrilite Corporation to only a legal partnership status with his financial backer. Soon Rehnborg's only partner, Calcote, was the sole associate in Rehnborg's business and its only financial backer. A short while later, after his wife's departure and the discovery of the sales manager take-over plot, Rehnborg and Calcote "drifted into a relationship."[46]

During this time, Rehnborg sued to gain custody of his son. With his divorce finalized, Rehnborg and Calcote married in Las Vegas, purchased a 3.6-acre alfalfa farm, and enrolled his son into a private boarding school. An accidental fire destroyed the company's inventory and laboratory equipment. Rehnborg had not purchased fire insurance but, with Calcote's resources, production was fully and quickly restored. The position of sales leader remained open.

Shortly after the fire and restoration, and less two years after the wedding, the marriage between the business partners came apart. With the divorce, Nutrilite's financial backing also ended. Rehnborg and his son moved into a single room near the plant, and Calcote returned to real estate investing. Apart from references to her in the Rehnborg biography, no other entries are to be found in a current Google search for Lela H. Calcote.

In 1945, one year after dissolution of Rehnborg's third marriage and loss of financial support, the bleak status of Nutrilite was clear. Thirty-three years since his ill-fated quest for gold in Alaska, and a quarter-century after his failed mission to bring canned milk to lactose-intolerant China, Rehnborg, now 60, was far from fulfilling his latest dream of selling vitamins to Americans on a scale grand enough to make him rich and famous. Yet, Rehnborg's quest would soon take him to a new business he could not even imagine. It had not yet been invented. Greater than anything he'd attempted before, this new business would claim to be "the greatest income opportunity in the world."

Pseudo-Truth

The stark business picture of Nutrilite might be the ordinary and expected fate of a startup vitamin company a few decades earlier. But, by this date, in booming southern California, and after vitamin mania made such headway into American culture, it cannot be attributed only to market conditions or public awareness. This period — the years Rehnborg returned from China and into the mid 1940s — is described by health writer Catherine Price as "arguably the most exciting time vitamins had ever known."[47]

By the end of World War II, the vitamin and supplement market was broadly established and ubiquitously promoted. Vitamins made by The Watkins Company, a marketer of various health remedies, were supplied to U.S. soldiers during the war.[48] Miles Laboratories (now part of Bayer) introduced the "One A Day" brand in the early 1940s that was offered in retail stores nationwide.[49] Ads for vitamins were in all major newspapers and magazines. Vitamins were even sold door to door as Forrest C. Shaklee, later founder of the Shaklee Corporation, had done decades before.

As Catherine Price's history and analysis argues, the mania for vitamins in Rehnborg's time — and today — is largely a result of advertising, public relations, marketing, and salesmanship. What scientists had discovered, advertisers and marketers remade into their own image, creating a mythic commodity that barely resembled the nutritional component of the laboratory. Commercially promoted vitamins and supplements, offered as pills, tablets and liquids, are, arguably, the perfect product for advertising, unsurpassed in suitability for what anthropologist, Jules Henry called advertising's "pseudo-truth and pecuniary logic."

"Pseudo-truth in advertising," Henry wrote, "is a false statement made as if it were true but not intended to be believed literally." No proof is offered, nor required. "Proof is that it sells merchandise; if it does not, it is false." Informing people that the normal diet of the times made taking vitamin "supplements" unnecessary became "false" — because it does not boost sales. Stating that vitamin pills provide "energy" (which is impossible as they contain no calories) and "boost immunity" (for which there was no evidence) became "pseudo-truth" — because it does lead to sales.

Pecuniary logic, Jules Henry explained, employs pseudo-truths "to prove something that is not true or real for commercial purposes." Thus, giving children vitamin pills, once a day, to ward off devastating diseases that are unrelated to diet, becomes perfectly logical and reasonable to millions of people. As Henry explained, people not in the habit of critical thinking commonly use pseudo-logic in everyday life.[50]

For the general public, the facts about vitamins are either unknown or misunderstood, or in their absence, vitamins are treated as invisible and near mystical life forces. Millions of people who take them daily do not know the difference between a vitamin and a mineral. Their value when taken in pill form for people with normal diets in America is a matter of faith, not evidence. The spikes and dips in popularity of certain vitamins over others, such a C or E, correspond to fads and marketing hype as are sudden surges in sales of various foods that are said to contain certain vitamins.

Vitamin pills are obviously in great "demand" by a public that also does *not* demand quality control over them even as they put them in their mouths. There is no public outcry for proof of the ingredients listed on the packaging or any call for hard evidence of value and efficacy for health purposes. If claims of vitamins' capacity to cure diseases such as the common cold are not accepted by nearly everyone, then belief that they may *prevent* the cold is held by the others, though repeated valid studies consistently show neither claim is true. Such has been the effect and the power of advertising in shaping the public mind around vitamins.

Though vitamins are associated with food and medicine, unlike actual foods or actual medicinal products, the vitamin supplements are exempt from governmental oversight. Quality control and the matching of ingredients with label descriptions are only self-regulated by the commercial promoters themselves. No government action occurs at all until the vitamin products are already on the market, and then only if the products are actually causing harm.[51] The creative advertiser is, therefore, largely free to cite scientific findings inaccurately and inappropriately without fear of correction, and to make claims that are worded as to be believed, even if "literally" untrue.

The only restrictions are against direct and explicit claims to cure or prevent diseases, which any creative copywriter can easily circumvent. With widespread public acceptance of the pseudo-facts about vitamins, presented in bombastic and circuitous verbiage that Jules Henry called "para-poetic hyperbole," the advertiser can elegantly construct a nearly impenetrable logic for purchasing vitamins for daily consumption. Merchandisers can demand and obtain exorbitant prices that cannot be evaluated for fairness or validity.

When Rehnborg was forming Nutrilite, the vitamin was arguably the hottest and most commercialized new technology of that period. Vitamin advertising and promotions not only led millions of people to believe they needed to buy and ingest them, but also to change what foods they ate on a daily basis. Many types of food, which had been processed, preserved, colored, and stripped of virtually all nutritional value, after being invisibly infused with synthetic vitamins, were magically converted — by advertising — into "healthy" and "fortified." The "enriched" foods, including some items that were unhealthy even before processing, were transformed into "good for you" with an advertised claim that they contained (synthetic) vitamins.[52]

Rehnborg kept up with the movement, selling vitamin-laced candy and even dispensing a vitamin product, called "Old Settler," in bars to be ingested with alcoholic drinks. The Schlitz Brewing Company in Milwaukee, for example, the nation's largest of that era, launched "Schlitz Sunshine Vitamin D Beer" in 1936, informing the reader, "Beer is good for you … but SCHLITZ, with Sunshine Vitamin D, is extra good for you."[53]

The American Medical Association ruefully characterized this period as a "gold rush." Between 1931 and 1939, when Rehnborg launched California Vitamin Company, the market for vitamin sales had already grown from $12 million to about $83 million a year. By 1943, about the time Rehnborg and Calcote were married, vitamin sales had grown to $180 million ($2.5 billion in today's dollars), with one out of every four Americans already taking vitamin pills.[54] Yet, Nutrilite had been unable to significantly grow or geographically expand beyond the Los Angeles area.

In Rehnborg's latest pursuit of wealth and fame in the California vitamin venture, the market conditions were nearly perfect as was his timing. Situated in the epicenter of the market, he personally devoted himself to his work to such an extreme that three wives left him.[55] Yet, as of August 1945, the company's total gross revenue was "just a few thousand dollars," per month, which had to cover his facilities, all manufacturing costs, supplies and raw materials, salaries, and sales commissions.[56] In the midst of a vitamin sales "gold rush," Nutrilite was a vitamin still looking for a customer.

Pseudo-truth catapulted the invisible and barely understood vitamin into a massive new market. It was insufficient for Nutrilite but it would provide a bridge to a much grander scale of deception in Nutrilite's impending future.

Subtleties will soon be replaced by what became known as the "Big Lie," and associated infamously at the time with dictatorial propaganda. As Nutrilite morphs into multi-level marketing, it will pioneer a distinctly American version of the Big Lie, not a government order but a business opportunity, delivered not sternly but with a beaming smile. It will promise "wealth beyond imagination."

Sales Personality

The primary channel of distribution for vitamins in that era, as it is today, was conventional retail. By the end of World War II, retail selling had vastly expanded as nationally advertised brands made coast-to-coast distribution of health-related products feasible and profitable. Itinerant sales of medical "nostrums" were replaced by "branded" medicines and over-the-counter remedies advertised in national magazines and newspapers. Advertising usurped the power of the salesperson to drive buyer preferences. Fictional advertising characters, such as "Betty Crocker" and "Aunt Jemima," became folkloric figures, along with meaningless but evocative phrases, like Carnation's "contented cows," catchy tunes, and stylized images that psychologically target specific groups.

Rehnborg had tried virtually every type of sales and distribution model, including direct selling, retail stores, even bars. But his brand, Nutrilite, was almost totally unknown and he had no revenue for a significant advertising campaign. He was competing with a growing number of national retail brands on store shelves and at much lower prices. His channel of "distributors" consisted of only a few dozen individuals, all of them local. Personally, he recognized that he lacked expertise or even aptitude for sales.

In 1940, searching for revenue growth and with Lela Calcote's financial backing, Rehnborg had hired an advertising consultant who advised an ad campaign in the *Los Angeles Times* to increase distributors. It produced no results. The consultant then advised Rehnborg to enroll in a Dale Carnegie course. Calcote also thought the training program would help Rehnborg "deal with distributors who were from the hard school of sales."[57]

Rehnborg's attendance at one of America's first large-scale "self-improvement" programs might harken to his early practice of making lists of habits for developing a "dashing personality." But a momentous encounter at Dale Carnegie's program, and the historical point at which it occurred, gave the event greater meaning. Again Rehnborg was swept up in a broad cultural and economic movement in America along with millions of others. But, this time, Rehnborg and Nutrilite would soon play a leading role.

Historian Richard Huber referred to this cultural shift as an evolution "from character to personality." The personality becoming distinctly *American*, and which Rehnborg was personally adopting by attending a Dale Carnegie program, was that of archetypal salesperson. As Huber wrote, "… what was once considered a separate occupation … was rapidly becoming … a way of life … America was becoming a nation of salesmen."[58]

Pre-World War II, few people were in "sales" work; those who were often endured public scorn or were even despised for their traits of feigned good will and devious manipulation. Now, the reviled salesperson's way of being was becoming the norm. This was driven first by the extreme scarcity of the Great Depression and then the over-capacity of the post-World War II consumption-based economy. Sociologist C. Wright Mills observed the growing influence of sales upon American society in the late 1940s and early 50s, tying it to the new economy in which, for the first time, "demand" had to be created:

> *The bargaining manner, the huckstering animus, the memorized theology of pep, the commercialized evaluation of personal traits — they are all around us; in public and in private there is the tang and feel of salesmanship.*[59]

At issue on the personal level, as this cultural shift took effect, were traditional values and concerns of honesty and deceit. Huber singled out Dale Carnegie as a key national figure who helped rationalize and advance the transition from "character to personality." Carnegie's book, *How to Win Friends and Influence People*, published in the depths of the Depression, 1936, taught a way of survival — not by forming labor unions, supporting social safety nets, or seeking full employment — but by privately reshaping one's own personality to get along and succeed on an individual basis. Other writers wrestled with the moral dilemma of this new type of salesman's personality, fearing a "cesspool of deceit" in which one could become a success but would be "unable to stand the smell of yourself." The resolution of this existential challenge was for persons with the newly adopted "sales" personalities to truly believe they are sincere even as they engage in calculated manipulation. "No! No! No! I am not suggesting flattery," Huber quotes Dale Carnegie. "Far from it. I'm talking about a new way of life."[60]

The new way of life advocated by Dale Carnegie, Huber wrote, was really a "new way of looking at life where people are used for the purpose of profit." The salesman's traits, designed for commercial success in crass promotions, financial negotiations, and covert persuasion, would be employed in all facets of life, including family and social relations.

Like Rehnborg, Dale Carnegie was an aspiring actor, but later found extraordinary success in teaching public speaking. When the public reputation of industry magnate Andrew Carnegie shifted — from widespread hatred for his ruthless strike-breaking and wealth building, to public admiration for giving away hundreds of millions to libraries and other good causes at the end of this life — Dale Carnegie changed his real surname, spelled Carnagey. A&E referred to Dale Carnegie's name change: "A brilliant, if perhaps somewhat disingenuous business tactic, the new spelling made people associate his classes and books with the storied Carnegie family, to whom he bore no relation."[61]

The most famous novelist at the time, Sinclair Lewis, characterized Carnegie's book about "winning friends" as "how to smile and bob and pretend to be interested ... precisely so that you may screw things out of them ..."[62] That *How to Win Friends and Influence People* is not at all about real friendship can be quickly ascertained from the subtitles, "Fundamental Techniques in Handling People, How to Win People to Your Way of Thinking, How to Change People Without Giving Offense or Arousing Resentment."

At the time of Dale Carnegie's death in 1955 at age 67, his publisher, Simon & Schuster, stated that Carnegie's book had already sold 4.8 million copies.[63] Today, more than 30 million have reportedly been sold worldwide.

Whether or not Rehnborg gained public speaking skills or learned how to "influence" people is not reported. However, at Dale Carnegie's program, self-promoted as a "new way of life," Rehnborg met a future accomplice for creating their own program to offer a new way to use millions of people for profit. This would also, finally, make Rehnborg rich, the goal he had sought his entire life.

Doublespeak

Rehnborg's new associate, a radio show psychologist named William S. Casselberry, and his future partner, a veteran of cemetery plot sales named Lee Mytinger, would soon take over sales and marketing responsibilities from Rehnborg and also facilitate his dream of making history. But it didn't play out quite like Rehnborg envisioned.

Under Casselberry's and Mytinger's marketing plan, Rehnborg's Nutrilite company would become forever known as one of the first and the most notable "supplement" companies to be prosecuted by the U.S. government for deceiving both consumers and salespeople. The case would go down in history, litigated all the way to the U.S. Supreme Court, which ruled against Nutrilite. From the training and the association Rehnborg gained at Dale Carnegie's program on "influencing people," his business would develop a culture of deception far exceeding his earlier exaggerations about his products or his background. It would also be based on the exploitation of friendships for profit, the first business ever designed to convert all social and family ties to commercial relations.

In 1948, soon after Rehnborg signed an exclusive sales contract with Casselberry and Mytinger, the U.S. Food and Drug Administration raided Nutrilite locations and seized inventory, charging Nutrilite, Casselberry and Mytinger's distribution company, and Carl Rehnborg personally, with making false medical claims to sell vitamins and recruit thousands of salespeople.

The FDA case described extraordinary and utterly false claims made by Nutrilite in sales literature regarding promised benefits of ingesting Nutrilite vitamins.[64] The Nutrilite distributors had been trained to repeat the falsehoods both to consumers and, more importantly, to all prospective distributors, vastly multiplying the deception. The claims and statements were documented in a sales booklet, presumably written by psychologist Casselberry, which the government cited for prosecution. But, as part of its legal maneuvering, Mytinger and Casselberry reworded the booklet so that the case eventually opened the doors to today's misleading or meaninglessly worded promotions by vitamin and supplement makers that promise miraculous health benefits without directly claiming to provide any therapeutic value at all.

William W. Goodrich, former General Counsel of the FDA, who served in the agency from 1939–1971 and was directly involved in the Nutrilite prosecution, described the duplicity used to market Nutrilite's products and its campaign of deception. Referring to the Nutrilite recruiting and sales sessions the FDA had recorded, Goodrich recalled,

> *They were going wild; they were making every kind of a claim you could possibly make. We knew that was so, and Mytinger and Casselberry denied it under oath and on their word to God that it wasn't happening, but we knew it was.*[65]

In the decade before signing on with his new marketing managers, Rehnborg acknowledged that the value of his concoctions was "speculative." Like all makers of vitamins, he did not have to disclose the full contents or prove they would cause no harm. Yet the FDA's charges were not about inherent worthlessness, disclosure of contents, or potential toxicity of the products. Rather, the case focused on how Mytinger and Casselberry were deceptively using the products to enroll distributors and sell the goods. Biographically, the FDA case shows how far Carl Rehnborg had descended as Mytinger and Casselberry were making him very rich.

Repeated in the bright and fact-based light of a federal lawsuit, Nutrilite's preposterous lies appeared almost comical. The lies were not hidden or imbedded but put forth with assumed scientific authority in a company booklet circulated to hundreds of thousands with an official-sounding title, *How to Get Well and Stay Well*, an echo of psychologist Casselberry's own book, *How to Use Psychology in Everyday Living*.

As the case proceeded, the FDA contended that Nutrilite's deception did not decline but actually escalated from deceiving consumers and would-be salespeople to also deceiving the government. The charge referred to what Nutrilite itself called a "new language." In the "new language," astounding, life-changing claims were made while simultaneously denying them categorically.

Mytinger would have been very familiar and adept with the crafted misuse of language. In the funeral and cemetery sales business where Mytinger had worked for decades language manipulation was central to its business model, as Jessica Mitford explained in *The American Way of Death*. Among the invented euphemisms: "funeral director" for mortician and "coffins" for caskets. Most important for profit purposes was to depict the dead person as if still living and therefore able to observe and judge the family's choices for their repose, including the "view" from the gravesite.

Nutrilite's new language, however, went far beyond euphemisms. It produced a special vocabulary and way of speaking that cover over facts by authoritatively asserting their opposite. It was a precursor to what would evolve in "MLM" into an Orwellian *doublespeak*, in which controlled and manipulated contractors became "independent business owners," quota purchasing became "selling," wholesale was designated "retail," distributor morphed into "end user," and 99% loss rates were proclaimed "the greatest income opportunity in the world." The term "doublespeak" is associated with George Orwell's famous novel, *1984*, published in 1949.[i]

---

[i] The term *doublespeak* is not used in the Orwell's novel. It is derived from two other linguistic devices described in the book, doublethink and Newspeak. Orwell's earlier masterpiece that also addresses the destruction of truth, *Animal Farm: A Fairy Story*, was published the same year Rehnborg signed his contract with Mytinger and Casselberry, 1945.

The absurd but audacious lying employed by Nutrilite in its sales booklet is detailed in the government's case:[66]

> *[the booklet] represented without qualification that Nutrilite is an effective therapeutic agent [for] low blood pressure, ulcers, menstrual depression, pyorrhea ... faulty vision ... high blood pressure [and] irregular heartbeat. At another point the booklet implied that 'cancer, diabetes [and] tuberculosis ... would respond to Nutrilite treatment....*

Government prosecutors then described how Nutrilite claimed it revised the booklet and corrected deceptions to avoid a criminal proceeding:

> *To convey to the public the false and misleading impression that Nutrilite Food Supplement will cure every ailment and disease afflicting mankind, and yet avoid mentioning any specific disease names, the defendants ... inaugurated a subterfuge, which they call "new language." ... The "new language" insists that Nutrilite will cure nothing — the patient merely gets well through the use of Nutrilite.*

The *doublespeak* that Nutrilite developed around products to escape prosecution would later expand to an all-encompassing, proprietary vocabulary, covering MLM's pyramid structure, false marketing claims, money-transfer pay plan, and would conceal or obscure the roles of recruiters. It would be taught with propaganda techniques involving constant repetition of thought-stopping aphorisms, e.g., "only quitters lose and only losers quit," resulting, as Orwell explained, in an inability for followers to hold contrary thoughts or to formulate questions. It constructs a parallel reality with alternative facts. Some would later call it brainwashing.

THE PLAN:
BLUEPRINT OF A PYRAMID SCHEME

Cemeteries and Psychology

When William S. Casselberry first encountered Carl Rehnborg at the Dale Carnegie course about 1940, Casselberry was promoting himself on local radio in the Los Angeles area with a 15-minute "psychology" show. He dispensed free advice to attract paying clients for his psychological counseling services. According to Rehnborg's biography, when they met, Casselberry was "desperately short of cash."[67]

Rehnborg was also desperate. After 10 years of operation, Nutrilite had 40 distributors, all in Southern California. There had been no growth in the sales channel since mid-July 1938, when Rehnborg reorganized the sales program, adopted the new company name, and moved to a larger facility thanks to Calcote's funding. He even offered overrides to distributors on sales volume of distributors' they recruited for the company, but this did little to help grow business.[68]

Rehnborg's first impression of Casselberry was dismal. But after the Dale Carnegie program, Casselberry signed up as a Nutrilite distributor, and began recommending the Nutrilite potions and recruiting his clients.

The practice of health professionals leveraging patient trust to recruit and sell them MLM products has since become a pervasive national pattern among medical doctors, psychologists, physical therapists, dentists, and chiropractors. A 1999 *New York Times* article, "Doctors' Offices Turn Into Salesrooms," reported that the American Medical Association was unable to resolve the division that had spread through the ranks of the medical community.[69]

Casselberry was already 48 when he met Rehnborg, 53. Both had begun their current careers later in life. Neither had found much success after years of struggle, yet still held lofty aspirations. In the midst of the nation's worst economic downturn, Casselberry had gone back to school to gain an advanced degree in psychology and called himself "doctor." His credentials were academic, but he also had a background in the hard knocks of sales where survival depends on "psychological" persuasion and sometimes heavy-handed manipulation. Casselberry sold kitchenware door to door and also had real estate experience. The sales orientation carried over as a lettered professional. In addition to using radio exposure to sell counseling services, he also hawked his book, *How to Use Psychology in Everyday Living*, a 324-page treatise that presents "psychology" as a set of "scientific" rules for living. The theme of moral precepts and authoritative guidelines provided by the "science" of psychology is made even more explicit in his later book published in 1969, *How to Work Miracles in Your Life, the Golden Secret of Successful Living*. The use of "psychology" as a "secret" tool for achieving financial success and happiness would later become prominent in all MLM programs modeled on Nutrilite.

Very similar in tone and published just two years after Dale Carnegie's famous work, *How to Win Friends*, Casselberry's *How to Use Psychology* was an early example of the "self-help" genre that was previously directed at salespeople for teaching commercial persuasion techniques, but would later go mainstream for effectiveness in all areas of life. Casselberry's book offers similar platitudes and homilies as Carnegie's, and it even recommends Carnegie's book for further reading, but Casselberry's is wrapped in the authority of psychology and his Ph.D. title. Yet, after more than eight years on the air as an advice-dispensing "doctor," Casselberry's radio show was "not hugely popular."[71]

Urgent need for money may explain why Casselberry signed on as a vitamin pill salesman with a struggling and unknown "health" company whose owner had no academic degree or any training in nutrition.[72] As events unfolded, however, and consistent with Rehnborg's past experience of attracting backers and managers with ulterior or even nefarious motives, it is more likely that Casselberry saw a larger opportunity in Nutrilite and Rehn-borg. The opportunity would require ramping up the already un-founded claims about Nutrilite's alleged health benefits to boost the pills' marketability. The deception required for such market-ing falsehoods proved no barrier to Casselberry. Beyond increas-ing the level of deception for the products, the opportunity that would soon be seized by Casselberry and a future cohort also required getting Nutrilite's sales operations out of Rehnborg's hands and securing complete control. Rehnborg would then be recast in the fictional narrative as a nutrition expert with formal training. (Later, he would be promoted as the father of the entire vitamin and supplement industry.) This opportunity to gain con-trol over the business and reposition the company and its owner in a fictional narrative became apparent to Casselberry during early conversations with Rehnborg, who confessed deep frustra-tions, a history of failures, and longtime search for sales manag-ers to deliver him to his rightful destiny of fame and wealth.

As a Nutrilite distributor, Casselberry was not very successful. Almost three years after signing up, Casselberry was still work-ing part-time at an aircraft company.[73] Rehnborg's own fortunes deteriorated significantly; the company had no sales growth, and his marriage ended.

At the Douglas Aircraft factory, Casselberry met his future part-ner, Lee S. Mytinger, described as "burly and flamboyant" who "resembled a classic salesman." He had experience "selling tires, insurance, kitchen utensils, and burial plots from Maine to Cali-fornia."[74] Casselberry and Mytinger were both nearing age 50. The men — opposites in appearance but sharing a common interest in sales — became fast friends.[75] Casselberry told Mytinger about what he knew of Rehnborg, Nutrilite, and the vitamin pill business.

Given what we know now about the FDA's prosecution of Mytinger and Casselberry for deception when they took over Nu-trilite's sales — and considering the decades of fraud allegations related to the unique sales plan the two subsequently invented — Mytinger's business background warrants attention. His sales training and history — its values, practices, and ethics — add yet another thread woven into "the plan" he and Casselberry formulated, which is known today as "multi-level marketing."

In the mid-1930s in Glendale, California, Mytinger was a sales trainer at a mortuary service and cemetery, Forest Lawn, where he managed a team of more than 100 salesmen.[76] Census Bureau records say Mytinger was a 35-year-old bond salesman with an eighth grade education. He and his wife and two children lived in Glendale in a $35 per month rental house. Ten years later, a few years before he met Casselberry, he reportedly made $4,150 a year (in 1940 currency). This appears to be his last sales job before working at the factory and beginning his collaboration with Casselberry and Nutrilite. The 1940s income, "highly lucrative" at the time, was likely from selling car tires, a profit opportunity probably created by wartime shortages and abruptly ended when price controls were instituted in 1942.[77]

Forest Lawn in the 1930s was, as it is today, America's most famous cemetery. It covers more than 300 acres. Best known as the "cemetery of the stars," it attracts more than a million visitors per year. Uniquely, it is also a site for weddings. Ronald Reagan reportedly married Jane Wyman there in 1940.[78] Celebrities including George Burns and Gracie Allen, W. C. Fields, Tom Mix, Sammy Davis Jr., Walt Disney, Lon Chaney, and Nat King Cole, made Forest Lawn in Glendale their final resting place.

From its earliest days, Forest Lawn was seen by authors and social observers as an extraordinary business and cultural phenomenon, distinctly American — a new force that reshaped how Americans perceived and defined one of the most significant aspects of any culture, the meaning of death. Hubert Eaton founded Forest Lawn after a transformational moment of "miraculous compassion" in which he vowed to change America's view of death. Eaton even claimed to have a special business partner. "Christ in business," he told members of a Rotary Club, "is the greatest thing that happened to business. We must in return give business to carry on for Christ."[79]

"The plan" Casselberry and Mytinger would go on to create would have a similar impact on another fundamental element of American culture: the meaning and purpose of "success." Just as Forest Lawn's interpretation and trappings sold at exorbitant profit overwhelmed traditional views of family, faith, loss, and grief, Casselberry and Mytinger's legacy would hijack and overwhelm traditional views of livelihood, success, and the boundaries separating social from commercial relationships.

In a 2010 article in the *Los Angeles Magazine,* author Ben Ehrenreich said Forest Lawn came to represent America's "euphoric approach to mortality, making it sunny, cheerful, lifelike."[80] A decade and a half after Forest Lawn was established, Mytinger was teaching Eaton's blissful and providential sales philosophy at Forest Lawn to sales agents, getting a commission every time one of them could translate the view of death as a "beginning," manifested in real estate, monuments, purchased ceremonies, and other trappings offered for sale. Mytinger's sales agents were selling an entirely new way of thinking about life and death.

In a 2016 article, "Los Angeles Is Killing Us, Finding the Secrets of Mortality at LA's Most Legendary Cemeteries," writer Adrian Kudler shows how the new philosophy became reality in Forest Lawn, not just with lofty words, but with audacious displays of copied European art and sculptures, facsimiles of famous churches and cathedrals, and hundreds of acres of lush green fields and ponds with fountains, in an arid region that perennially struggles for water. The "eternity" promised to the dead mirrored the American Dream, in which higher social status in the afterlife could be acquired in reserved areas of the cemetery, exclusively for the great and famous or any willing to pay a higher price.[81]

The 1948 novel, *The Loved One*, by English writer Evelyn Waugh, parodied the sales and marketing of Forest Lawn as symptomatic of America's "endless infancy." Distinct sections of the cemetery, based on sales approach and customer profile, have dreamlike, fantasy names, including, Babyland, Graceland, Inspiration Slope, Slumberland, Sweet Memories, and Dawn of Tomorrow. "I am entirely obsessed by Forest Lawn [and] plan a long short story about it," Waugh wrote to a colleague while working on a screenplay in California. "It is an entirely unique place — the only thing in California that is not a copy of something else."[83]

Forest Lawn also played a central role in Aldous Huxley's satiric novel, *After Many a Summer Dies the Swan*. Huxley's impressions of American culture exemplified at Forest Lawn have been described as "narcissism, superficiality, and obsession with youth."[84] His Forest Lawn-inspired book was published seven years after his famous dystopian novel, *Brave New World*. Huxley wrote *Brave New World* after an earlier visit to the United States in which he encountered a new culture, with predominantly narcissistic personality types exuding "commercial cheeriness," while ruled by the rigid requirements of mass manufacturing and marketing.

Multi-level marketing did not offer cemetery plots among its array of lures. Yet, the culture of the in-home cemetery-plot sales world carried over. The adept use of charging fees based on immeasurable time and undefinable benefits — "perpetual care" and "eternal" peacefulness — are mirrored in MLM's promises of "infinite" expansion, "unlimited" income, and "total" success. The psychological manipulations of personal grief or fear of death were copied in MLM's claims to provide lifetime security and a safe haven from economic downturns or obsolescence. Mytinger's experience recruiting, motivating and replacing an ever-churning cemetery plot sales force carried over to a plan based on 60-80% annual attrition with near total loss rates.

Inventing a Business

Jessica Mitford's classic inquiry into the funeral and cemetery business world, *The American Way of Death,* published in 1963, provides the greatest insight into the sales and marketing culture Lee Mytinger would carry over to Nutrilite. Her journalistic exposé, necessarily softened at times with ironic humor, shocked the country for the cruel manipulations and the extortionate profitability she revealed. But perhaps even more disturbing was the harsh mirror she held up for America to see itself as it succumbed to fantasies and frauds.

One chapter is dedicated to the legendary and industry standard-setting Forest Lawn. Portending the invention of "multi-level marketing" partly based on Mytinger's experience at Forest Lawn, Mitford explained that selling cemetery plots for profit was an invented business. It existed only for a decade or so when Mytinger made it his career. Prior to 1920, the vast majority of all cemetery plots were provided at low cost by churches, local governments, and the military — not businesses. Plots were not for profit and were usually not purchased until time of death. The modest costs were covered by savings, family contributions, churches or, very often, small life insurance policies or death benefits provided by employers and fraternal organizations.

The new for-profit business stealthily maintained the traditional "non-profit" identity, thereby exempting it from taxes and expropriating the tone of religious piety and public service. This new business model drastically increased the cost of burial, grabbed up the pool of death benefits and family savings, and added billions in consumer debt. It did this while producing almost unheard of profits to the developers, "spectacular beyond the dreams of the most avaricious real estate subdivider," Mitford found.

A key element in the transformation of burial from a simple faith-based and public function into a highly commercialized and wildly profitable marketing scheme was the fielding of thousands of door-to-door salespeople promoting "pre-need" purchases of plots and a host of related services. Forest Lawn was among the first to offer funeral and cremation services along with burial plots, all purchased decades before buyers needed or had planned them. The sales pitch replaced tradition while claiming to be its fullest and highest expression. The famously high-pressure and manipulative sales program added at least 50% to all charges just to cover the salespeople's own commissions. This was where Mytinger learned "direct selling."

The amazing profitability unleashed in commercializing an intimate and spiritual realm of life was revealed in data Mitford researched, showing the price per-cubic-foot for a cemetery "crypt" to be twelve times greater than the cost of family homes. Teams of invasive door-to-door sales representatives were used not only to increase dollar volume per sale, but also to offset the greatest of all barriers to moneymaking in cemetery sales: the actual death rate. By using installment plans, far more plots could be sold each year than would be used for actually deceased people. The system was so profitable that it naturally led to more and more for-profit cemeteries being established. As Mitford explained, the developer of new commercial cemeteries could start selling plots long before the cemeteries were developed. Salespeople trained in the new business often moved from one new development to the next, just as later "king pin" MLM recruiters would as MLMs spread across the country.

In most other businesses, the relative value provided by salespeople is weighed against existing product demand and the company's established brand. Advertising and marketing programs might also offset calculations of the actual value provided by the sales force. But, in the field Mytinger trained in, it was clearly understood that the personal delivery of the sales message by high-pressure representatives in prospective customers' homes was responsible for virtually the entire business. Customer "need" was *created* by the sales presentation. No demand had ever existed for the ostensible product of a cemetery plot, to be purchased years before the customer passed away. But Mytinger's sales reps were not selling just real estate. They were offering a way to remove the sting of death, purchase eternal bliss, and even gain higher social status, replete with music, statues, and vistas of mountains and valleys to be appreciated for eternity.[85]

The absence of immediate need for a burial plot, even one described by promoters as "a place of infinite loveliness," was overwhelmed by talk of factors implying urgency, such as, obligation to lift a future burden from family, gaining the exalted status of land ownership (for many people the only "real estate" they would ever own), protection from "inflation," and securing "perpetual" care. The "selling" factor in the new industry was praised by the president of a leading sales organization for increasing the price of lots at one cemetery from $150 to $380. Industry data showed "four to ten times more is spent for direct selling (by the commercial cemetery promoters) than is spent for the total cost of planning, development and landscaping."[86]

This experience in an invented field — based almost totally on sales pitches, not intrinsic value or consumer need —would prove crucial when Mytinger and Casselberry launched their new sales plan at Nutrilite. There was no demonstrable need or consumer demand for Rehnborg's vitamins. Indeed, the need for and value of all vitamins of this type had not been demonstrated for virtually all Americans eating a traditional diet. But the marketing plan devised by Mytinger and Casselberry was not aimed at customers merely seeking better health any more than cemetery salespeople were merely selling burial plots to perfectly healthy people. The real product message planned for Nutrilite was to be about "unlimited income" and "total financial security," escaping the dreaded destiny of "loser" and achieving "complete success."

The sales position at Forest Lawn and other cemetery sales operations Lee Mytinger occupied was termed "memorial counselor," presaging the nomenclature adopted in multi-level marketing of "coach, consultant, associate, distributor" — anything other than salesperson or recruiter.[i] In this "counselor" capacity, the range of services recommended could extend far beyond a plot of burial soil, to include "vaults, bronze grave markers, flowers, postcards, and statuary and the collection, control and management of huge 'perpetual care' funds." Mitford revealed that cemetery plot salespeople could add a surcharge from 10% to 25% for "future care" even on concrete mausoleums.[87]

Such non-quantifiable services and products as enhancing "motivation," sales leads of unknown source and value, registration fees at "recognition" events, books offering instructional advice on living "positively," and inspirational audio-visuals for upholding an optimistic view despite dire financial results, would eventually be added to the sales portfolio in Mytinger's future MLM plan. Certificates are issued by some MLMs at formal ceremonies in which the recruits wear "caps and gowns." Some of the "educational" programs are actually called "university." These ephemeral services would formalize into the teaching of "laws of attraction" and "secrets" that ensured financial success and an economic and political ideology based on extreme individualism.

Mytinger was trained in a then classic but now largely extinct setting for generating business: the face-to-face struggle between

---

[i] Mitford characterized the misleading and disguising terminology adopted by the cemetery and funeral sales business: "as ornately shoddy as the satin rayon casket liner."

trained and weaponized sales representative and unarmed but formidably resistant customer. To the customer's great disadvantage, the battle occurred *inside the customer's own home.* The customer might be vigilant while the sales rep stood outside the front door. But once inside the home, the sales rep became, by social custom, a guest, and thereby accorded civility and deference, coffee and pie, even as he moved in for the financial kill. The salesperson's very survival was on the line, fortifying him with fierce determination while armed with finely tuned techniques of persuasion and domination. Every objection had a rehearsed and logically unassailable answer. Writer Ben Ehrenreich characterized the Forest Lawn marketing scheme and narrative as "a sophisticated strategy for lubricating the checkbooks of the grieved."[88]

So prevalent is deception in the cemetery plot business that the FBI lists it as a specific category among "the most common scams that the FBI encounters."[89] The magazine, *Consumers Digest* called the cemetery industry "treacherous for consumers."

Today, the U.S. Securities and Exchange Commission (SEC) warns, "Pyramid schemes masquerading as MLM programs often violate the federal securities laws, such as laws prohibiting fraud ..."[90]

Getting "Cuts"

Casselberry and Mytinger's invention of a new sales and compensation model, "The Plan," was apparently hatched by the two between 1943, when they met at the aircraft factory, and September 1945, when they signed a contract with Rehnborg to take over all sales and marketing rights.

While at the aircraft factory, Casselberry and Mytinger frequently discussed the "mechanics of sales." Reflection and analysis may have been prompted by the fact that Mytinger was not doing any sales work after so many years of accumulated experience. Casselberry was nominally still a Nutrilite salesperson but apparently gaining little or no income from it. His marketing efforts on the radio for his counseling services and book sales were also not bearing much fruit. Their talks would have included classic tales of triumphs and failures, hopes, complaints, and near successes that veteran salespeople have always engaged in. Mytinger likely recollected and reflected on his past work, which spanned as many as 20 years, and included selling cemetery plots. Yet their talks — perhaps guided by Casselberry's orientation to the psychology of persuasion as outlined in his book — moved beyond swapping war stories to a deeper inquiry.

Mytinger saw his most productive salespeople promoted to sales management, costing him personally by losing "his cut of the man's sales," and requiring him to "search for, recruit, and train a (replacement) salesman."[91] In conventional sales management, promoting the more productive salespeople is believed to incentivize them. In the same view, "recruiting and training new salespeople" is thought to be the sales manager's primary role, for which a "cut" of the other salespeople's labors is his additional compensation.

Mytinger had a different interpretation that apparently came from a deep well of frustration, resentment and disappointment.

Promoting higher performing salespeople, the veteran informed Casselberry, had only "limited (Mytinger's) incentive to expand the business."[92] Mytinger went on to proclaim that if he ever got his "own deal someplace," he would figure out a way so that "I keep the income from the people I develop."

Yet, if the manager would get a "cut of their sales" forever, how would the recruited salespeople benefit? If sales management were not replenished from among the ranks of higher performing salespeople, where would it come from? If the sales manager's role and income were vested and protected, how would the company prevent resentment from the rank and file salespeople? Most important, in protecting the sales manager, what incentive would be provided to the salespeople who, after all, are the ultimate engines of all sales revenue?

Mytinger's vision of a perpetual and ever-expanding base of income, gained from more and more salespeople's work, could have just been a vision of someday having a highly secure position at the top of a growing sales organization with steadily increasing income, a sales manager's utopia. Hardened field experience would preclude such an idealistic aspiration. In any event, Mytinger's dream of a never-ending font of income produced by other salespeople was expressed in the larger context of the "mechanics of sales," and while discussing a new type of sales organization that might be applied at Nutrilite.

As the Mytinger-Casselberry "plan" was later implemented at Nutrilite, the puzzle of incentives, commission flow, and management security would be resolved by offering every successive salesperson the same opportunity to get his own cut off his own recruits, *forever*. Effectively, *all* salespeople were offered the same incentive to become managers if they could recruit new salespeople below them. But most important for Mytinger's dream of a protected position, the plan would not reduce the income of the upper level managers — the position he would occupy — if he ever got his "own deal someplace." In his plan, the incomes of their upper level managers would not be displaced, but also be increased. Even as underlings aggressively added more people and revenues grew from their labors, the upper position would not be threatened, but would instead be enhanced and enriched also.[i]

These were the banal beginnings of an "endless sales chain," the primary element of what is now called "multi-level marketing." It was formed out of the common clay of door-to-door selling so often promoted as a field of dreams, yet experienced as drudgery, rejection and, most notably, disrespect. By 1945, it was also already becoming an obsolete model as retail locations reached virtually every town and village and mass advertising replaced the persuasive peddler.

"The Plan" differed radically from traditional door-to-door sales. In Mytinger and Casselberry's view, if you worked for Avon or Fuller Brush, popular door-to-door selling opportunities of that time, you were, for all practical purposes, an employee. You had a regular job. If you did well, you might become a district manager, but you never got much more than a salary or bonus. The Plan, as it eventually developed, "changed all that." It allowed "industrious" distributors to build their own distribution chain. It was a system bound by "personal links" and limited only by one's ability to forge them, offering a "huge incentive" to expand a network of agents as quickly as possible. Mytinger joked to Casselberry that if the first 10 agents each recruited two agents, there would be 20 more agents. And if they, in turn, each recruited two, there would be 40 more agents, and if they worked hard enough, "everyone on earth would eventually be selling the product!"

---

[i] As the plan was later formulated, the proportion of the "cut" paid to the top managers increased as purchases made by the entire chain of recruits increased, transferring most of the total commissions to the top-ranked.

The vision of an "endless chain" of salespeople was born not out of a grand plan for a vast new industry, which did develop, or as a plot to cause losses to millions of people, which it did; it emerged from the mundane experience of a seasoned old cemetery plot sales manager who dreamed, as all sales managers have, of a protected and growing income. It was conceived out of a longing for a safe haven from the insidious competition of younger upstarts, from the brutal realities of market limits and fluctuating demands for commodity products. It was imagined as a form of deliverance from the humiliating circumstances endured by sales managers the world over, a transformation of a thankless role as custodian of a churning sales force into the captain of a regenerative money machine.

In the new plan, the deserving sales manager could finally accrue equity. This equity would not be issued in company stock. It was also not dependent on the value of the product or the larger market conditions that limited a product's marketability. This newly created equity would be based on the only true currency known in the sales managers' world — the labor and expenditures of recruited salespeople. The real commodity to be marketed under the new "plan" would not be Avon-type cosmetics or Fuller Brush gadgets. *It would be the salespeople themselves*, the clay of the sales manager's craft. Appropriately then, new managers would all be called "independent business owners."

This new form of "ownership," unlike real estate or shares of stock, would *infinitely* and *perpetually* increase. No longer would the manager be bonded to the fortunes of the sales force. The sales force would be perpetually bonded to their "upline" managers, in what would later be termed "lines of sponsorship." Breaking free of decades of disrespect, the managers would be "exalted," the term later universally applied in sales training of "multi-level marketing." Casselberry's psychology precepts would provide the rules and values for the salespeople not just of business but also of living, and "the business" would become a "way of life." The sales managers' profligate wealth and conspicuously displayed lifestyle, gained from his elite position at the top of the chain, would be presented to all below to envy and to emulate as the ultimate achievement of life, proof of "total success."

In the coming decades, hundreds of millions of people all over the world would avidly, and some desperately, plunge into a multitude of "MLMs," each a direct descendant or clone of Nutrilite. The potential of an exponentially expanding recruiting chain would become their beacon of hope for a better life. All would be shown charts and videos explaining that if they just recruited a few others who duplicated the process, they would soon have thousands in their chain, all providing "cuts" to them every month.

Playing a Math Trick

Despite the fact that "The Plan" offered a huge incentive for "the most industrious to expand his or her sales," it had a devastating, inherent flaw. This would be obvious to anyone with basic math skills. Mytinger would have possessed those skills, even with only his eighth grade education. Before launching his sales career, Mytinger worked as a bank clerk and cost accountant.[93] As a sales manager for cemetery plots and automobile tires, his competency would have involved budgets, sales goals, commission schedules, forecasts, and averages.

That Mytinger fully understood the flaw and likely informed Casselberry of it, in case he did not, is disclosed when he "joked" that the number of salespeople would expand even to "everyone on earth." This projection shows an understanding of exponential expansion, which many people can hardly believe even when it is shown in hard numbers. The nearly universal unawareness of

If you double a penny every day for 30 days:

Days	Dollars
1	$.01
2	$.02
3	$.04
4	$.08
5	$.16
6	$.32
7	$.64
8	$1.28
9	$2.56
10	$5.12
11	$10.24
12	$20.48
13	$40.96
14	$81.92
15	$163.84
16	$327.68
17	$655.36
18	$1,310.72
19	$2,621.44
20	$5,242.88
21	$10,485.76
22	$20,971.52
23	$41,943.04
24	$83,386.08
25	$167,772.16
26	$335,544.32
27	$671,088.64
28	$1,342,177.28
29	$2,684,354.56
30	$5,368,709.12

the phenomenon is dramatized in the example, often told as a riddle: *Which would you take: One million dollars in cash right now, or, one penny now that doubles each day for just 30 days?*

Few people would pass up the million dollar instant windfall, being unable to grasp the exponential math. *The Answer: The one-penny choice would become more than $5 million dollars on the 30th day.*

However, the riddle has one other surprise that is particularly relevant to Mytinger's recruiting plan. *Doubling each day, it takes 25 days to amount to just $100,000 ($167,772.16). Then, the total explodes to $5 million in the last five days.* Applying this to the recruiting plan envisioned by Mytinger, only the people in the top or earliest levels would ever benefit because the total begins to "explode" only after many levels have been assembled. For those at the end, however, the math works in reverse — their potential to build more levels would never be possible due to obvious demographic and market saturation factors. For them, the chain would break or never expand significantly. They are doomed by their bottom-level position.

In practical sales terms, the plan would inundate the market with salespeople and massively outstrip the available customers. For example, if one person recruited five others who continued the "plan" four more levels, there would be 3,905 salespeople recruited. Yet, as math shows, those at the bottom, 3,125, would need to find 12.2 million more "salespeople" (3,125 × 3,905 = 12,203,125) to duplicate the "success" of those above them, which would be presented as a feasible model to follow. Not "everyone on earth" would need to sign up before the plan blocked the fortunes of later recruits.

Behind the impossible math and the demographic limits was an even deeper *economic* defect in Mytinger's "mechanics of sales." His engineering violated the elemental physics of the marketplace that all door-to-door and other retail sales plans have been governed by since the first sales were ever made among humans. As the biography reports, the Mytinger plan "changed all that." The plan financially incentivized recruiting salespeople, *without regard for demand for the goods themselves.*

Whereas the traditional direct selling model used by Avon, Fuller Brush, encyclopedia sales, and all others at the time, depended on each salesperson's personal retail sales volume, the Mytinger-Casselberry "plan" was not based on personal retail sales volume but on "personal links." This unrestrained recruiting actually destroyed the potential for individual retail profitability. In direct selling, retail profits (the difference between what the salesperson pays or is retroactively charged for goods when sold and the price ultimately paid by the retail customers) cover the direct seller's costs of selling and provides the compensation for labor and skills in making sales. Maintenance of a retail profit margin is inextricably tied to a limitation on the number of salespeople in any market area.

The previous 10 years of effort by Rehnborg indicated there was little actual market demand for his branded products at least at the prices he was charging and in the "direct selling" method he was using. But, under the "plan" envisioned by Mytinger, it would not matter at all whether the market needed or wanted Nutrilite products or whether any individual salesperson could make a retail profit selling them.

While the incomes of the future top level managers — imagined by Mytinger and Casselberry as *themselves after they gained control of Nutrilite* — would become vested and perpetually growing, the people that were subsequently enrolled would be cast into chaotic, cannibalistic competition without connection to an external market. For as long as recruiting was carried out, profitable "cuts" would flow upward, but the people below, on whom the cuts were inflicted, would become ever-mounting financial casualties.

Last Ones In ...

To the mathematically adept, an even more insidious flaw than demographic saturation and dilution of retail markets for retail sales would also be recognized in "the plan." This flaw is also rooted in basic math. The vast majority of all the recruits that would ever join — *the last ones in* — were *prevented* from benefitting from the "cuts." The doomed fate of the majority is demonstrable and predictable even before the first recruits were thrown into the unsustainable, self-destroying folly of relentless recruiting and futile attempts at retailing.[i]

In the "five-get-five" plan, or some similar version of it, which was to become universal in MLMs, each person would theoretically produce a total chain of 3,905 new recruits within the first five recruiting levels. (1 + 5 + 25 + 125 + 625 + 3125 = 3,905) Each would, in theory, get a "cut" on all those below. However, those in the bottom level would get no cut at all because they have no others below them. That bottom level includes 3,125 of the total of 3,905, or 80% of the total. (3,125 ÷ 3,905 = 0.80)

While the bottom level, 80%, could earn no cut at all, the next level consisting of 625, which is another 16% of the total, would also gain nothing or nearly nothing after time and sales costs are factored, because each member of that rank only has five others below. Profit would only begin perhaps at the next level above, in which each would have 30 in their respective "downlines." In the transcendent realm of infinite expansion, imagined and designed

---

[i] Using Mytinger's own example of 10 initial distributors recruiting just two each, producing 20, and so on, simple math reveals the onerous consequences for the majority: The bottom level will always be 50% or more of the total that are ever recruited, denying the total majority the promised benefits, by design. In real terms, not only would the dead-bottom level not get any "cut" but the next several levels would get so little as to be unprofitable, when other costs are factored in, making the true percentage of the plan's losers more than 90% of the total, all "doomed by design."

by Mytinger and Casselberry, 96% or more were doomed to "fail." The profit from "cuts" would be denied them, *by position*. These fatal proportions of "losers" would remain fixed, regardless of how large the recruiting chain would grow, how long it would run, or how many people would join and quit in the duration.

It is likely, though, that Mytinger and Casselberry were not focused on or even concerned with the plight of that 96%. They were far more likely to have been transfixed by the income that could flow to the top level, where they would sit. This fortunate position would have almost 4,000 recruits in just the first five recruiting cycles and then would grow explosively, almost beyond imagination. The 3,125 at the bottom of the fifth cycle could become almost 10 million five cycles later. The planners would have also taken note of the next level below them made up of just five members who would each have almost 800 right from the start, the original "black hat" upliners.

Regardless of the aggregate effort expended and the intensity of hopes that "the plan" would elicit from new recruits, the bottom 96% would never gain a profit from the magical source of benefits — the cut — while the top few percent would become kings, or as they were later to be known, "kingpins."

Mytinger and Casselberry were, of course, designing a novel version, never before seen in the sales world, of the classic pyramid scheme. Using marketplace terminology of commission sales and aiming the plan at people who might seek an income from selling goods, "The Plan" amounted to nothing more than an unsustainable money transfer from later participants to the earliest ones. The "money" paid in by later recruits and passed upward would consist of inventory purchases and the value of their time and labor to sell goods and recruit others.

Since the plan destroyed retail sales potential, the greatest and surest contribution to the money-transfer fund would be the recruits' own purchases, making the plan a closed market, the very opposite of a customer-based sales business driven by consumer demand. The incentives offered from recruiting — and then leading to inventory purchases by those who enrolled — would replace the need for retail demand. The salespeople supplied the "demand" but not for products. They would be enticed by the mythical "income opportunity" elevated in meaning and importance as the benefits Mytinger had previously sold in the cemetery field, "a garden that seems next door to Paradise itself, a place of infinite loveliness and eternal peace."

Industrious, in this plan, would mean the *unscrupulous* whose incomes would only be the losses suffered by those later recruited, often close friends and family members.

From Selling to Swindling

As Casselberry and Mytinger secured total control over Nutrilite's sales and marketing in September 1945, Rehnborg's role in the MLM genesis fable was more or less completed as the fated company owner and producer of the product used in the original MLM plan.

"The Plan" was put in place involving the "endless sales chain;" multiple ranks, volume purchase quotas to remain qualified for "cuts;" basing "cuts" on recruits' *purchases*; and the formulation of "commission" payments, so the majority were passed directly upward to the top 1-4%. These elements fit into an integrated, rationalized and camouflaged system that succeeded spectacularly in its goal of enriching Mytinger, Casselbery and Rehnborg.

Insight into the groundbreaking moment when "multi-level marketing" was created requires looking closely where few have explored — the similarities and the boundaries between *selling*, which was the primary bond between Mytinger and Casselberry, and *swindling*, which is what they conspired to create. Mytinger and Casselberry crossed the line from selling — generally defined as voluntary agreements for commercial transactions between parties based on adequately disclosed information and resulting in a reasonably equitable exchange — into swindling, generally defined as calculated deception, withholding of information necessary to a voluntary agreement and — by design — resulting in loss to one or more parties at the hands of the other.

This nexus of sales and sales scam, where Mytinger and Casselberry's new "plan" was born has seemingly been shunned by academia, including law schools or even denied, this despite the obvious similarities to pyramid fraud and the many prosecutions, warnings, and rules that have surrounded the field of "multi-level marketing."

One renowned academic and legal scholar, however, did make precisely such a study. In his 1976 book, *Swindling and Selling*, Yale law professor Arthur Allen Leff parsed the blurry and unexplored boundary. As he explained, all selling is not swindling but "all swindling is selling and ... one can understand much of selling only by seeing it as a response to the same problems of customer resistance faced by professional bunco artists."[94]

Leff identified two specific elements that must be present in all swindling and selling alike. These are the need to show:

1. *an explanation of an external source for the alleged benefit to the customer in a sale or to the "mark" in a swindle; and*

2. *an explanation that that both parties are needed for the supposedly advantageous transaction in which both will benefit by agreeing to do the deal together.*

The external source of reward, whether it is a vast pool of promised money, as in some swindles, or merely a special reduction in price as in a common variety of sales promotions, must be explained. Where does the money or the savings come from and how is it that the salesman or swindler is able to make it available to the sales prospect or mark? No one believes that money is given away for free. In sales, the bargain might be portrayed, for example, as "limited time," implying that the regular prices paid by the unfortunate later buyers provide the funding for the discounts *today's* wise or lucky buyer could enjoy. The salesman is the only person who can offer this special deal now. In a swindle, a similar claim must be established to explain how the swindler is able to make the offer and how the mark benefits financially by getting into the deal with the swindler.

Leff acknowledged that few involved in sales schemes and sales-related swindles "know what they are doing and why they are doing it," a justification he made for writing his book. Selling and its illicit cousin swindling, he explained, have been "almost ostentatiously neglected by almost all scholars in almost all pertinent disciplines ..."[95]

Not coincidentally, his study led him to look specifically into the field of "multi-level marketing" just as it was beginning to explode across America in the late 1960s and 1970s. Leff referred to this new model as "Pyramid Selling," calling it, "America's top swindle." He worked as a consultant to the U. S. Federal Trade Commission, which had just begun to recognize the spread of "MLM" and had begun to prosecute them. This was the period just before the federal government, for political reasons, chose to allow MLMs to operate.

Leff unequivocally defined pyramid selling, aka multi-level marketing, as a swindle and a "big con," (also called a "long con"). He also, however, recognized that MLM's use of purchased products as the mechanism for transferring money and the employment of door-to-door "retail" sales as an identity, placed it on the "borderline between what most people would distinguish as those different realms (of swindling and selling)."[96] In his analysis the two domains appeared nearly identical, making MLM distinct and perhaps unique among frauds, not a sales business engaged in swindling but a swindle engaging in sales.[97]

The close proximity *in appearance* between "direct selling" and the newly invented "pyramid selling" accounts, partially, for how millions of otherwise honest people plunge into the scam and lure friends and family as well. Mytinger and Casselberry's pyramid scheme, launched in the late 1940s, took advantage of exploding needs and hopes of millions of people in post-war America whose lives and livelihoods in the modern era were increasingly defined by sales and marketing. Those needs and hopes have not diminished and the defining imprint of sales and marketing has only become stronger, swelling the "market" for MLM recruits decade after decade.

As Leff noted, in swindling — as in selling too, but more important in the swindle —the swindler needs to show that he needs the "mark" in order to gain a benefit for himself. He cannot just claim to already have access to funds that he could enjoy on his own but capriciously chooses to share. He must also show that the mark's participation is necessary for his own benefit and *for the mark's*. In selling, the benefits to the seller are often self-evident, but the rationale for offering a discount or a bargain must be declared by the seller so the seller is shown to be benefitting even while reducing his own profit.

The pyramid selling scheme Mytinger and Casselberry invented promised a stupendous benefit to the mark, the potential of "unlimited" income to each and every new recruit, but this "unique" income opportunity is presented as a joint benefit to the recruiter and the person recruited. Each solicitation is therefore not just a proposition to buy, but also to join the recruiting chain. Mutual benefit gained from the transaction is firmly established, or at least appears so.

There must also be a plausible explanation for how such a benefit is possible. In MLM, the reward to the recruit for paying to join and recruiting others to do the same is described as potential wealth of such plenty that it makes ordinary salaries look like wage slavery. It is said to be not only "unlimited" in volume, but also "perpetual" in duration.

Only when the actual identity and source of MLM's promised cornucopia – where the money comes from – is discovered can the insidious swindling nature of multi-level marketing become clear and obvious. In the swindle, the reward is never delivered. The swindler does not have it to give. It does not exist, and so too, as will be shown, in MLM.

Ponzi's Triumph

In 1920, the world learned of a financial fraud run by its namesake, Charles Ponzi. Ponzi was eventually arrested, imprisoned and then deported, and the "mechanics" of his scheme were widely publicized. Ponzi's "profits" were not actually profits at all, as prosecutors revealed, making his entire "investment" enterprise a swindle.

The claim of returns of 50% every 90 days came merely from later investors' funds deceptively transferred to earlier ones. His plan, which appeared to his investors to be valid and trustworthy, was destined to fail his investors from an inevitable point when he could no longer find enough new investors, or if existing investors in large numbers withdrew their investment capital that was being depleted by his payouts. In the interim, before the reality would be revealed, the investors lived with the happy delusion that they had discovered a secure and lucrative opportunity, a deal of a lifetime.

Ponzi deceitfully claimed that the extraordinary profits came from the purchase and resale of international postage coupons. He said he was ingeniously leveraging differences in currency values among countries, yielding a great profit margin on behalf of the investors. In fact, he did not do any such trades, at least that have been recorded. But his claim to be making highly profitable postage coupon trades provided the alleged source of the benefits for his investors.

By claiming he was a trader of these coupons, he made the case that he needed the investors to supply him with funds to make the lucrative trades. He benefited from using investors' funds, while they benefited from his specialized trading knowledge and expertise. Mutual need was established for mutual benefit and an external source for the benefit was provided. The basic requirements for a sale or for a swindle, as explained by Arthur Leff, were met. Even more pertinent to Leff's analysis, Ponzi had found a wellspring of money enabling him to operate the scam: the investors' own funds. Payments delivered as promised at the beginning drew in flocks of excited new investors, extending the life of the scam. The awesome power of the "endless chain" money transfer was demonstrated, sparking a mania of excitement and hope.

When the Ponzi hoax occurred in Boston in 1920, Census records show that Lee Mytinger was living in Brooklyn, New York, and working as an "accountant." He was 25 years old and married. It would have been difficult for him, especially as an accountant, not to hear about the scam. Ponzi's outrageous claims to offer Wall Street-sized profits to his Main Street investors struck a chord in America, where popular resentment against the wealthy was rivaled only by envy. Mytinger later lived in Maine, and likely knew about Charles Ponzi's trials and eventual imprisonment in Massachusetts.

The mysteries of capital gains, margin lending, compound interest and dividends, available to "preferred" shareholders and the elite, were now opening up to the benefit of the laboring masses, Ponzi seemed to claim. His assertions were bolstered by the support he gained from at least one major newspaper. Several local banks backed his scheme and managed his funds. And, mirroring the power of wealth itself, regardless of its source, Ponzi's vast fund, about one-quarter billion in today's currency, caused many to believe it was legitimate on its face. In truth, few on Main Street USA understood how any of the established rich and powerful in America gained their fortunes. The sheer scale of their fortunes exceeded the experience, understanding, or imagination of most people who typically subsisted month to month. Ponzi's sudden and enormous financial success therefore provoked no special suspicions among his investors, only awe. Further, month after month, Ponzi did indeed fulfill his promise to pay the extraordinary returns to his investors, *using their own money.*

As to where Ponzi himself came up with the idea of his now iconic fraud, biographer Mitchell Zuckoff connects the scheme to an earlier experience Ponzi had working as a bank manager in Montreal in 1907.[98] The bank owner, Louis Zarossi, was found to be operating a "robbing Peter to pay Paul" fraud. He used customers' funds intended to be sent back to Italy to their families as the source for paying out coveted higher interest rates on customer savings. The normal rate paid on savings accounts was 2%. Zarossi announced he would pay 6% and customers flocked to his bank. To make up the difference, he began tapping into the money his customers entrusted the bank to send to families in Italy. Zarossi expected enough of a time interval between funds not arriving in Italy and the local customers making a complaint during which he could refund the "lost" funds with new deposits coming from other customers. Zarossi's scheme was exposed, costing Ponzi his job. Ponzi was investigated for possibly being a part of the swindle.[i]

Even if Charles Ponzi were not inspired by the Zarossi bank fraud of 1908, his work experience in banking might have also provided some basis for his own scam. Banks routinely and legally make loans in excess of the total funds on hand. They back their loans with funds that amount to only a fraction of what they loan out. Banks' sustainability depends, as did Zarossi's and Ponzi's, on a time factor and other contingencies. Banks rely on depositors not seeking withdrawals in large numbers, and the margin of reserves needed for expected withdrawals and interest

---

[i] Another possible inspiration was Charles Ponzi's chance meeting with Charles W. Morse, whose fraudulent scheme to take over a sector of industry is cited as one of the triggers setting off the financial panic on Wall Street in 1907. In January 1910, Morse was convicted of misappropriating bank funds and began his sentence at the federal prison in Atlanta. Ponzi was at the same prison at this same time, serving a two-year sentence for sponsoring illegal immigrants. See Bruner, Robert F., *The Panic of 1907* (p. 183). Wiley. Kindle Edition.

payments being always replenished by current or new depositors. The system also depends on the expected ability of debtors to repay their bank loans. If a large number of loans were not repaid, the bank would collapse as it would in the face of large or sudden withdrawals. At all times, loans are not secured with full cash and all depositors' cash is not actually available. The ever-astute Charles Ponzi, as a bank manager, may have observed that banks legally rob Peter (a margin of deposit funds they don't actually possess) to pay Paul (interest payments and profit-making loans). Though some economists consider the model unsustainable and unfair, it is the predominant legal form of banking across the world.[99]

For his 1920 scheme, Ponzi was never charged by federal authorities for operating a "robbing Peter to pay Paul" scam. He was arguably the first financier to operate such a scheme at this scale. Lacking a clearly defined violation of existing law, federal authorities found evidence that he had used the postal service in a deceptive manner. The charges were minor against the scale of his scheme but sufficient to destroy public confidence. Ponzi was forced to plead guilty, leading to several years in federal prison. But on his release, the state of Massachusetts brought "larceny" charges against him, which required more direct proof that his investment proposition, which he advertised as the "Ponzi Plan," really was a fraud. Ponzi could not afford legal representation and he was not an attorney. He represented himself. A jury of his peers found Charles Ponzi innocent on all counts. The state brought a second trial, resulting in a hung jury. He was finally found guilty only when the state persisted with a third trial.

Whatever else the Ponzi prosecution disclosed about a new type of financial fraud, the larger revelation was about the minds of its victims and the response of the public at large, including some jurors. Ponzi's proposition of lucrative and unending returns both captivated and confounded the public's imagination.

Ponzi had found an external source of wealth that he could promise to his investors, and in fact deliver for a time. As Arthur Leff explained, all successful sales and swindles must be able to explain the source of the benefit being offered. The money for current investors, as the authorities sought to explain to the public, was an illusion. Overall, it was merely a portion of the investors' own money being returned to some of them as illusory "profit." The inherent fraudulence of such a transfer plan seemed to elude many people.

Proof of the cultural influence of Ponzi's new form of profit-making — transferring funds from later investors to earlier ones in an "endless chain" — is undeniably demonstrated in the many new opportunities and venues for this same fraud today. Bernard Madoff's fraudulent "hedge" fund was essentially a carbon copy of Ponzi's 1920 scheme, except that Madoff claimed to be trading Wall Street stocks using a secret strategy called "split strike conversion." In fact, just like Ponzi, he was not making any trades at all, just transferring money from later investors to earlier ones. The "payments" were coming from the investors' own funds in aggregate. Madoff's Wall Street Ponzi, 80 years later, was able to draw in professionally managed pension funds, large institutional investors, and his own friends and family members.

Reflecting the gathering momentum of Ponzi's influence, Madoff's fraud continued to operate for 15 years. In his book, *The Ponzi Factor: The Simple Truth About Investment Profits*, author Tan Liu *debunks the widely held misconception that Ponzi schemes are inherently short term.* Liu persuasively argues that much of the stock market today is defined and characterized by what he calls the "Ponzi Factor," an internal money transfer model, disconnected from true profits gained in the external marketplace. Share price depends on continuous infusion from later investors.[100] Liu notes that many of the highest valued stocks, such as Tesla, have no recorded profits at all. Many stocks, even when they are exceptionally profitable, such as Facebook and Warren Buffett's fund, do not share the profits in dividends distributed to shareholders.

Madoff's scheme was better executed than Ponzi's but was still vulnerable to the threat of sudden and significant withdrawals. When the overall stock market crashed along with real estate values in 2008, many of Madoff's investors suddenly needed cash and asked for withdrawals, prompting the scheme's exposure and collapse. Madoff's alleged source of funds, ingenious stock trading, was invented. It was as financially impossible for Madoff to have delivered consistent, above average returns from making actual trades in the stock market year after year as it was for Ponzi to pay 50% quarterly from trading postage coupons.

It was later revealed that, even if Madoff operated his fraudulent "hedge" fund entirely by himself, many of his peers and colleagues on Wall Street facilitated the fraud with their complicit silence, rationalizing that exposure might shake confidence in the entire financial system. Ponzi's legacy extended to the wider securities market presumed to be legitimate.

As for law enforcement against the Ponzi phenomenon, many, such as writer Matt Taibbi, who exhaustively researched the scandal, conclude, inescapably, that the SEC must have known Madoff was operating a Ponzi scheme, or at least an insider trading fraud. Many now believe the SEC bowed to institutional and political forces, purposefully ignoring the massive fraud for fear of triggering a wider panic.[101] Whereas authorities relentlessly pursued Ponzi once his fraud was suspected, now regulators, many believe, had become integral to cover-up.[102]

Ponzis and Pigeons

While getting much less attention, the Ponzi phenomenon on Main Street, including small and rural communities, is expanding as calculated frauds and as desperate speculation such as real estate "flipping," lottery ticket buying, day trading stocks, gold and silver trading, and crypto-currency buying. One of the more tragic and illustrative instances was the "Pigeon King" Ponzi that ravaged family farms in Canada and northwest USA in the early 2000s.

Canadian businessman Arlan Galbraith began selling breeding pigeons and offering to buy back the offspring. With his plan's legitimacy seemingly upheld by authorities, Galbraith's offer was seen as too good to pass up by small farmers struggling to survive selling poultry and pigs. Though the price Galbraith charged for breeder pigeons was as much as $500 a pair, he contracted to pay $50 per offspring. Within a year, the entire initial investment in breeders could be nearly recouped, with later years' operations yielding almost 100% profit. Galbraith was hailed as the farmers' salvation.

Excited farmers took the proposition to local banks for loans to buy in, putting up farmlands and buildings as collateral. Bankers looked no further than the prices paid by the farmers for breeder pairs and contract prices Galbraith would pay for the offspring. Galbraith's plan, "Pigeon King International" spread across Canada like a mania and started also to enter the USA. One "salesperson" for Galbraith personally brought in more than 100 farmers. Some farmers unwittingly lured neighbors and family into the swindle. Contractual long term obligations of Pigeon King were exceeding a billion dollars.

Galbraith's plan, like "the plan" of the inventors of multi-level marketing had the same lethal flaw. The business was not based on market demand for the products, pigeons in his case. Rather, it depended on an "endless chain" of new investor-breeders. Where was Galbraith getting funds to buy back the newly bred pigeons at such high prices? Bankers did not ask that question, just as few have asked where MLM gets its funds to pay "unlimited income" to its "endless chain" of recruits. Canada's Competition Bureau, equivalent to the FTC in the U. S., which regulates business opportunity schemes, apparently saw no cause for inquiry into the Galbraith's amazing income offer.

Ontario-based freelance fraud investigator, David Thornton, publisher of *CrimeBustersNow.com*, immediately saw the implausibility of the scheme. He began calling out "Pigeon King" as a Ponzi scheme. He warned banks and farmers of the flawed business model. He called on Galbraith to reveal his external market for the multitude of pigeons he was contractually bound to buy. He also alerted Canada's Competition Bureau. Thornton was threatened with lawsuits by Galbraith and called a fear-monger by farmers. He was dismissed by the news media, and ignored by Canadian law enforcement.[103]

His questions finally led to a news investigation not from Canada's news media but *Better Farming*, a small trade magazine. Mainstream news inquiries then followed. As became evident, Arlan Galbraith had no market for pigeons. The money to pay "returns" came from one place – from the investment money of the later farmers. Every new breeder/investor generated the absolute need for many more breeders in order for Galbraith to pay for their pigeon offspring. Meanwhile, the total number of pigeons being bred was multiplying exponentially.

Tragically, when the plan collapsed, the farmers were financially ruined with some suffering foreclosure by the banks. Millions of pigeons faced starvation. Having a true market value of about $2 each, many were gassed or just released. Television news scenes of farmers personally wringing the necks of hundreds of pigeons serve as an unforgettable metaphor for the inevitable outcome the "last ones in." It also revealed the irrelevance of "products" and other props used as money transfer vehicles in pyramids and Ponzis.

In December 2013, five years after he declared "bankruptcy," Galbraith was sentenced to seven and a half years in prison for fraud.[104] In July 2016, a loophole was found in Canadian law enabling Galbraith an early a parole release.[105]

As Arthur Leff argued, the newly invented "industry" of multi-level marketing, now raking in as much as $30 billion a year from a churning base of as many as 20 million U.S. households, is the direct descendant of the original Ponzi scheme, with minor mutations, as are all the various Ponzi formats in stocks, pigeons, and mortgages. The 2008 banking collapse that destroyed Main Street equity, the Madoff fraud that exposed the rot of Wall Street and pigeon fiasco that wiped out farmers in Canada could be seen as the revenge of convicted and deported Charles Ponzi, and the global MLM phenomenon his triumph.[106]

Salesman's Joke

To whatever degree they were aware of the 1920 Ponzi fraud and its reverberating influence on business practices in later decades, there were powerful lessons offered to Mytinger and Casselberry in 1943 as they formulated "the plan" for Nutrilite. Not the least of the lessons was a popular belief gripping America's imagination: a business model actually existed, somewhere, that was capable of producing perpetual and extraordinary income for all participants, delivering to the common man what was once available to only the elite, thus fulfilling the promise of the American Dream.

It was clear that such a plan could provoke a national mania in which tens of thousands of people will throw their money and hope into it with virtually no due diligence. Most people do not grasp, or are *willfully blind* to, the mathematical trick in the endless expansion model, which Mytinger understood well when he made it the mainstay of his new Nutrilite sales "incentive." The capacity of the endless chain scheme to escape discovery was demonstrated when, even when Ponzi's fraud was exposed, many of the victims blamed the government, banks, and Wall Street elites for the collapse, while continuing to hold Ponzi innocent and maintain faith in the scheme's promise of wondrous returns.

In the official account of "the plan" to convert Nutrilite into the first "multi-level marketing" business no provision was made by Mytinger and Casselberry to conceal the factor of unsustainable, impossible expansion. No cover story was invented such as postal coupon trades as Ponzi had concocted for an external funding source. Between Mytinger and Casselberry, and later to millions of new recruits, the mathematical impossibility of the Nutrilite plan would be openly acknowledged. *Each new investor's profit would always come from future level's investments and expenditures, to be called "teams" or "downline." Aggregately, most or all "commissions" — the only possible source of profit — would come from the salespeople's own investments in the form of some sales and, most important, their own product purchases and fees paid to participate.*

Far from concealed, the inherent implausibility of Mytinger and Casselberry's plan and the financial harm it would cause were treated merely as a *salesman's joke*, as related in Rehnborg's biography when Mytinger explained it to Casselberry. Gained from the cruelest of economic schools, door-to-door cemetery plot sales, the "joke" reflected their mutual understanding that in sales there is *always* inside information not available to the customer or the public at large. No matter how lowly, every salesman carries this information as his power, his payback for the rejections and disrespect he endures.

Without having examined the sales "dramaturgy," or dissected the role-playing as Yale Professor, Arthur Leff would do 20 years later, both men fully understood that the benefits promised by the salesman, whether in exaggerations of qualities or attributes related to the product or in some other aspect of the sales promotion, are mostly a chimera. The external source of reward, facilitating the "bargain," and the narrative about mutual need and mutual benefit if the deal is done, are just part of a carefully directed and contrived tale. The customer's belief that that they are making rational decisions is, the salesman knows, mostly an illusion. In reality, the salesman makes it happen with information he does not share. The salesman's joke, therefore, is always on those who are not in possession of that key information and who can be directed, even controlled, by scripted promises, logic and benefits. This is the universal secret knowledge salespeople hold, the tools of their trade.

In sales management ranks where the battle-weary Mytinger had worked so many years, the inside joke is first played upon hapless new salespeople whose labor and expenditures are key to the manager's profit. Part of this trickery is to divert the new salesperson by telling him of the great profit he will gain by carrying out this same type of subterfuge on his customers.

During the recruiting and training process and in the early stages of work, freshmen salespeople do not know about their future sales costs, time requirements, the actual value of "leads," if there is any, (dramatized in David Mamet's play and film, *Glengarry Glen Ross*), how the commission schedule pays out in practice after time and costs. They don't even know the truth about product they try to sell. They can be maneuvered to expend time and resources that profit their managers with little or no benefit to themselves, to work through sales leads that may provide minimal profit opportunity, but carry costs managers cleverly transfer to their own accounts. The salespeople, especially the newest ones, can be directed to say things about the products that may be blatantly false but which, when exposed, only the lowly salesperson will be held accountable for telling the customer.

In the Casselberry-Mytinger discussion, the electrifying hope that a Ponzi expansion and transfer plan would ignite among unwitting new sales recruits, giving them all the apparent chance to become "kingpins," is deeply appreciated. Indeed, its wondrous benefits were the stuff of Mytinger's own fantasy based on a lifetime of frustrating, inconsistent and, for the most part, barely profitable sales work. He would know that his own hopes and fantasy would be shared by every other salesperson who ever knocked on a door. The promise of unending expansion and unlimited profit was told as a "joke" by Mytinger because he knew that those who got excited by the promise would be those who did not realize its impossibility or ultimate consequences.

In 1943 to 1945, when Mytinger and Casselberry sold Rehnborg on "the plan," Nutrilite remained marginal, barely surviving. Rehnborg appears to have little to do with the formulation

other than to buy into its potential for vastly expanding production of his potions. He may be viewed, historically, as the first
person to be sold an MLM endless chain proposition. In his case,
he would be the "first one in," guaranteed to be rewarded. He
will be followed by legions of losers — brunts of the salesman's
joke — from whose losses he ultimately benefited. They would
become the proverbial last-ones-in, destined to lose.

Conning Friends and Family

Charles Ponzi exhilarated thousands who initially invested their savings with him and millions of others who only heard about it.[i] Then Ponzi became a legendary villain, thrown in jail and later deported. Ponzi's plan had a major flaw that led to exposure.[107]

There was one element of Ponzi's venture, however, that was thoroughly repugnant even to those who longed for his income promises to be true. It was that he had solicited or accepted funds from personal associates who lost it all when his plan imploded. This revulsion against Ponzi for having cost family and friends their life savings reflected a shared value that certain areas of life were non-commercial, off limits to business, and literally more important than money.

As Arthur Leff explained, among families and social networks, persuasion is fundamental to the viral spread of "pyramid selling," aka, multi-level marketing, resulting in the defrauding of closest associates. Trust and love then become carriers of the toxic proposition, igniting a person-to-person epidemic.

Today, MLM solicitations, presented as personal or even intimate conversations or invitations, are everywhere on the Internet and experienced by virtually everyone almost daily. Who can escape them at family gatherings, in the office, at places of worship, on Facebook, or in the dreaded call, text or email from a nearly forgotten classmate suddenly and inexplicably wanting to "have coffee and catch up?"

---

[i] The long reach of news and excitement about Ponzi's amazing "returns" was historically referenced in the BBC drama, *Downton Abbey*. Lord Grantham considers investing the family fortune with Ponzi. "There's a chap in America, what's his name, Charles Ponzi, who offers a huge return after 90 days." (https://getyarn.io/yarn-clip/97cd631d-3c20-48d3-9f5c-4ee00e29f073)

Somewhere in the 25 years between Ponzi and Nutrilite, the latter of which was to become America's first pyramid scheme operating on a national scale as a chartered sales company, the public aversion toward profiteering on intimate relationships greatly diminished and, for many, ceased to exist at all. Overall reactions to these devious financial intrusions into personal spheres of life — worship, friendship, family — have declined from moral outrage to mere annoyance or grudging tolerance. For many others, there is no longer any boundary at all. Even a funeral is a setting where the rawest human feelings and the deepest blood connections offer special recruiting "opportunity."

Between 1920 and 1945, a cultural phenomenon would be needed to build upon Ponzi's mythical promise of Wall Street profits for Main Street but which also would make the solicitations of money from family and friends permissible and legitimate. Ponzi and all his descendants tapped into a hidden treasure trove among the poor and working classes. It was their own money and that of all their social connections. The Ponzi money transfer mines the collective investments of hundreds of thousands of people and promises the aggregate wealth to each and every person as an "unlimited income." They would be taught to solicit it, as Dale Carnegie instructed, with "a real smile, a heartwarming smile, a smile that comes from within," person to person, among their closest relations, explaining to all how the magic of "exponential expansion" will work for everyone.[108]

Arthur Leff identified two historical phenomena, largely forgotten or diminished in public understanding today, that set the stage for a Ponzi-type swindle based on commercially exploiting intimate and social relationships. Both of these phenomena serve as harbingers and markers of the hurricane social force on the horizon. Both are swindles in their own rights. One is a devious technique specific to direct selling, Mytinger's and Casselberry's shared milieu, and the other was a grassroots delusion that spread like a virus in the heartland of American civil society, in neighborhoods, factories, churches, clubs and offices — captivating the very same people who would later become candidates for Mytinger and Casselberry's newly invented version of "direct selling."

The two phenomena are the money chain letters and referral selling. Each promises great rewards whose bounteous source is not fabricated, like Ponzi's and Madoff's were, but openly acknowledged, and the reward, at least for some, is real, spendable cash. Reward money is to be gained from the expenditures and investments of one's friends and family. Ponzi's need to concoct the bogus income source would be eliminated. The referral selling scheme and the money chain letter mania were bridges from Ponzi to Nutrilite.

Money chain letters preceded the referral selling schemes, though the referral trick may have been in informal use in door-to-door selling before being officially identified and outlawed in the 1960s. The money chain letter exploded in America starting in 1935, when Mytinger was immersed in the cemetery plot industry, traveling between Maine and Southern California. Casselberry had just gained his "doctoral" degree and begun offering counseling services. His book, *How to Use Psychology*, was just a few years from publication. Dale Carnegie's book, which advocates commercial selling techniques to "win" friends, would appear just one year after money chain letters set the country on fire with hope.

In a successful "sale" just as in a workable swindle, the source of the enticing reward or savings must be external, not owned and offered by the swindler or the seller himself, as explained in *Swindling and Selling*. Further, the narrative must explain how the swindler and the victim need each other, that is, why should they enter into a transaction *together*. In Mytinger's plan, the seller offered enrollment in "the plan" that promised "unlimited income." The buyer provided the needed access to his friends and family for recruiting purposes. The ensuing money stream, sourced from those intimate relationships, would supposedly flow upward to the benefit of both recruiter and his mark.

In the midst of America's worst economic downturn, with almost one in four out of work, and thousands of farmers losing their land and livelihood both to foreclosures and a climactic disaster, a mysterious event occurred that promised not merely financial relief but a life-changing windfall for all. It did not come from Roosevelt's New Deal. It did not come from churches that had set up soup kitchens and temporary housing or from any popular political movements that promised to fairly redistribute wealth someday.

From an unknown source, thousands of people suddenly began to receive letters in the mail inviting them to join an amazing plan in which an expenditure of just one dime, $0.10, would quickly and certainly provide a return of more than $1,500. In today's dollars this would be an offer for less than a $2 investment to produce more than $27,000. The people receiving the letters could not know that they were part of an exploding national phenomenon, leaving the impression that fortune had come just to them, fulfilling the American Dream myth that success is always gained individually, not in collective action. Each letter contained the names and addresses of six individuals. The letter instructed the recipient to send $0.10, one dime by mail, to the person at the top of the list, then to take that person's name off the list and add one's own name to the bottom, making the total of six again. The letter was to be copied then with the new list, including the recipients' own name at the bottom and resent to five other people, whom the recipient would know — friends and family — and want to benefit also. The text of the letter explained that as the process continued just five more cycles, the recipient's own name would rise to the top position on the list and at that point

15,625 others would each send a dime, providing the windfall of $1,562.50 arriving in the mail in dime currency.

$$(1 \times 5 \times 5 \times 5 \times 5 \times 5 \times 5 = 15{,}625) \times (\$0.10) = \$1{,}562.50$$

Historians believe the "send a dime" money chain letter originated in or near Denver, Colorado, also the first place where news articles reported the strange occurrence and where the postal inspector quickly issued warnings that it was a fraud. The warnings were not heeded. To the contrary, the letters — and perhaps the government warnings played a part also — ignited a mania, spreading across the country. Millions of people soon joined in the hope and faith that financial deliverance had arrived. When the mania subsided, the U.S. Postal Service reportedly was left with 2–3 million letters in its dead letter office.[109] The volume of mail that wound up in the government's dead letter office increased as much as 1,500% during the craze. Up to 200 letters a day were mailed to President Franklin D. Roosevelt.[110]

Six years into the deepest period of economic depression in American history, few established institutions held any popular credibility, causing people to take the mysterious chain letter seriously and enabling the money-chain letter to escape common-sense analysis. The mania also gained validity from firmly held beliefs, even if never consciously examined, such as faith in the American Dream and the widely held notion that positive thinking can manifest prosperity. The arrival of these letters seemed to many the fulfillment of their hopes. The chain letter's anonymous and mysterious origins seemingly added to its authenticity.

Though few people today know the details, background, or scale of the send-a-dime mania, and it is seldom included as part of America's economic history, almost everyone has heard of chain letters. They have largely disappeared in their earlier formats but they left an enormous imprint on the public, made indelible by the time of Depression hardship in which they occurred and the intensity of hope they aroused.

A review of the chain letter hysteria in the late 1930s reveals where major elements of Mytinger and Casselberry's new plan could have originated, almost as a rehearsal for formalizing the chain letter into a durable commercial format. "The Plan" they would invent would also have the friends and family as prime recruiting prospects and require a payment to participate (much more than a dime). It would add the feature of *continued* payments. Like the chain letters, "the plan" would make an astonishing and electrifying income promise based entirely on expanding, multiple "levels" of new people also joining and paying and bringing in others to do the same. A key difference, which satisfied Mytinger's desire to "keep the income from the people I develop" and never lose "his cut of the man's sales," would be that the person's name on the top, as long as that person kept paying, would *never be taken off*. New people could lengthen and expand the chain forever, and for as long as they kept paying, the "cuts" would keep flowing upward.

Daniel W. VanArsdale, a retired mathematician and self-described amateur folklorist, recently assembled a history of this strange and largely forgotten chapter in Main Street economics. His enormous archive of records of the chain letter movement is referenced as an authority on the subject by the well-respected Snopes.com resource for authenticating or debunking popular claims and beliefs.[111] VanArdsdale describes the public response following government warnings against participation.

He documented how mailmen could hardly bear the weight of a massive increase in letters, each containing a dime. The seemingly spontaneous event was quickly organized into commercial enterprises to increase the financial returns while also creating new ways to financially profit from the delusion. Movie theaters attracted viewers by offering send-a-dime forms. "Chain letter factories" appeared, he reported, "that supplied cheap printed forms ... and often the services of typists and notaries." His research details how, under warnings by state and federal law enforcement, the chain letter also evolved to evade postal laws.

VanArdsdale's tracking of the send-a-dime frenzy shows the direct line leading from the anonymous chain letter phenomenon into related commercial pyramid schemes. The income opportunity, represented by the official letter, were "sold." Purchasing the letter, rather than just accepting one for free in the mail, actually added authenticity. Selling the letter further validated the sense of legitimately creating a viable "return." The absurdity of the endless chain proposition was covered over in seemingly legitimate steps that mimicked the real marketplace, promising to lead, somehow, to extraordinary returns of the scale often reported in the stock market among the moneyed elite.

The developments in the chain letter mania of 1935 are an eerie precursor to Mytinger and Casselberry's plan concocted just eight years later. After signing up and buying required products, Nutrilite "distributors" would then be "authorized" to recoup initial investments by recruiting other "distributors" who would join "the plan" and buy products, with the potential of returns being generated by thousands of more recruits, perhaps millions in successive "levels." What was made to look like a normal direct selling business in truth was a payment scheme entitling the participants to get in on the *main chance* of "unlimited income" based on the "endless chain."

The send-a-dime craze, brief as it was, showed the inevitable direction the "friends and family" pyramid scheme would take of formalizing into businesses. The price soon escalated from dimes to dollars and the promised returns catapulted proportionately. Makeshift "factories" emerged during the episode, adding efficiency and organization to what began spontaneously and spread virally. A Cincinnati, Ohio, newspaper during this time reported police closing down one such chain letter "factory" whose operator claimed to employ 125 people.[112]

VanArdsdale shows that although the send-a-dime program withered quickly under government threats, negative news, and the plain realities that few people ever actually gained any benefits, the chain letter phenomenon did not disappear but rather proliferated and evolved into new forms. He directly connects the send a dime scheme to the first "gifting schemes," appearing in 1978 and continuing through the present time in which hundreds of these schemes have spread across the country and other nations as well, enrolling millions of people, far more than ever joined in the chain letter outbreak of the mid-1930s. The "gifting schemes" are a non-business pyramid scheme phenomenon operating as a close relative to the hundreds of "multi-level marketing" companies that also emerged after 1979.[ii]

The chain letter mania reinforced the dark truth — on a much vaster scale — that the trick of "exponential expansion" had enormous potential for swindlers. Most of the original money-chain letters included the electrifying figure of $1,562.50 that would come back to the senders. Did people understand the absurdity of this proposition or the math behind it? In hindsight and considering that the money chain letter lives on as "gifting schemes" and other iterations, and continues to vex and dupe millions of people, it is apparent that few people did understand the realities of the chain letter math. As designed, only one out every 15,625

[ii] The 1978 "Circle of Gold" scam has been followed by scores of others. It was in one of the earlier ones, called the "Airplane Game," that I had my first and fateful encounter with pyramid schemes and led to my writing the book, *False Profits*, published in 1997. All of these may be called "person to person" chain letters that do not use the mail. All of them today are generally referenced as "gifting schemes," all essentially identical, distinguished only by different names and occasionally by minor variations in structure or dollar amounts. More than 30 states have issued warnings or have prosecuted Gifting Schemes. See https://pyramidschemealert.org/gifting-schemes/

could possibly be compensated. These long odds were multiplied to even greater absurdity by the preposterous condition that everyone would faithfully follow the instructions through five successive mailings. Even one break in the chain reduced the reward significantly. Yet millions participated and banked lifelong hopes in it.

The letters of 1935, just as in the "gifting" and "multi-level marketing" schemes that were its legacy, adeptly play upon this blind spot in popular consciousness and awareness. Behind all the various money chain letter formats that were invented was the same illusory source for the promised rewards. It was as close and real as your own family and next-door neighbors. Their money would be your gain. As *Ponzinomics* evolved, critical judgment was not only diverted but would be banished by dogmas, values and specialized language, pretenses of a viable and beneficial economic model. The national chain letter hysteria confirmed that almost no one understood the fraudulent proposition behind the belief system and its dire consequences. It also formally broke the barrier of commercializing "friends and family." Ponzi's sin was pardoned. Now, everybody was doing it.

On the foundations of door-to-door sales deceptions honed in the cemetery plot business, Ponzi's famous fraud, and the national chain letter delusion, the new Nutrilite emerged. It would sell vitamins but its true product was a hyper-commercialized parody of "success," reserved only for a few at the top while held out to all seekers as a fulfillment of the American Dream. Hidden beneath its garb of economic pretenses and "direct selling" identity was a monstrously distorted anatomy. Only by removing the disguise and dissecting that anatomy — as undertaken in the next chapter — can the ugly reality be made plain.

Anatomy of a Pyramid Scheme

Just a Few Questions

On a regular basis, confused and frustrated reporters who have examined MLM for an assigned story call on me for quotes but mostly to help them understand the business. Despite years of examining various industries and with college or advanced education they confess they just don't understand what they have seen. Outwardly, MLM looks like a sales company, they admit. There are products, purchases, commissions and profit margins. Yet, they cannot grasp fundamentals, such as who sells the products and who the customers are; how the demand for the products is generated; and, most confusingly, how they pay rewards. The "compensation plan," they note, is particularly unfathomable, a jumble of quotas, ranks, rules, percentages, all with bizarre and theatrical titles. They just have a few questions for me, they all say, not realizing those question will lead to answers they cannot print.

I always begin my analysis by trying to turn their confusion into the most important fact to report: If seasoned, well-educated journalists can't figure out MLM, what chance does an ordinary consumer have? I remind them, maybe too early in the conversation, that such confusing terms and details are the classic hallmarks of flimflam, scams and sophisticated cons.

They all tell me the same story — an online search turned up scores of websites promising independent reviews and analysis or even warnings about MLMs. But following these links led only to promotions and solicitations. Many sites are click-baits or bots. Other sites are unabashed enrollment pitches with over-the-top praise, excitement and ridiculous claims of income. In confusion and frustration, some reporters tell me, just for a moment, they themselves wondered if MLM might be good to join, given their own pay and job insecurity.

A multi-million dollar enterprise with millions of salespeople, a business so popular it is all over social media, yet there is almost nothing useful for due diligence or research purposes on it on the internet, nothing in the business press and nothing about it from government sources? Reporters are assigned by their editors to report on whether certain companies are "legitimate MLMs" or pyramids (or at least show people how to tell the difference). Their searches eventually turn up my website, *Pyramid Scheme Alert*, or a news story about some MLM in which I am quoted.

Here we go again, Groundhog Day for me. "What is the difference between 'MLM' and a pyramid scheme?" they all want to know.

I begin the analysis, a dissection of the MLM anatomy, starting not with a question but by pointing out the reporters' own research experiences: whatever MLM is, you can't know it until you have removed the outer costume, the hype, the claims and presentations, which are demonstrably useless or misleading. Relying on that outer costume, you cannot possibly understand it. And none of those millions of consumers who did rely on those presentations understood it when they signed up and paid.

As for the pay plan the reporters tried and failed to calculate, they could not possibly understand it. No one could. There are far too many variables, each affecting the others. Without systematic study it is beyond comprehension. But even then, the only way you could actually understand how it works out in practice is to join. That way, you would see how the all the variables interact *from experience*. But then it is too late.

I make a feeble stab at ironic humor on the pyramid question. To answer the question about the difference between MLM and a pyramid scheme, I ask the reporters to first define "MLM," the subject of their story? A pyramid scheme, robbing Peter to pay Paul, with unsustainable expansion, is understandable. But they asked me to distinguish MLM from a pyramid scheme. So, I ask them, please, explain what they mean by "MLM."

Silence, then a realization: OMG. The reporters actually do not know exactly what MLM is. A type of direct selling, right? You sell and you recruit a team to sell, right? *Do* they sell, I ask? And aren't they recruiting their own competitors for sales? Have they ever seen any MLMers selling? Why would anyone need a personal salesperson for skin cream? Ever bought something from a MLM "salesperson" without also being recruited to *become* a salesperson for the scheme? No. No. All have been recruited directly and online various times. It always felt weird and sleazy.

I point out that they did not realize that they did not know what MLM is until after I asked. They just *thought* they knew. Like millions of others, if they enrolled, they would have joined a business they couldn't explain and with pay plan they didn't understand. That's how it works for everybody. So let's first define MLM, and then we can compare, I say. This won't take long, I promise. *Great!*

> *Spoiler alert*: Despite the reporters' initial excitement at finally unravelling the mystery of MLM, the stories that are later published do not address the startling fact that what the reporters thought MLM is was only a vague and erroneous notion, not based on facts. The stories that are published in my Groundhog Day experiences do not say that the MLM pay plan, the key to its claim of "unlimited income," is unfathomable and anyone signing up for "income" cannot possibly know what they are getting into. To have written that people have either no clue how MLM works or have a wrong impression of what MLM is would reveal MLM as a massive and carefully-set consumer trap, causing tens of billions in losses each year due to deception or at least to key facts being purposefully withheld. It might mean a dis-information or cover-up by the MLM industry, ignored, perhaps deliberately, by law enforcement.

I plunge on. I say, MLM's financial proposition cannot be understood without accurately *defining* it, which requires separating it into defining parts. Then, the truth becomes obvious, in plain sight. This is not rocket science. But its obviousness is also why MLM promoters use extreme persuasion and diversion measures of emotion, fear and utopian promises. It's why the reporters encountered the fake websites and false testimonials — to prevent a deeper examination. But I get ahead of myself. I walk the reporters through the defining elements of what is called "multi-level marketing." There are only four.

1. Endless Chain

Everyone knows, in theory, an endless recruiting chain, with each level larger than the one before is mathematically impossible and unsustainable. With each person recruiting just 5 others, the earth's population is exceeded after just 13 levels. Markets are limited. There are only so many people to sign up. That obvious fact dooms most to lose because most are always at the bottom. If one person recruits five who recruit twenty-five who recruit one hundred twenty-five, etc., the bottom levels will always be over 80% of the total and that percent never appreciably changes even if the chain grew to one hundred twenty-five *million*. Last-ones-in *always* lose and they are *always* the vast majority.

So, how could MLM operate with such a defining structure? All of them do. That is how they promise "unlimited income." Some have as many as 12 or more defined ranks or levels. And always, the last person to join can recruit an endless number of more salespeople, *ad infinitum*. What would be the "sales" purpose for such an impossible structure? For management? An entire country can be easily managed with three management levels with one or just a few people in each position — national, regional, district — overseeing the local sales force. Is there not some limit to the number of salespeople an area can bear or needs? The reporters agree that MLMs are defined — uniquely — by their endless recruiting chain of salespeople in which everyone is also a recruiter/manager and there is no level that is defined only as "sales," without also being authorized to *recruit*. We agree from a sales and management perspective this seems to make no sense, and nearly all that join have to lose *based on their position*.

2. Pay to Play

We observe that to work in an MLM as a sales contractor, you have to pay an enrollment fee. Then, to benefit from the bonuses flowing up to you from your recruits, you have to keep paying — buying a quota of stuff monthly. But, why? You are not told where you are on the chain or how many others are already operating in your area or have ever joined before you. You have no protected territory. You cannot use media advertising. You don't have the benefit of company advertising or sales leads. The company keeps adding more and more salespeople in your area and encouraging you to recruit your own competitors. You cost the company nothing. You pay for marketing materials, fees for motivation events, even business cards. On the other hand, you have severe restrictions under the MLM contract you must sign when you first enroll. You can't recruit for several MLMs at the same time. You can't even criticize the company or its products. You can't sell your products on eBay or in a store. You can't participate in a class action suit. Yet, all MLMs require payment to join, payment to renew and quotas of purchases or recruiting or both to gain overrides on your own recruits.

The reporters agree that from a business perspective, required payments and quota purchases seem unjustified and would likely result in many people soon quitting, under the burden of monthly costs, if they were not successful in recruiting enough people. And, we already figured out that it is mathematically impossible for the majority to be successful recruiters.

3. Recruiting Mandate

No one needs a Ph.D. to know this one. All recruits figure this out in a matter of days. To gain the promised income in MLM, you have to recruit. Selling door-to-door at a marked-up retail price is absurd in the era of eBay, Amazon and Costco. Selling online when thousands of others are selling the same products at the same pricing is similarly fruitless. Trying to develop customers while the company keeps adding competitors and offering your customers the wholesale price as "preferred customer" or "discount buyer," is also absurd. MLM is "direct selling" in name only. In reality it is all about recruiting. The people on the stage at motivation events that make the big bucks are not door-to-door salespeople, but black hat, top gun recruiters.

The reporters agree that if you don't recruit, you don't make money. The endless chain income proposition only makes sense if you are a recruiter. The exponential math (5 recruit 25 who recruit 125 who recruit 625, etc.) that is shown during the presentation only works if you recruit the first five and all of them do too. And, we had already figured out that it is mathematically impossible for everyone to recruit more people. From a business perspective, we also had already figured out that required payments seemed unjustified and would likely result in many people soon quitting, under the burden of monthly costs.

4. Extreme Money Transfer from Bottom to Top

And then we come to the defining element of MLM that caused the reporters not only confusion but also momentarily inclined them away from hard facts and toward MLM's dream-visions and fake-testimonials of happiness and wealth. This defining element dumfounds and diverts new recruits. It involves the incomprehensible pay formula with its charts and rates, titles, rules, points. In John Oliver's famous exposé of

MLM on HBO, he played an actual — and typical — video clip of a slick MLM promoter explaining how extraordinary and "simple" the pay plan is. Within three sentences the listener is lost in complexity and incomprehensible variables. This guile of claiming simplicity of something hopelessly complicated is to get the listener to abandon due diligence and just accept the wondrous assurances of the promoter, without understanding anything. *He said it is simple, so it must be my fault for not under-standing the explanation.*

But, here's the thing, I assure the reporters: you don't need to go through that torture or fall for the diversion. Right on the surface and without need of algebra, the most significant aspect of the MLM recruiting pay formula is visible and un-derstandable. The formula, I remind them, is only based on overrides gained from having recruited a "downline" and we already determined that recruiting is the only actual way to make money. In MLM, "sales" means recruiting; retail means wholesale, the price paid by the "downliner;" and, since ev-eryone on the chain must meet a purchase quota, salesperson means buyer. Got it? I further remind the reporters that we had already determined that the pyramid structure always places the majority at the bottom. This is all in plain view or can be figured out pretty quickly.

Just beyond the pyramid shape of the plan in which the great majority of recruits are positioned at the end of the chain, and before you get to all those rules, quotas and ranks there is a ba-sic calculation. It's simple arithmetic. It is the allocation of "com-mission" rates to each level. Just add them up and you will im-mediately see that the pay plan designates that the lower level recruiters — the majority — benefit the least when and if they do make a "sale." The reward plan for "sales" has been turned upside-down. So not only are most people in the bottom, where they have little or no "downline," and therefore little or no income, but even when individuals do recruit some others, they still won't make a profit. The money they might have gained is transferred to the upper levels *in extreme.*

This payout formula, unique to MLM as is its "endless chain" of salespeople, contradicts all conventional sales compensation plans. In real sales businesses, the highest rate *on each transaction* is allocated to the persons making the sales, with diminishing and much smaller rates paid to each layer of managers above. Overall, in true sales companies, the great majority of the total commissions paid on each transaction goes to the lowest levels of the chain where the sales are actually made or directly managed. Collectively, the upper management receives a much smaller proportion of total commissions. Individually, upper managers may earn more in total each year due to their position and responsibility but they never get more of the total commission *on each transaction.*

In MLM, the opposite occurs. In MLM, I remind them, "sales" means *recruiting.* Money is made by recruiting new "salespeople" who then buy product based on a quota for eligibility in the pay plan. In a research report published in 2008, I examined the payout disclosures of 11 multi-level marketing companies that serve as representatives of the industry. It showed that all the companies transferred more than 50% of total payouts to the top 1% in the network in a single year and much more than that for the top 4%. The true percentage of profitable participants in a multi-year time frame shrinks to a tiny percentage. The vast majority gains nothing at all because they failed to recruit anyone or not enough and soon quit. John Oliver's HBO show showed one major MLM in which over 95% of all the "salespeople" received no commissions at all, zero. Those near the bottom who do try to recruit get a pittance of the total commissions paid on their "sales" (purchases made by their new recruits, after being enrolled).

As Senior FTC Economist (retired) Peter Vandernat wrote,

Unbeknownst to general participants the terms of the pyramid compensation plan secure the result that the vast majority will fail to obtain monetary rewards.[113]

Consumer advocate Dr. Jon Taylor[i] analyzed the pay plans of most of the larger MLM companies. He called the typical MLM pay plan "top-weighted," a gentle way of describing a classic system of transferring most of the money from the bottom, the proverbial "last ones in," to recruiters and owners at the peak of the pyramid. The trigger for the higher payout rate is the total purchase volume of the entire "downline" of the enrollees. The more they work, the more is transferred out of their hands directly to those at the top.

This upside-down, top-weighted formula was present in the Nutrilite plan, the very first MLM, and it has never changed in 75 years for all the MLM that were created. In that first MLM, the lowest rank qualified to gain a monthly bonus would receive 5%, which is the difference between his lower price and the higher price charged to his new recruit. On that same purchase transaction in which the recruiter gained 5%, the levels above him received 20% collectively. Four times more is paid to those that did nothing at all than is paid to the one that actually made it happen. The pay formula also added in special "bonuses" when higher volumes were reached by a recruiter's downline. The result is just to add more payment, per transaction, to the top ranks. At

---

[i] Jon M. Taylor was an author, consumer advocate and educator was one of the few researchers in the world to examine the business model and compensation plans that typify and define "MLM". His deconstruction of "MLM" into its defining components made the terms, "multi-level marketing" and "pyramid scheme" synonymous. Taylor's work required more than the usual fortitude. As a Mormon living in Utah, where MLM is now most concentrated and has become identified as a Mormon-based scam, he withstood special forms of social censure. Jon Taylor died in August 2018.

this point, I email many reporters a graphic showing how this all works in a simplified format, entitled "The Perverse Proportions of a Pyramid Pay Plan" based on the work of the late Dr. Taylor.

Fascinated but now also horrified at the picture that is emerging — and still clinging to the identity of MLM as "direct selling" — reporters typically now ask *why* the formula for recruiting bonuses is turned upside-down? By now, most understand the absence of retail profit opportunity, the impossibility of the endless chain, the absolute and impossible requirement for recruiting and how the pyramid puts most at the bottom, where they can't make money. But why would MLM also turn the recruiting pay-formula upside-down, they ask?

We are now descending into the deepest level of the MLM scheme, the point where the other steps of deception trigger the money-transfer swindle. I explain that the upside-down reward plan is *essential* and it fits tightly and integrally with the other elements we discussed — the unsustainable structure, the unjustified payments and purchase requirements, and unrelenting and impossible recruiting mandate. As we already determined, there is no sustainable retail customer base, no real demand for the goods, no need for a personal salesperson and therefore little to no retail selling. But there is a *tremendous* market for "income opportunity." That market has been drawing in more people since MLM was begun in 1945 and then grew tremendously since the mid 1970s. Today, it includes students with college debt, seniors facing mountains of medical bills and disappearing savings, families with unbearable rents, people already working two jobs, immigrants trying to survive, and military spouses facing multiple deployments, among others. The income-opportunity market is exploding!

It's just that, unfortunately, and fully known to the owners and top promoters of MLM, the MLM income opportunity, the one based on recruiting, does not exist. It is a phantom, a lure. It is the promised reward that cannot and will not be delivered.

The actual plan results, by design, in more than 99% of partici-pants losing money.[ii] Such a plan can only reward a tiny number, the owners and the few at the top of the recruiting chains. But for them to reap their reward, all the others must lose. It is the losses of those countless others that are transferred up and called "income" for owners and the top levels. Those losses are prede-termined, baked into the plan and structure. The fourth defining element is called "money transfer" to distinguish it from justified rewards based on creating value and producing true profit.

The upside-down pay plan, I say frankly now that we have laid out the whole picture, may seem to be a kind of insult piled on injury. It is not arbitrary, though. It is necessary. It is based on the most basic fact about the plan — that the last ones in cannot be successful. They are doomed by the "endless chain" design. They lost when they signed up. Why would the company lighten the hit? It would make no sense to waste commissions on them. They will be quitting soon — as many as 80% of the latest recruits do quit within the first year of joining. But they are replaced. Some move on to other MLMs, replacing dropouts at those companies. The object is to get them to buy as much as possible (that's why there are purchase quotas), for as long as possible (that's why they are promised "unlimited income" if they keep buying and if they miss even one month, they lose everything), and get as much from them (the extreme money transfer formula) as possi-ble while they are enrolled and buying.

The lost investments of new recruits who are seeking the leg-endary income opportunity are the primary revenue source of the MLM company. The top-weighted MLM plan rewards those that do the enterprise's *most valuable work* toward gaining that reve-nue. They *add the most value* to the enterprise, as it is designed.

[ii] See "The Myth of MLM Income Opportunity" at https://pyramidschemealert. org/study-of-ten-major-mlms-and-amwayquixtar/

That value they add is not measured by their individual "sales" or even the sales of their recruits; those "sales" come after a person is persuaded and enrolled. Value is measured by their contribution to the company's mission.

But, what is that mission, I am asked hesitantly, betraying a dread of my answer?

It's to deceive all the new recruits about the non-existent income opportunity. It is to get them to *believe*. MLMs seek to capture the mind of the recruit. Money will follow. The more they believe and the longer they believe, the more money the company gets from them. The Top Gun recruiters audaciously repeat and act out the Big Lie on stage, on videos, with their lifestyle, their politics and their claims of "success." The Top Gun recruiters orchestrate the recruiting campaigns and serve as the role models for all who, desperately, hope to get to the top where they too will have "success," not understanding that only a percent of a percent can be there. The Black Hat recruiters and the company owners play the roles of guru, the holders of ancient secrets to success, totally fulfilled and enlightened persons. They persuade recruits that they must become like them or be doomed to live as "losers."

Inevitably, at this point in the calls that had begun so blithely, I sense a line has been crossed and the mood has shifted away from further inquiry. Questions stop. A point was reached earlier where the reporters already realized that this story, regardless of its veracity, would never be published.

I finish it off anyway. So we can see, I say, the four defining elements of MLM, endless chain, pay-to-play, recruiting mandate and money-transfer, are exactly the elements of a pyramid scheme. A portrait of one is a replica of the other. Both rely on deception. Both cause the "last ones in" to lose. You pay to join an endless chain; you find others to also join, to get some of their money for yourself; you falsely promise every new person they will make money when they bring others in and, if they don't, they lose out; and the money from the new people is the money the earlier people receive.

Though I am not asked but just to round out the portrait, I explain that most naked pyramids eventually collapse when not enough new people join, resulting in others not getting their rewards. The chain breaks. But MLM is not recognized as a pyramid scheme because its true anatomy is disguised. It's endless chain keeps breaking but is repaired as new people replace the "losers." MLM is officially designated as "direct selling." It is "legitimate." So people keep joining, lured by deception, and driven by hope and need. Even though the data exist showing the 90+% loss rates — it was even explained, comically, by John Oliver on HBO — few people believe it. Because how could that be true and it also be "legitimate?" MLM, they are told, sits at the head table of the Chamber of Commerce. It has the support of Congress. Its shares of stock are traded on Wall Street. The courts and the FTC affirm it is legal. Top celebrities and star athletes endorse it. Even President Trump promoted several MLMs. So the losses, they conclude, must be "market based," the fault of the "losers." Buyer Beware. Work harder. Be positive. Losses only happen to "average" people. The opportunity is real. It's the American Dream and all that. Now, the reporters usually thank me sullenly and quickly end the phone call.

The articles that are published almost always quote the Direct Selling Association about the popularity of direct selling, about "average" incomes of "direct sellers" and how those that don't make money just didn't want to or didn't try hard enough. They just enrolled to get the wonderful products "at a discount." A photo of a "winner" is featured smiling in front of a display of skin lotions. Six figure incomes are cited as possible. I am quoted as a "critic" claiming that MLMs operate as pyramid schemes but the article also notes the FTC says MLM is legitimate.

The Perverse Proportions of a Pyramid Pay Plan

This illustration shows a plan that expands with each rep recruiting just two others to qualify for company bonuses. Each rep purchases or "sells" just $1,000 a year or about $80 a month (a conservatively typical MLM figure).

The pay plan shows the "bonus" increasing from 5% to 15% only when the downline reaches 10 levels. So, when level 9 recruits someone in level 10, level 9 gets 5% of the sale. But the person at the top gets 15% and the other levels collectively get 30% on that same sale. Additionally, the 15% will be paid on the deepest level, which always consists of 50% of the entire organization, increasing the total payout to the TOP tremendously.

Levels	Cumulative Total in TOP's Downline	Total in Each Level of TOP'S Downline	Percentages of Total by Level or Groups of Levels in TOP'S 10-Level Downline	Residual Commission Rate for each Level that is Paid to those Above	Income per Sales Rep (Assuming $1,000 of Annual Purchases by each Sales Rep)	Percent of Payout Received by TOP and each level of TOP'S 10-Level Downline (Rounded)
TOP					$204,700	20%
1	2	2		5%	$51,100	10%
2	6	4		5%	$25,500	10%
3	14	8		5%	$12,700	10%
4	30	16		5%	$6,300	10%
5	62	32		5%	$3,100	10%
6	126	64		5%	$1,500	9%
7	254	128	Levels 1-7 = 12%	5%	$700	9%
8	510	256		5%	$300	7%
9	1022	512	8-9 = 38%	5%	$100	5%
10	2046	1024	10 = 50%	15%	$0	0%

- Total Purchases by 10-level Downline: $2,046,000

- Total Residual (Override) Payments to Top Position and 10-level Downline: $1,024,100 (50% of Wholesale Revenue)

- 50% of all "sales" reps will always be at the bottom level regardless of how large the organization becomes.

- The one person in the TOP position purchases or sells no more than any other rep but makes approximately as much money as all the people in Levels 7-10 combined, which is 1,920 people or 94% of the entire organization.

- The one person in the TOP position represents 1/20th of one percent of the total organization and the total purchases but receives 20% of all company bonuses.

- The TOP Position and Levels 1-3 receive 50% of all the company bonuses but represent only 3/4th of one percent of the total organization.

- 15 people receive as much money as 2,032 combined, though each purchased the same amount of product.

SECRETS OF THE PYRAMID

Secrets, Ancient and Modern

The ancient pyramids famously hold archeological and architectural secrets related to their massive scale, near-perfect symmetry, and mysterious alignment with stars. For answers, many people consider mystic knowledge, alien intervention or supernatural powers over the plainer explanations of mathematics, physics and astronomy known and practiced by the priestly leaders.

What *is* a genuine mystery, however, is exactly how the pyramids were viewed by the unnamed masses who built and paid for them. How were so many mobilized? How were the funds obtained for projects that aggrandized so few at the expense of so many? Archeologists say the public was led to believe the pyramids were monuments to sacred beliefs and that working on them would lead to divine rewards.

Modern pyramid beliefs, *Ponzinomics*, have spread to many areas of finance and pubic life, such as housing speculation and unpayable debt. Yet, it is the institution of multi-level marketing that truly permeates American society, enrolling one-in-six American households every year and explicitly teaching *Ponzinomics* dogma. MLM is America's monument to *Ponzinomics*, as the ancient pyramids were to the beliefs of that era.

Holding ceremonial spectacles in enormous stadiums and posing on stage as high priests possessing sacred secrets, MLM promoters tout their schemes as the fulfillment of the mythic American Dream. They flaunt their own wealth as proof they can align the stars, so to speak, to deliver success and happiness to followers. They gain enormous wealth and near worship from awe-struck followers who suffer financial loss, debt and social alienation, building the MLM pyramids with their own money and free labor.

Behind the MLM myth and rituals, hidden from view, are the mundane tools and techniques to create illusions for deceiving and dominating the MLM workers. Uncovering MLM's pyramid secrets requires piercing the symbolic façade in the same way archeologists expose the math, physics and astronomy behind the mysterious pyramids that struck wonderment among people of their times and incite imaginations even today.

In particular, two of the modern pyramid's secrets that will now be revealed bear special notice. They are basic aspects of pyramid scheme architecture, well understood by designers Mytinger and Casselberry, yet, for the millions who were enrolled — like the countless souls who built and paid for the ancient pyramids — remain obscured by diversions, deceptions, and magical beliefs.

The Saturation Secret

In a pyramid scheme, the "marks" are "roped in" with a pitch that seems true enough and entirely feasible: *Surely you know five other people? And they will each know five others, right? Now, you already have 30 on your team!*

Only if the math is continued does the plan show its absurdity. The last 30 will also have to gain 30 each in the same way, adding 900 new people, and those 900 will have to find 27,000 who will need 810,000 ... Very soon, those at the bottom will not find their own 30, maybe not even one.

As Lee Mytinger privately explained to his future partner William Casselberry when they formulated the blueprint of all future MLMs, it would lead to "everyone on earth" eventually selling for Nutrilite. In Carl Rehnborg's biography, Mytinger described the plan's electrifying promise of an expanding chain, transferring "unlimited" income to each new recruiter, as a "joke."

He knew full well that finding just five others who are actually interested and will pay is not "sure" at all. And if the five are found, their "five others" often turn out to be each other or their *mutual* friends. Long before overall saturation arrives, local and individual network saturation breaks the chain.

The awe-inspiring vision of a pot of gold — money from an enormous pyramid of social connections — blinds people not only to the reality of saturation and chain breakage but even to the funding source itself — their own money. All that is occurring is money being moved around inside the chain, a closed market. Virtually nothing is generated in the real, open market. The MLM money transfer in the recruiting chain is equivalent to promising 10 people that if they each invest $10 into a common fund, each and every one of the 10 people could get the fund's total of $100.

From Mytingers' perspective, the illusion of "everyone on earth" signing up was just part of the inside story, the secret knowledge that the company would possess and that the newly recruited salespeople — the target for revenue — would *not* know or understand. As Nutrilite was rolled out with the new plan and began to draw in hundreds of thousands of hopeful adherents, its "saturation" secret would mesmerize and confound those being propositioned even as they lost money and quit in vast numbers and were replaced by their recruits who experienced the same predetermined outcome. It would also confuse regulators who were asked to recognize inevitable saturation as the blatant red flag of the *inherent* deception of a pyramid scheme swindle.

Staying One Step Ahead of Attrition

Before the plan was enacted in late 1945, Nutrilite continued to languish, leaving Carl Rehnborg with little bargaining leverage yet still driven by his life-long ambition to become rich and famous. When the contract was signed, Mytinger and Casselberry, still working at the munitions factory, gained complete control over sales and marketing, the sector that controlled the company's and Rehnborg's future. With their pooled psychological persuasion methods and sales manipulation techniques, Mytinger and Casselberry grasped that the "endless chain" plan would cause an explosion of sign-ups.

With insight into the plan's skyrocketing power and its outcome of massive losses for the recruits, Mytinger also foresaw that the challenge facing the new pyramid selling company was not going to be a scenario of total market penetration. Rather, it was how to sustain the recruiting when the illusion of "unlimited opportunity" lost its mystique, and people discovered that virtually no one actually is making the promised money. The marketing challenge is to keep the expansion illusion vivid and commercially viable and never to give away the pyramid's secret that saturation prevented unending expansion.

With this realization, Mytinger understood that the only way company revenue growth could be ultimately sustained would be to keep opening new territories or to target new population sectors. He needed to go where the reality of loss rates was not yet known and the illusion of unlimited expansion was still believed.

The teams of sales canvassers Mytinger had previously managed selling cemetery plots faced the local saturation scenario regularly; their customers seldom needed more than one gravesite and funeral plan. This is why he and his sales teams were constantly traveling outside the local area. In the pyramid plan, local saturation and a growing local awareness of consumer losses continuously eroded the base, as if it were built on sand.

Nutrilite, the first — and for several years the only — multi-level marketing company, was able to forestall a saturation phase by moving sequentially to every state in the country, facing no competitor and therefore no advance knowledge among consumers about how pyramid selling worked. By 1954, after an eight-year recruiting run, a decline had finally begun *for the company*. In the future, as more "MLM" companies were formed, this process would shorten in time.

The plan was promoted as capable of expanding *ad infinitum*. But just two and a half years after launching, Southern California was already becoming saturated with Nutrilite distributors, making further growth for the "industrious" new recruits very difficult.

The question of saturation often is reduced to absurdity by asking whether a person could find even one new recruit, presuming if just one more person could be recruited, that saturation — and therefore the existence of a pyramid scheme — is absent.

In reality, as the experience of Nutrilite recruiters in saturated Southern California revealed, the challenge is not to find just one new person. To be successful, many, perhaps thousands must be found. Factoring a 50% or more annual dropout rate, or a dropout rate over 75% of the newest recruits, the income proposition requires a vast population of prospects for each person.

In the confusing debates and legal wrangling over "saturation," it is often forgotten that wherever the "industrious" recruiters go, even to other countries, they will only benefit themselves at the cost of virtually all others they rope in who will be doomed to financial loss. The saturation secret protects the Pyramid's bigger secret: it causes its harm *the day it is launched.* The percentage of "losers" is more or less fixed from the start.

The Secret of 'Growth'

The Carl Rehnborg and Nutrilite story reports that on September 1, 1945, Rehnborg signed the exclusive agreement with Mytinger and Casselberry "that was drawn up in anticipation of rapid growth, addressing contingencies relating to size and volume."

The story does not explain why there would have been cause for "anticipation of rapid growth" except to imply that, all along, it was just more effective sales management that had been needed for Nutrilite to suddenly become an exploding sales phenomenon.

Even if the sales management factor were that important, the story does not account for why it would have been assumed that a former cemetery plot salesman who had not done sales work in five years and a psychology counselor with two part time jobs warranted a presumption of stupendous success. "The plan" — the only new element in the business — is not referenced as the cause for this presumption of growth, yet as events quickly unfold, a monumental expansion — in accordance with the plan's explosive mathematical design — does indeed ignite.

"The plan," in theory, could cause 40 agents to expand to a point where "everyone on earth would eventually be selling the product!" as Mytinger was quoted. In fact, 40 agents worked for Nutrilite at the moment of signing on September 1, 1945. In the first eight months of 1945, prior to the contract signing

Nutrilite's Reported Retail Revenue	
1944	$24,000
1945	$50,000
1946	$750,000
1947	$2,096,000
1948	$4,584,000
1949	$5,968,000
1950	$9,740,000
1951	$10,567,000
1952	$12,425,000
1953	$16,319,000
1954	$25,222,000
1956	$26,514,000
1958	$19,145,000

and implementation of the plan, Nutrilite averaged monthly revenue of about $2,000, indicating a mean average sales volume per distributor of $50 per month in 1945 dollars. The highest estimated commission paid, based on sales volume, was 40% or $20 per month on average, before deducting all expenses. The Nutrilite product offering had clearly never demonstrated much of an income opportunity for Rehnborg or for his 40 distributors.

Suddenly, in the four months following the contract signing between Rehnborg, Mytinger, and Casselberry, revenues increased to more than $8,500 per month, resulting in 1945 annual revenue more than doubling from the previous year to $50,000. But this was only a spark for the firestorm of expansion that followed.

In gross data, the first nine years of Nutrilite's explosive launch under "the plan" appeared to show powerful organic growth on a foundation of year-after-year success. In reality, Nutrilite was not "growing" in the sense most people understand how a large company develops by building a larger and larger base of loyal customers. Nutrilite's explosive increase in revenue merely reflected that pyramid recruiting was strongly outpacing the rate of quitting.

In just 16 months, Mytinger and Casselberry's "plan" catapulted Rehnborg's little business from monthly retail revenue of $2,000 to more than $60,000 per month. It did this without changing the line up or the pricing of the company's products or carrying out a significant advertising program. And, despite a scandal that engulfed the company starting in 1949 when it was prosecuted by the U.S. Food and Drug Administration for making false health claims, Nutrilite's sales just kept growing explosively. By 1950, sales reached $9.7 million, then $12.5 million in 1951, hitting $25.2 million in 1954.[114] The expansion was unrelated to the product, pricing or its sullied reputation.

In the annals of sales, this is an astonishing event, but especially so for those involved in labor-intensive door-to-door selling and the vitamin businesses. Predictably, the plan was quickly carbon copied with the similar amazing growth results for imitators. How or why becoming a Nutrilite distributor would suddenly become so appealing to so many, is not addressed in the mythic account. Rehnborg's personal life blossomed with the business and he quickly found a new wife, put his son back in private school, and bought a new house.

An avoidance of the pyramid factor in explaining Nutrilite's overnight success is the likely reason Rehnborg's biography documents the growth figures of Nutrilite only up to 1954. In these first nine years after implementing the plan, Nutrilite's revenue exploded an astounding 50,000%! But court data from a government prosecution of Nutrilite show that immediately after that period Nutrilite's growth drastically slowed and then steeply declined. From 1952–1954, revenues went up more than 100%, but in the next two years, 1954–1956, revenue rose just 5%. In the next two years, 1956–1958, revenue declined 28%, wiping out the previous five-year's of increases.[115]

The trend of decline continued at Nutrilite another six years to where revenue in 1964 was less than 1950. Factoring inflation, Nutrilite's reported retail revenue in 1964 was less than one-third what it had generated in 1956. When the company was sold to Amway in 1972, factoring inflation, Nutrilite's reported retail revenues at the time were half what it generated 18 years before.

The revenue pattern of Nutrilite, showing almost unheard of and inexplicable growth followed by a similarly inexplicable steep decline, is now known as "pop and drop," a universal phenomenon among multi-level marketing enterprises and one of the telltale signs that MLM bears no resemblance to direct selling. What appears to be "growth" is an illusion. There is no underlying foundation of customers or sales force. The extreme pop and drop phenomenon is inherent to the math and the mechanics of "the plan," making the pattern inevitable, one of the secrets of the pyramid to be militantly guarded with diversion and rationalization.

The promise of "unlimited" rewards created a chain letter mania of Nutrilite recruiting but built no foundation of stable salespeople or steady retail customers. When the salespeople quit, generally their customers, if they had any, were lost also. There were no "territories" to take over when the new recruit joined the business and no existing customer list to build upon. The company could not stay viable without relentless recruiting to replace an enormous turnover of the "losers" it manufactured with assembly-line precision. The recruiting process of pyramid selling, unlike that of direct selling was not a factor of "labor" related to the storied hardships of personal sales. There was no broad base of salespeople gaining modest but viable income. "MLM" recruiting was, instead, an existential function to offset continuous collapse as the lower ranks, which sourced most of the revenue, disappeared each year and never returned.

It was not surprising, therefore, that soon after Nutrilite's decline set in from the late 1950s, two of Nutrilite's top recruiters defected and started a new company, directly copying Nutrilite's now proven "plan." That first defection and duplication of Nutrilite set the pattern that has not changed to today and has produced thousands of new "MLMs." All of them are copies of Nutrilite.

The defectors broke off to form a new company that was to be called Amway, destined to become the world's largest "MLM" and the progenitor of many more MLM clones. In 1972, Amway would acquire Nutrilite, absorb its diminished force of recruiters and incorporate the Nutrilite potions into its product mix. The role of Nutrilite ends in the MLM drama. Amway quickly takes center stage.

Most important to the untold story of multi-level marketing, and as will be shown in the next chapter, it will be Amway's founders that make MLM "legal," the most important development in MLM's worldwide spread. As top recruiters for Nutrilite, the Amway founders witnessed how Nutrilite, using clever legal maneuverings, survived the FDA prosecution for making dangerously false medical claims — without actually changing its false claims. Using its own legal maneuverings and powerful back-room lobbying, Amway will survive pyramid fraud prosecution — without actually changing its pyramid practices.

THE LORE OF
LEGALITY

Conning the Court

In the mythology of multi-level marketing no aspect is more consequential than the contention that MLM was tested in the federal court and found to be perfectly legal. In 1979, Amway, the largest and oldest existing MLM, was exonerated by a judge of a charge brought by the FTC that it was an illegal "endless chain."[116] In the MLM legend, this court ruling is enshrined like Scripture and referenced by MLM promoters as the ultimate judicial authority. Without a hint of its extreme irony, the first line of legal defense among all MLMs against questions of deception, cultism, or a bogus income opportunity is, "We operate like Amway."

The reality of this court ruling is radically different from the tale. The ruling of 1979 was not made in a federal district court, an appeals court or by the Supreme Court, or any court presided over by a presidentially appointed federal judge, as might be supposed from the great status accorded the ruling. It was made by an Administrative Law Judge (ALJ), James P. Timony. ALJs are paid by the agencies for which they hear cases. Timony was brought in a year after the FTC's pyramid scheme case against Amway was already underway.[117] Judge Timony had never before adjudicated a pyramid scheme case.[118] Prior to becoming an ALJ, Timony had worked in the FTC's "Restraint of Trade" division and in the General Counsel's office. After the Amway case, Timony heard cases from 17 different government agencies. He retired in 2003 and has never made a public statement or been publicly interviewed about his famous decision. There has never been an academic review of the ruling or an assessment of the validity of his conclusions in which real-world sales experience, actual loss rates and retail sales data are measured.

Officially, ALJs are part of the executive branch, not the judiciary. They are appointed after passing a test and an interview in front of a panel. There are twice as many ALJs as there are federal court judges and they hear twice as many cases.[119] The majority of cases are individual disputes with the Social Security office. The cases are called "trial-like,"[120] but there is no option for a jury. Enforcement of their rulings requires formal acceptance by the government agency bringing the case. The agency has the option to appeal to an actual judicial court and it could reject the decision. If the agency accepts the decision, the ALJ ruling, unlike a federal court ruling, is not binding on future actions of the agency. It is not necessarily applicable to any other case against other companies. ALJ decisions do not require the agency to use the rulings for general guidance to other similar companies regarding boundaries of legality. Today, in consumer protection cases, the FTC has essentially abandoned using ALJs in favor of litigation in federal court.[121]

Despite the low status and non-binding nature of the ALJ decision, the FTC accepted the pyramid scheme exoneration in the Amway case without appeal. Ever since, the FTC has referenced the ruling as the model on which the entire multi-level level marketing industry is defined, making "MLM" legal, fair, and legitimate (not inherently deceptive and harmful), unless an MLM company might be determined to operate otherwise.

The formal acceptance was written by Commissioner Robert Pitofsky, one of that special class of attorneys and academics that moves back and forth between the regulatory agencies and law schools and politically-connected law firms representing corporate clients particularly affected by regulation. Pitofsky led the FTC's Consumer Protection Bureau (1970–1973) when President Richard Nixon named Miles Kirkpatrick FTC chairman. Pitofsky was made an FTC Commissioner (1978–1981) under Jimmy Carter, and later Commission Chair (1995–2001) under Bill Clinton, during which term he oversaw the FTC's approval of the merger of America Online (AOL) and Time Warner. Pitofsky also served as counsel to the well-connected D.C. office of the law firm Arnold & Porter, and taught anti-trust law at Georgetown law school.[122] The anti-trust backgrounds of both Judge Timony and Commissioner Pitofsky are reflected in the ALJ's ruling and Pitofsky's written acceptance for the Commission at the cost of the consumer protection elements of the case.

Imaginary Retail, Fabricated Rules

Judge Timony's opinion that Amway was not an "endless chain" in violation of FTC law against "unfair and deceptive" trade practices was based on the unfounded and implausible claim made by Amway that its entire business was "retail-based." The judge chose not to verify the retail sales claim with data or field research inquiry, relying instead on the accused company's word. Accepting "retail selling" as the company's primary activity, much of the rest of the case then dealt with "competition" and "pricing." In reality, and as Amway *later* disclosed, virtually no profitable retailing occurred, making pricing and competition with true retailers like Procter & Gamble irrelevant.

The most memorable and consequential part of the ruling was based on Amway's claim that it had "rules" that ensured that revenue would always be based on retail selling and that all salespeople were chiefly gaining their income and earning profits from retail selling, directly with their own retail sales or indirectly from the retail sales of the genealogy of their recruits, called a "downline." The "rules" were invented by Amway. They were not referenced by FTC attorneys in the initial complaint. They entered the case as "evidence" and "proof" that the company was "retail-based." These "rules," according to Amway, *required* every salesperson who received a "bonus" to have at least 10 retail customers monthly and to have resold 70% of all products ordered monthly to retail customers *or to other salespeople.*

If the rules had been enforced, those who did not sell the goods they purchased received no bonuses — which the FTC found were the great majority. The payments to the recruiters were made by Amway and only to those that successfully recruited consumers to join the chain or purchased a quota of goods. No data were produced, however, to show how many "customers" — other than the people inside the closed recruiting chain — ever bought Amway goods on the open market. No data or evidence were presented showing average pricing or profit to the salespeople or the total volume of open market retail sales. Using raw data of company revenue and total number of recruits cited in the case of $200 million in revenue with 360,000 recruits, the monthly purchase per person among people on the recruiting chain was about $45 a month, impossibly small for retailing.

Even though Amway paid its recruiters before retail sales were made, if any occurred at all, Judge Timony accepted Amway's word that the rules guaranteed that people on the recruiting chain were never induced to buy goods as the cost to join the recruiting chain or maintain eligibility for recruiting-based rewards.[i] The claim that after the recruits made the purchases, retail sales occurred was accepted without verification. After the Judge's ruling, the claim to include the "Amway rules" in their own policies became the primary defense of every MLM against pyramid scheme charges.

Neither the judge nor the FTC inquired whether or not the "rules" *actually* prevented the deception and harm *inherent* to

---

[i] From the ruling, "Thus a sponsoring distributor receives nothing from the mere act of sponsoring. It is only when the newly recruited distributor begins to make wholesale purchases from his sponsor and sales to consumers, that the sponsor begins to earn money from his recruit's efforts." (In fact, the upline of recruiters is paid immediately when the recruit makes a wholesale purchase and earns nothing more or less if the recruit subsequently retails the goods or not. The entire bonus system is disconnected from subsequent retail selling.)

a pyramid recruiting plan. The deception would include being falsely induced to sign the contract and make purchases in the expectation of gaining income from retailing or recruiting. Neither the judge nor the FTC looked at the business directly, as it operated on the street.

To this day, the validity of the rules to ensure retail selling and to prevent deception and harm has never been verified and the FTC has made no inquiry. Yet, in the acceptance of the ruling, Commissioner Pitofsky wrote and quoted from the ruling,

"… Amway's (10 customer rule) makes retail selling an essential part of being a distributor… Specifically, the Amway Plan is not a plan where participants purchase the right to earn profits by recruiting other participants, who themselves are interested in recruitment fees rather than the sale of products."

Apparently neither the Judge nor Commissioner Pitofsky considered the possibility that the "rules," which Amway itself invented and made part of its defense, might be fake, ineffective, or just irrelevant to the deceptiveness and harmfulness *inherent* to any "endless chain" income proposition. They did not ask, for example, what sales company would ever *need to require* its salespeople to make sales if the plan had not falsely induced them to buy the goods or if they believed they could gain income in some other way. They seemingly saw no cause to suspect that inducing recruits to purchase goods with quotas might be tied to receiving recruiting rewards. They appeared to believe that thousands of people were signing up to reap minimal rewards from unverified retailing of Amway commodities, rather than from the "unlimited" wealth that Amway promised from recruiting. In the same vein, they apparently saw no contradiction in salespeople personally retailing and then being rewarded for signing up their own retail *competitors!*

The Judge and the FTC Commissioner even cited data showing a potential of perhaps $3 a week in average retail profit per person, before selling costs and taxes are deducted, if all the products were *actually* retailed. The court also cited evidence that much of the products purchased by the recruits was never sold but was personally "consumed."[123]

Still, the Judge saw nothing amiss in this picture. Nor was curiosity awakened by Amway's phenomenal U.S. revenue increase from $4.3 million in 1963 to $169.1 million in 1976, an increase of 3,800%. The question as to why almost 200,000 people a year would sign up to gain average "retail" profit of less than $3 a week — before expenses — from selling laundry soap seemingly did not occur to Judge Timony or Commissioner Pitofsky. The two antitrust attorneys showed more concern about mythical retail pricing and allowing Amway to "compete" with Procter & Gamble, which the Judge Timony called an "oligopoly."

Flaming Red Flags

For every red flag of deception and a pyramid scheme cited by the FTC staff attorneys in the original complaint or during discovery, Amway had a "business" or "direct selling" answer that persuaded the Judge. These red flags included:

- false income claims of life-time residuals;
- sudden and extraordinary "growth;"
- promises of great income based on "duplication" and "multiplication" of recruiters recruiting recruiters;
- three-fourths of the newest recruits quit within one year;
- overall annual turnover rate of 50–60% of all participants yet the hundreds of thousands of departing recruits left no repeat retail customers behind for the new ones to build upon; month to month revenue tracked directly with recruiting levels and average revenue per recruit remained constant;

- all recruits signed "sales" contracts though they underwent no formal sales training and no evidence was offered that most ever sold any product at all;

- only 25% of the entire sales organization gained any of the lucrative recruiting-based "bonuses" and most of them made almost nothing, yet a few at the top of the recruiting chain received enormous payments;

- largest expenditure of the company was for payments to recruiters;

- business was said to be based on retailing, but retail selling was not company-verified, company-managed and the company did not compensate for retailing;

- recruiting chain had no territorial restriction and every salesperson was encouraged to recruit more salespeople, yet all were told market areas could never have too many salespeople; and

- the company advertised an extraordinary income opportunity but, in fact, virtually no participants gained any net income.

Psst, Buddy

The Amway story to recruits that it is a "direct selling" business run by pious and conservative executives offering "opportunity" to sell household products served as an innocuous and plausible introduction. But it was "the plan," that would later be explained, the one invented by Mytinger and Casselberry at Nutrilite and which Amway copied, that enabled Amway to make the electrifying claim it had special access to "unlimited rewards" it could offer recruits. The Plan was the basis on which Amway could make the astounding promise of "wealth beyond imagination." These are claims that no other "direct selling" company could plausibly make. The cruel rigors, the human limits, and sheer loneliness of real direct selling were all too well known.

This "direct selling business" story provided the rationale for soliciting enormous numbers of marks to sign "sales contracts," and charging, in advance, for "sales kits" based on an "income" proposition. This was the equivalent of what legal scholar Arthur Leff called the "Psst, Buddy" approach. The story also convinced the Judge that although almost no recruits ever made a net profit, Amway's extraordinary references to "unlimited" income were not callously deceptive and capable of causing a mass mania. Rather, in the tradition of Dale Carnegie courses, these references were merely "inspirational and motivational."[124] The FTC agreed with this and the Commissioner affirmed the view that "generalized" income claims by Amway were not misleading, calling them "vague 'puffs,' which few people, if any, would take literally..."

The green magistrate had apparently never attended one of Amway's "opportunity" rallies, seen the expressions on the faces of attendees, and watched the ecstatic responses to Amway's income promises. He was apparently unaware of the hysteria an "unlimited income" promise can produce. This was the same fanaticism historically associated with the famous tulip mania, periodic real estate bubbles, gold rushes, and other popular delusions. In 2004, *NBC Dateline* took hidden cameras into Amway recruiting events, including a mass rally in South Carolina. More than 10,000 people gathered in a huge, darkened auditorium. Each attendee held a lighted candle as they followed an Amway promoter in a thunderous chant, "Freedom, Freedom, Flush that Stinking Job!" Based on Amway's claim to offer them "unlimited income" the recruits were exhorted to quit (flush) whatever work or profession they were doing.

From my own experience running a consumer education website for 19 years and serving in more than 30 court cases, I have personally and repeatedly seen instances of MLM victims divorcing spouses, neglecting children, and bankrupting themselves and their families in the quest for the "unlimited" income that Amway and other MLMs promised. Some have committed suicide as their dreams were not fulfilled and they had "flushed" all other career pathways and social relationships. In the final ruling of the Amway case, 1979, Judge Timony dismissed the entire phenomenon later to be identified by cult experts and psychologists as "undue influence" and mind control and by others as the classic "Big Lie."[ii]

Judge Timony and then the FTC accepted Amway's claim that business was not based on rewarding recruiting, but on retailing, even though Amway increased payments to recruiters — per transaction — based on increased recruiting.[iii]

Any experienced door-to-door salesperson in the tradition of Fuller Brush or Avon of that time would likely have seen the model as unworkable as a retail sales business and would have found the incentive to recruit your own competitors in your own sales area incomprehensible. Experienced salespeople in any field would quickly see the entire pay plan was oriented to recruiting because the high incomes, indeed any net income at all, could only be gained from recruiting.

The contradictions and impossibilities of Amway's story were fully grasped by the government attorneys, led by FTC staff attorney Joseph Brownman. In the initial complaint filed in 1975, FTC staff attorneys had argued the obvious, "The greater

---

[ii] Wikipedia defines the Big Lie, "A big lie is a propaganda technique. Adolf Hitler coined the expression when he dictated his 1925 book, *Mein Kampf*, about the use of a lie so "colossal" that no one would believe that someone "could have the impudence to distort the truth so infamously."

[iii] The pay formula awarded higher "discounts" and more "bonuses" the greater the total volume of purchases by the recruiter's entire "downline." The escalating percentage paid to the top results in transferring the largest share of the total commissions paid on all transaction to the few at the top, even though they are furthest from the point of transaction.

the number of distributors or dealers previously recruited, the lower the chances of a profitable distributorship or dealership operation."

Apparently, the FTC attorneys did not believe that it required significant explication. They did, however, support the premise with carefully gathered research data showing saturation in the specific areas where Amway recruited. In 1970 the U.S. Census showed only 71 million households. In 1977, at 360,000 salespeople currently enrolled, each Amway distributor would, therefore, have had less than 200 households on average to recruit or even to sell to. Factoring all the millions unable and uninterested to buy and more than one million ex-Amway distributors, the true per capita market for the hapless new Amway recruits was pitifully insufficient.[iv] Even Amway's own disclosed data showed massive losses and turnover at the lower levels of the chain and extraordinary rewards gained by a few at the top.

Just as Nutrilite's attorneys had baffled the FDA with diverting disclaimers while still managing to promote its potions as miracle cure-alls, Amway's attorneys led Administrative Law Judge Timony and Commissioner Pitofsky into a rhetorical labyrinth linking "infinite" expansion to "free enterprise," and turning the doomed pursuit of income in an endless chain scheme into an "American Dream" story.

Timony's ruling and the FTC's affirmation written by Commissioner Pitofsky established an entirely new economic paradigm, *a legalized pyramid scheme*. Under this newly ordained model, previously viewed as *prima facie* fraud based on its physical and commercial impossibility, financial rewards could be legally promised to paying participants based on the astonishing claim of a genealogical marketing chain that extends *forever* and is capable of generating money to all who join, *without limit*.

INTERLUDE:
THIS IS NOT A PYRAMID SCHEME!

I have a fantastic *opportunity* for you. It's like a job but a lot better. It's an opportunity to make *unlimited* income.

Pay only $399 for a starter kit, and then you can work as an independent salesperson for our company, selling the company's great products on a commission basis.

Why should you *pay* for this job, you ask? Okay, I realize paying for a job might seem unusual. But, you see, this opportunity is *unique*. By paying your $399 you gain not only the right to sell our products to the general public but also the right to recruit other salespeople to sell for the company. When you sign up new salespeople and they buy some of our products, you'll get a commission on all their purchases, month in, month out. It's like becoming CEO of your own sales company.

Best of all, you can make money *right away* by enrolling people you already know and who already trust you. *Everybody* is a candidate for this job. Who doesn't want to make *unlimited* money?

What's that? Personal relationships? Oh, I see! You're uncomfortable recruiting friends to sell for the company when you haven't made any money yourself, at least not yet. Is that it?

First, let me assure you that this business is *very profitable — beyond your wildest dreams*. You *will* be profitable — when you recruit a lot of your friends. I can tell you about some of our people who've quit their 9-to-5 slave jobs. Now, they make money while they sleep.

Still worried you could mislead friends to get payments for recruiting them?

Well, let me make one thing perfectly clear! You will *never* be paid one penny for recruiting! That would be *illegal*. That would be *wrong*! It would be a *pyramid scheme*. This is not a pyramid scheme!

Let me tell you more about the rest of the opportunity. After you hear it, I think your worries about relationships and honesty may go away.

Now, if you sign up five of your friends, for example, and they each buy $100 a month of products, you'll get …

What? Commissions on the $399 sign-up fees?

No, No, No! You will *never* get paid a commission on the $399 sign-up fees. That would be payments directly from the people you recruit. That would be getting paid to recruit. That would be wrong! That would be a pyramid scheme! This is not a pyramid scheme.

You don't get paid on sign-up fees, but you get money *after sign-up fees are paid.* Your recruits have to pay the sign-up fee in order for you to start making money on them. The company gets money from your recruits' sign-up fees and your recruits' product purchases. You will get commissions from each recruit who pays the sign-up fees, but I assure you the money you receive is not from the sign-up money they paid. It's from the product purchase money they paid. Understand?

No? Money is money, you say? How do we separate the two piles of money?

Okay, let me spell it out. You never get paid *to* recruit but you always get paid *after* you recruit. The more you recruit, the more money you make. The less you recruit, the less you make, but you are never, *ever*, paid to recruit! Paying people to recruit others who are paid to recruit others who are paid to recruit others, and so on — that would be *wrong*. That is a pyramid scheme. This is not a pyramid scheme.

Now, let me get back to the *income opportunity*. You will get commissions on the purchases of as many new salespeople as you sign up. There's no limit! Five, 10, 50 — there's no cap. The more the better, *for you.*

Too many salespeople? No, there could *never* be *too* many. The market of people wanting extra income is always growing and our products fit everyone's needs. But no matter how many more join, you would be making money on all of them, so you would want as many more as possible. Doesn't that make sense?

You're *still* worrying about profits from your *personal* sales? Just wait, I'm getting to that, but let me remind you again that the commissions from the salespeople are from *sales*, not from recruiting.

Why would the *salespeople* buy the products?

They don't have to, of course. It's totally optional. But, listen, what kind of salesperson sells something he or she wouldn't buy themselves? Anyway, salespeople always need samples and giveaways. And, they need to show their customers that they *believe* in the product. So, the salespeople are also *customers*! In fact, they are your very *best* customers!

Why? Well, that takes me to the really *unique* part of this opportunity. This will answer your first question about why you should pay $399 for this income opportunity.

Like I said, you're getting commissions from every new salesperson you recruit, based on their purchases, and every salesperson will make *a lot of purchases*, more than a regular customer will and for a much longer time. No customer is more loyal than a salesperson.

But then, you'll also get paid when your new recruits go out and recruit other salespeople. Yes, that's right, the people you sign up will be able to sign up salespeople too! Each one, just like you, gets the right to recruit as many as they can, and every time the person they sign up as a salesperson makes a purchase, they get paid, just like you do, on *your* recruits' purchases.

But, here's the kicker! You'll get a payment on the purchases of *their* recruits! Think about that! If you sign up five new salespeople and they each do the same, you have 25 more salespeople working for you, a total of 30. Remember, you didn't get money from the sign-up fees, only on the purchases made after the sign up fees are paid, and you didn't get paid to recruit, but you got paid because you recruited. Is that perfectly clear?

But wait! There's more! When their recruits (the 25 additional salespeople) each recruit five more, you'll get paid on *their* purchases too! That's *125* more! Now, you've got *155 salespeople*, each one making purchases and you're getting a commission from every one of them. How's that sound? All you need to do is find five new salespeople.

Why would all those people sign up as salespeople? Because each one has the same opportunity as you to build their *own* 155-person sales force. The income is unlimited because *the opportunity is unlimited*. We call it *network marketing*.

Now do you see why you pay $399 to become a salesperson for this company? And since the friends that you recruited have the same chance to also make money while *they* sleep, can you see why it is *good* to recruit them, even *before* you start making money? No need to wait. You're giving them the opportunity of a lifetime! That's really what you are selling — the opportunity!

No, it's not just the opportunity to sell products! It's the opportunity to sell the opportunity to others to sell the opportunity! *Ain't it great?*

What *about* product sales? Well, let me be sure you understand something. Product sales are the foundation of our company. We are a product *sales* company. Our *products* are how we define ourselves. We are very proud of our products. The more products your salespeople — from first level to the last — buy, the more *you* make.

Their *personal* sales? You're asking about sales *by* the sales-people, not sales to them or between them? Oh yes, that's *very* important. You get paid on the basis of the *purchases* of each sales-person, right? So, the more each one sells, the more he or she purchases or is credited with selling. So, when I say sell, I really mean buy. When I say buy, I mean sell. Get it?

How much does each salesperson sell on average? Well, that's up to each person. We don't track that. But I will tell you this. Anyone who buys our products from a salesperson is also a per-fect candidate to sell them! So, any customer of any of the sales-people could become a salesperson too! Always remember, the salesperson is the best of all customers.

But, we go even further than that! We *require* each salesperson to sell to at least five customers every month!

If it were so profitable, why would we have to *require* our salespeople to sell? Well, only because we would not want even the appearance of a *pyramid scheme*. This is not a pyramid scheme. So, we would never want anyone to join our company and just focus on recruiting.

What's the catch? Well, there aren't any, really. Of course, to get these commissions all the way down to the end of your network, you have to maintain a quota of purchases or sales. We couldn't keep paying you on the work of your network if you aren't per-forming too, could we? Everybody in the network has to maintain their quotas of buying — I mean selling — to remain qualified. But, here's the good part. If any of the people below you fall short and don't buy or sell enough to remain qualified, whatever com-missions they were going to receive are transferred to those above. You could actually make more when someone below you quits! That's called *compression*. And, it only gets better from there.

How? Well the bigger your network — that is, the more sales-people you and your sales network *recruit* — the more the whole group *buys*. The more they buy, the higher the commission rates that we'll pay *you*. Higher *group* volume means a higher commission rate to you on every *purchase they make*. Because you're at the *top*, the more your group buys, the bigger your share of the pie on each transaction!

There are even *more* rewards! For example, the larger your group is, you get paid on deeper levels. When you reach our executive levels, you get paid on *all* levels of your group, all the way to *infinity*. Think about *that*! As the chains extends, while you sleep, you get paid more *per sale* from the entire group, and you get paid on more levels, which means, *on more total sales*. So, you win *two ways*. Everybody in your network is motivated to recruit more people into your network because they are also always recruiting for theirs too. Each salesperson is always at the top of the group they build. That's why it's called *multi-level* marketing.

No! Of course that's not paying people to recruit! I thought I made that *clear*. Paying money for the chance to get paid to recruit people would be *wrong*. You get paid on sales and purchases of those you recruit and those they recruit and those *they* recruit, and so on. You never get paid for recruiting. Understand now?

Where does it end? What do you mean *end*? This is an *unlimited* opportunity. You have the chance to get paid *forever*. *Everybody* in the network does too. It all starts with finding just five others who also want to make unlimited money. Who can't find just five others? More people are being born every day and our company is expanding to more and more countries. Soon, we'll be in China! So, the last people who join your network, many levels below you, can always recruit more. And you'll get paid on *all* of them.

So, are you ready to sign up? Great! Sign the contract right here. You can read it at home. $399. Thanks. You'll never regret it.

It's the greatest business in the world! The only way you could lose is if you *quit* and the only people who quit are *losers*. You're not a quitter or a loser, are you? No, you're a *winner*!

So, of course, you'll want to join the Winners' Marketing Program. It's where you learn from the masters every month. There are *secrets* to success, and this is where you learn those secrets. It's not a cost at all. It's an *investment* that you'll get a huge return on; so it's really *free*.

No, paying for the monthly marketing program is not *required*. But then, neither is your success.

PONZINOMICS — PROPAGANDA

Ponzinomics: noun / pän-zē-ˈnä-miks/ a pseudo-economic, all-encompassing, delusional belief system that promotes the swindle of a Ponzi or pyramid scheme as a valid economic model *that promises believers a fulfilling and financially rewarding way of life, complete with mission, values, leadership and worldview.* The societal spread of Ponzinomics is necessarily accompanied by governmental collusion.

From Denial ...

In pleasing natural colors, the cigarette advertisement shows a healthy, sexy, young couple savoring a smoke together while sitting next to an idyllic stream in the countryside. In the corner of the ad, a terrifying warning is posted, starkly in black and white, that smoking causes cancer and birth defects. Alternative and harshly conflicting messages cannot be simultaneously processed. The dire, factual warning of death and deformity competes with positive and pleasing *imagery* of health, beauty, and enjoyment. The cigarette producers do not deny their product kills. They don't need to. They know the more powerful and reassuring *alternative* message — smoking is about pleasure — will prevail.

Less than three years after Judge Timony and the FTC ruled that saturation from Amway's unlimited recruiting was "immaterial," that false claims of high incomes were "inspirational," and that "retail rules" prevented harm, new factual evidence emerged that contradicted those reassurances. Realities of saturation, enormous consumer losses, and pervasive deception came to a forefront. As it turned out, the revelations did not matter. With enough power and presumed authority, and backed by FTC approval, these devastating facts and statistics would be blithely contradicted, reality reshaped by a dominant narrative that MLM is the truest pathway to the American Dream.

Live celebrity appearances, clergy and politician endorsements, countless testimonials delivered with smiles of joy, and proclamations about "income opportunity," made victim complaints and damning data virtually invisible. Like cigarette promoters who did not have to deny their products are lethal and could sell them with horrifying warnings right on the package, Amway moved beyond denial to rely on alternative facts to smother those truths.

In the aftermath of Judge Timony's ruling and as contrary facts emerged, MLM had already grown into a major political lobby with extensive connections in the National Republican Party. Rich DeVos, former Nutrilite recruiter and one of Amway's founders, served as the National Finance Chair of the GOP in the same year of the legendary "Amway Decision." To support the nomination of Ronald Reagan for the upcoming 1980 election, DeVos personally contributed and raised $145 million[i] (in today's dollars) from America's rich and powerful, of which the former Nutrilite recruiter now ranked as a member.[125] His Amway co-founder and Nutrilite colleague, Jay Van Andel, had simultaneously become the chairman of the U.S. Chamber of Commerce.[126] Big Business and the Republican Party were now arrayed with Amway's "endless chain" scheme, a financial proposition that had previously been understood by regulators across the country, including the FTC, as fraud.

By then, multi-level marketing was more than just a very large business with deep political connections gained from payments to politicians. It was also a mass movement on Main Street USA with millions of followers who displayed levels of zeal and obedience never before seen in American business. Some followers resembled addicts with fanatical behavior once reserved for certain realms of religious fundamentalism and political extremism. Now giving itself the legitimate-sounding name, "multi-level marketing," the phenomenon morphed into a syndicate of essentially identical enterprises. Amway, the direct descendant of Nutrilite, was the syndicate's ringleader.

The new cartel took its seat in the pantheon of American power alongside Big Tobacco, Big Pharma, the Military-Industrial Complex, Wall Street, and Hollywood. It used the tools and tactics of

---

[i] DeVos reportedly raised $46.5 million for the party's 1980 election cycle. To put this in perspective, Ronald Reagan's presidential campaign spent $29.2 million (both figures in dollars of those times)

all extreme power holders among them, to deny or ignore reality when facts posed a threat or inconvenience, and never to admit to errors or contradictions, even when verified and indisputable.[ii]

While most people fell in line under the presumed moral authority and veracity of Judge Timony's "Amway Decision" in 1979, Wisconsin's Assistant Attorney General at the time, Bruce Craig, did not. He was appalled and astounded by the decision. It defied common sense and the laws of economics. "How could what is *inherently* deceptive, an endless chain financial proposition, become legal?" he questioned. Moreover, in his youth, Craig had personal work experience in direct selling and so was able to grasp that profitable retailing in that field is impossible if the number of "retailers" is constantly expanding in any market area. With that basic experience and from his direct involvement in the earlier FTC actions against Koscot, another large MLM, Craig understood that retailing was impossible and irrelevant to the destructive outcome of any "endless chain."

Bruce Craig, it turns out, was one of only a few people in the world who paid attention and directly litigated against endless chain "business opportunity" schemes. He was one of the few who grasped MLM's innate deceptiveness and destructive power. As an attorney, he understood the *inherent* fraudulence of such a scheme, as a legal matter, could not be changed. Written law cannot conflict with commonly perceived reality. This commonsense view and overall regulatory perspective toward pyramid selling schemes were the bases for his state's anti-endless chain regulation, which he himself had written. That regulation, along with the similar statute in California, was adopted by other states, almost word for word. There was no controversy among law enforcement and in the regulatory community,

---

[ii] In *Origins of Totalitarianism* Hannah Arendt wrote that authoritarian regimes share in common "extreme contempt for facts as such … the chief qualification of a mass leader (is) unending infallibility; he can never admit an error."

until Judge Timony's 1979 ruling and FTC concurrence, which were then backed by national politicians and the larger business community.

In addition to his Wisconsin experience, Craig worked cooperatively with other Attorneys General offices and with the FTC in pyramid matters. He served a subpoena to close down MLM Holiday Magic on its CEO William Penn Patrick in California. In the late 60s and 70s, Craig worked with about 10 other AG offices that were investigating or prosecuting the new phenomenon variously called pyramid selling, endless chains, pyramid-franchising distributorships, and, eventually "multi-level marketing." Communications and leadership from the FTC came from FTC attorney, Gale P. Gotschall, who held the title of Deputy Director for Federal, State and Consumer Relations. Gotschall was instrumental in the drafting of legislation that gave states similar authority to that of the federal government to prosecute consumer fraud. The new outbreak of "pyramid selling" was an important factor in the creation of state consumer protection laws and regulations.[127] He retired in 1980, a year after the Amway ruling and months before the Ronald Reagan administration. From 1980 when Reagan took office through 1992, including the term of Reagan's former vice president, George H. W. Bush, the FTC launched almost no new prosecutions of pyramid selling schemes. Attention resumed in a limited way only in the second term of the Bill Clinton administration. During this period of regulatory silence, 1980–1996, the number of MLMs vastly expanded across the U.S. and into many other countries.

Reflecting on the general view of regulators in the 1970s, Craig said, "At one time, there was the general belief that pyramid schemes were quite similar to Ponzi schemes, chain letters, and lotteries …" He said the matter-of-fact view shared by many regulators was that MLM promoters were aware of their illegality and eventual prosecution and were merely trying to make as much money as they could before the schemes would collapse or be shut down by law enforcement. The massive and pervasive phenomenon, now called "multi-level marketing" was viewed as nothing more than a fast-money flimflam that would soon be stopped before it could further toxify the marketplace.[128]

Nevertheless, after the 1979 FTC endorsement of Judge Timony's ruling, he said "there developed a confounding legal standard where an unprovable premise (that "Amway rules" prevented deception and consumer harm) supported the myth that there are legal MLM companies (on the one hand) and evil pyramids" (on the other).

Almost immediately after the ruling, Bruce Craig and AG investigators in Wisconsin took notice of massive recruiting by Amway in their state; they started receiving reports and complaints of large-scale consumer losses. They eventually gathered data over the next several years on the incomes and tax records of all Amway operators in Wisconsin.

Craig found income deception, consumer harm, and demographic saturation. In July 1982, he filed charges against Amway and several of its top recruiters operating in Wisconsin. The Wisconsin 1982 lawsuit against Amway and its findings provided hard evidence that Amway's "rules" were irrelevant or ineffective. Retail profits were virtually non-existent, the recruiting was devious, calculated, and misleading, even to the point of hiding Amway's company name during solicitations. The income scheme based on the recruiting program, disguised as "bonuses," produced exactly the loss rates that are inherent to any endless chain. Only those at the peak, a small percentage of 1%, were making a net profit.[129]

Yet, the Amway ruling and the FTC's adoption of Judge Timony's alternative reality had the effect of building a protective wall. The truth was now struggling to be heard and believed.

Bruce Craig tactically chose to prosecute Amway only on false income claims and other forms of deception rather than as a violation of the state's well-worded endless chain regulation.[130] He made this prosecutorial call, not because of substance, but due to the new position of the FTC.[131] The self-evident truth of endless chain fraud on which the Wisconsin statute was written was set aside. This allowed Amway and other MLMs to sell an impossible income proposition, collect fees in advance, and then publicly blame the victims themselves for their losses. Pyramid Scheme prosecution was now "politically impossible."

In total, Amway's Wisconsin "sales force" that Craig was examining represented about one of every 18 Amway participants in the entire country. Craig's research showed 20,000 Amway distributorships, or one current Amway "sales" representative for every 82 households in his state at that time.[132] Wisconsin investigators made basic math calculations to show that demographics alone made Amway's income promises impossible. As the data showed, saturation was already in place,.[133]

Wisconsin prosecutors examined payout records and obtained and reviewed tax returns of all of Amway's "direct" distributors in Wisconsin. The "direct" distributors were at the top of the recruiting chain and accounted for less than 1% of the total. It also investigated how Amway presented its "income opportunity" to Wisconsin residents. At one large presentation by one of the defendants, the suit reported that consumers were told, "When you invite people, don't tell them much. The idea of products can turn some people off. Don't be a SAP, and mention Sales, Amway and Products."

The Wisconsin suit charged that the practices employed to lure people into Amway were "untrue, deceptive and misleading in that they falsely disguise the true nature of the presentation and the identity of the company involved to the extent that had the prospect known the truth, he would not have attended."

Amway's methods of solicitation were much closer — literally — to Arthur Leff's description of the classic swindler's approach, "Psst, Buddy."

Regarding the income to be gained from the recruiting chain, the lawsuit revealed a statistic so extreme that it could hardly be believed even by the prosecutors. The top 1% of Amway's sales force, on average, was suffering an annual net loss of almost $1,000 after expenses.[134]

As to Judge Timony's conclusions that Amway's pay plan was based on retailing, the tax return that Craig examined of Wayland C. Behnke, one of the three individual defendants named in the suit, is instructive. Promoted as one of Amway's great success stories, Behnke's "bonus" income, which was paid by Amway based on the volume of purchases made by Behnke himself and his entire "downline" of recruits, was twenty times greater than his gross profit from "sales." Personal sales on a retail basis in this proposition virtually became afterthoughts.[135]

Assistant Attorney General Craig was later interviewed on the 1982 *CBS 60 Minutes* exposé of Amway entitled, "Soap and Hope," about the findings of his Wisconsin prosecution of Amway. From the transcript of the *60 Minutes* broadcast:

> *MIKE WALLACE: ... after looking at the average income of the 20,000 Amway distributors in Wisconsin, Craig came to the conclusion that (Amway's income) claim was outlandish.*
>
> *[to Craig] Surely, SOMEbody's making that kind of money.*
>
> *BRUCE CRAIG: Yes. That's correct.*
>
> *WALLACE: How many? Percentage wise.*
>
> *CRAIG: About one percent.*
>
> *WALLACE: ... How much do they actually make?*
>
> *CRAIG: After business expenses, a net income of minus $918.*

The Wisconsin revelations and others did lead to the FTC taking Amway back to court one more time concerning specific "income" claims and promises that were prohibited in the 1979 ruling. Four years after Wisconsin documented pervasive deception, involving about 6% of Amway's entire USA operatives, the FTC fined Amway $100,000 and ordered it to disclose income data to new recruits, the equivalent of posting a cryptic cancer warning in a beautifully illustrated cigarette ad. Amway's version was a document it called a "Sales Aid," known as SA4400. The document disclosed that retail-based direct selling accounted for only 18% of sales, and the majority of Amway distributors never made even one sale.[136]

These baffling facts were largely ignored. MLM no longer denied its Ponzi money transfer. As the scheme spread globally, Amway and other new MLMs moved from denial to a more aggressive form of deception, the creation of an alternative reality with "alternative facts." Amway began proclaiming itself "the greatest income opportunity in the world."

... to Alternative Facts

The year after the pyramid scheme case against Amway ended, 1980, America chose a new president whose election Amway fatefully played a central role in financing and supporting. Amway's founders had fortuitously gained key roles in most of America's powerful institutions: the new U.S. president's own political party, and his main backer, the U.S. Chamber of Commerce. Federal prosecutions of MLM pyramid schemes disappeared.

The spread of *Ponzinomics* would move from American living rooms and courtrooms to the national and global stage where politics and propaganda prevailed. A campaign of "alternative" facts, replacing the reality the Wisconsin lawsuit revealed, would spread through news media using powerful PR backed by official government policy. The triumph of that decades-long campaign may be seen in the 2016 election of Donald Trump, a longtime MLM spokesman, and his appointment of a member of the Amway founding family, Betsy DeVos, to run America's educational institutions.

Many observers have noted that America has recently entered a strange new era, characterized by outrageously false rhetoric and absurd conspiracy theories. Verifiable, widely accepted, even scientifically proven facts now must officially compete with blatant lies, euphemistically called "alternative facts." In this new realm, dedicated liars have the extreme upper hand.[i]

MLM employed this perverse epistemology long before Donald Trump's administration gave it a public face. Corrosively operating at the very foundation of civil society in neighborhoods, churches, and workplaces, as well as professionally in the halls of Capitol Hill and on K Street, MLM has been, arguably, the spear

---

[i] "A lie can travel halfway around the world while the truth is putting on its shoes," —questionably attributed to Mark Twain

point on Main Street USA of the new culture of deliberate, outrageous and pervasive deception.

To sustain and spread the myth of Judge Timony's 1979 decision as *Supreme and Final Truth*, the keepers of the MLM legend have had to diminish or cover over a cascade of events that expose the ruling as a judicial snafu. Believing in the 1979 Amway ruling requires faith. Inquiry becomes heresy.

Beyond having to step over the *inherent* deception of any "endless chain" proposition, many other faith-challenging facts continued to raise their head after the ruling, starting with the Wisconsin prosecution of Amway for deception, then a criminal tax evasion case against Amway in Canada. The evidence continued unabated in court rulings against "endless chain" schemes, class action lawsuits charging deception, racketeering and pyramid fraud, occasional media investigations revealing near total absence of retail customers, self-published memoirs of cult persuasion in MLM, online videos featuring outrageously false income claims, and data analysis showing virtually 100% loss rates.[137]

In keeping with the well-known principles of propaganda making, MLM promoters employed the famous practice of repeating a lie, aka *alternative facts*, so often it is eventually perceived as the truth.[ii] Truth — actual truth — soon becomes stranger or more frightening than the comforting and constantly repeated lie.[138]

In an article about the baffling recent phenomenon of millions of American believing demonstrably false claims made by President Donald Trump, *Forbes* contributor Steve Denning referenced the writings of Hanna Arendt.[139] On the origins of authoritarianism, Arendt argued that the public (during the Nazi period), "do

---

[ii] "Repeat a lie often enough and it becomes the truth," is a law of propaganda often attributed to the Nazi Joseph Goebbels.

not believe in anything visible, in the reality of their own experience ... obsessed by a desire to escape from reality ... they can no longer bear its accidental, incomprehensible aspects. Totalitarian propaganda thrives on this escape from reality into fiction."

Current Main Street realities — low pay and limited job market, rising student debt, unaffordable housing, and bankrupting healthcare costs — provide fertile soil for the *Ponzinomics* fairy tale to take root. MLM's authoritarian character and suppression of critical thinking develop right along with its Big Lie to create an absolutist ideology on par with what George Orwell studied and wrote about.[140] MLM's endless chain deceptions are now ubiquitous on Main Street USA. Millions are taught at MLM events and recruiting sessions to deliberately manipulate friends and family and to swear success and happiness in the face of their own losses and social alienation.

Dismiss or Destroy Whistle-Blowers

In all extreme belief systems where deception and fairy tale legends replace history and fact-based reality, brutal enforcement measures are used when trickery and propaganda prove inadequate. Questioners, critics or opponents who challenge the lies face public lawsuits, smear attacks, even physical threats. MLM follows suit.

Procter & Gamble (P&G) encountered MLM extremism when a whisper campaign spread among Amway's army of participants throughout the 1980s and early 1990s suggested P&G was a "satanic" company and its logo was an evil symbol. Many Amway recruits, some of whom were traditional Christians and believed the vicious rumor spread informally and over Amway's corporate voice-mail system, hurriedly threw out products in their homes bearing the "evil" P&G logo and replaced them with Amway-branded goods, though many were much higher priced.

As a result, P&G protested in 1995 that Amway was involved in a smear of the company name, which led to Amway suing P&G and its law firm. The suit included a single whistle-blower, Sidney Schwartz, who maintained a home-based website that reported critical facts and negative experiences of Amway recruits. Schwartz was forced to abandon his consumer education efforts. P&G eventually won the case in 2007.[141]

In his memoir, *Spellbound*, former MLM recruiter Robert Styler narrated his own experience as a true believer in one of the country's fastest growing MLMs, Equinox International.[142] In classic MLM fashion — exemplified by the first MLM, Nutrilite — Equinox swelled in just five years to more than 100,000 recruits with revenue exceeding $195 million.[143] In 1996, Equinox was listed #1 on *Inc. Magazine's* list of the 500 fastest-growing private companies. But it was all a fraud. According to federal court records, more than 80% of all Equinox recruits earned less than $1,000 a year (before costs). In a letter to Equinox founder Bill Gouldd, some distributors also accused him of "sexual misconduct" and "fear tactics."

From his perspective as a successful recruiter for Equinox, writer Rob Styler described an even deeper level of cynicism, perfectly representative of the MLM culture of propaganda in which error or defeat are never admitted and whistle-blowers are marginalized into non-existence. Styler told me that after a devastating negative exposé by ABC's news magazine program, *20/20,* was broadcast, Equinox began promotions as if it had been praised and positively featured on the show, not excoriated and debunked.[144] Building on its #1 ranking from *Inc Magazine,* Equinox began to boastfully publicize itself, *"As seen on 20/20!"*

Gouldd continued offering "training" and "consultation" services to MLM recruiters and promoters, multiplying the deceitful methods that led to his prosecution. Gouldd also displayed another classic MLM trait shared with Big Lie propaganda. He blamed the victims themselves or a conspiracy of others, exonerating himself totally. His website offered an apology to anyone "misled, lied to or manipulated" but not by him. Rather, he shifted all blame to "leadership."

When hedge fund owner, William Ackman produced hard data, documentation and verified testimonials to support his thesis that MLM, Herbalife, is a pyramid scheme, he encountered — at a level he did not expect — a firestorm of false accusations, personal attacks and counter claims. Ackman was accused by Herbalife and allied MLM promoters of illegal stock manipulation and threatened with a libel suit. When the independent documentary, *Betting on Zero,* was made about his efforts, Herbalife publicly claimed Ackman was secretly financing the film and sought to destroy the reputation of the film director, Theodore Braun, an experienced and award-winning documentary filmmaker and University of Southern California professor.[145] When it was later disclosed that the true commercial backer of the film had no association with Ackman and no financial interest in Herbalife, still Herbalife claimed, without evidence, the producer was colluding with Ackman.[146]

Attacking, discrediting or marginalizing critics or whistle-blowers are defensive and enforcement aspects of Big Lie propaganda. To maintain strict control over believers and adherents, this level of deception requires even more unconscionable actions. People must be taught the equivalent of a heaven or hell destiny: a utopian future if they keep paying and recruiting, a hellish dystopia for the doomed quitters and losers.

Dystopia and Utopia

Just a few years after the "Amway Decision" in 1979, two individuals who threw away their old lives and followed MLM's alternative path to success reflected on their experiences. They offered vivid firsthand accounts of the relentless recruiting and extreme manipulations and deceptions employed to enroll people, induce them to buy product, and continue the recruiting program. They described tactics and behavior that the authors characterized as cultism. Both discovered they had entered the very dystopia they had hoped to escape. Phil Kerns's book, *Fake It Till You Make It*, and Stephen Butterfield's *Amway, the Cult of Free Enterprise*, were each published by small publishing firms that no longer exist.[147]

With two years' work and financial investment in pursuit of Amway's "compensation" plan, which he believed would provide a utopian lifetime annuity income and money "while he slept," Butterfield finally calculated the demographic limits of Amway's "endless chain" proposition. Using Amway's plan and income disclosure, he concluded that less than one-half of one percent of Amway recruits could ever reach the level of sustainable net profit, the so-called Diamond level. He calculated, "at least 2,083 new active people must be brought in, trained, motivated, programmed and supplied." Reflecting on the hundreds of thousands of new recruits lured into Amway's net each year with the promise they could become "Diamonds," Butterfield concluded, "(The business) is sold as the American Dream, but, for the average distributor, it's more like a nightmare."

By the time the Butterfield and Kerns books were published, Amway was already a major force in the National Republican Party in the U.S. Kerns's book opens with a description of the lavish dedication of the Amway Grand Plaza Hotel in Grand Rapids, Michigan, near the Amway headquarters and funded by Amway.

The event was presided over by former President Gerald R. Ford and his wife, Betty Ford. A year before that event, at the Amway annual convention, the guest speaker was presidential candidate Ronald Reagan.

Butterfield and Kerns's books each offered a portrait of how the scheme permeated individual lives, disrupted, families, and impacted social networks. Amway had become an evangelistic belief system, they both wrote, with its own rituals, hierarchy, membership, rules, enforcement, and extreme indoctrination. To those financially struggling and feeling left behind or forgotten in the global economy, it promised deliverance and fulfillment of the American Dream. To those who quit or even questioned the promised destiny, Amway's promoters predicted a dreadful life of unfulfilled dreams, regret and lost potential, a level of hell that Dante's *Inferno* might have included had Dante lived in modern America.

A decade and a half later, two more courageous individuals documented their own stories inside Amway, the prototype of all other MLMs, confirming and adding to the accounts of Butterfield and Kerns. Author and 10-year Amway participant, Eric Scheibeler, believed Amway's dystopian view of America as a land of mediocrity for those who do not seize opportunity when it is presented to them, with Amway as the greatest of all, the "opportunity of a lifetime." He dramatically quit his regular "job," mockingly called in Amway's parlance, "Just Over Broke," and based his livelihood on Amway. Like virtually all others who made that decision, he piled up debt and faced bankruptcy. In an *NBC Dateline* exposé of Amway, Scheibeler confessed he was "destitute." As he chronicled in his book, *Merchants of Deception*, he was a platform speaker at Amway recruiting events and, while falling behind in his home mortgage payments, he was hailed as a model of success in the Amway program and proof that "anyone can do it." New recruits sought his autograph. Scheibeler estimated he never made more than about $30,000 gross income from Amway.[148]

Writer Ruth Carter (literary pseudonym) also wrote a book about her long-term experience inside Amway. She described working for one of Amway's champions, a "Diamond" near the peak of the Amway hierarchy who was similarly promoted as a model for success and one of Amway's many "millionaires." She reported that this "Diamond's" entire presentation of being his own boss, enjoying generous time with his family, long vacations to exotic destinations, and an enviable life of wealth and lifetime security, was far more than a lie or exaggeration. Utopia was dystopia. He was almost dead broke, owed back taxes, was drowning in credit card debt, and traveled constantly to stir up new recruits and rally the defectors who dropped out of the program in huge numbers. He had no equity, and barely coped with family conflict caused by his long absences and constant financial pressures.[149]

The book-length accounts by Phil Kerns, Rob Styler, Stephen Butterfield, Ruth Carter, and Eric Scheibeler all revealed a lie so "colossal" they could not have imagined it. Not only did the promised utopia not exist, but also the pursuit of it led to the hellish dystopia they believed they were fleeing. Amway and other MLMs convinced adherents that happiness and fulfillment were found only at the peak of an MLM "endless chain" rather than in their own pursuits of happiness, shaped by their unique identities and founded on their personal values.

In their journey to that discovery, they each uncovered another secret. Not only was the promised Amway income unachievable for the new recruits, the famous recruiters proclaiming from the stage to have reached the utopia of "unlimited income" did not gain whatever money they were supposed to receive from selling Amway goods or from persuading others to join and buy.

In reality, the actual "income" source for the bragging and sanctimonious speakers at Amway's "motivation" rallies was the money the audience members paid to attend the events. Unsuspecting attendees were exhorted to "never quit," "believe," and buy the speakers' books and tapes. Scheibeler, Carter, and Butterworth realized that not only was the MLM goal unreachable, but the "tools" sold to them were a hoax as well. There was no secret to success in MLM, except to deceptively sell one.

DoubleSpeak Reinvented

As we've covered, the true notoriety of Nutrilite and its owner, Carl Rehnborg, was not gained as the first MLM, but rather for the FDA's landmark prosecution of the company, Rehnborg and his MLM inventors, William Casselberry and Lee Mytinger, for making dangerous medical claims for their vitamin nostrums. Nutrilite's true legacy enabled today's vitamin and supplement industry to proclaim itself "alternative medicine" while stating on all products, *"has not been evaluated by the Food and Drug Administration. This product is not intended to diagnose, treat, cure, or prevent any disease."*

Federal regulators proved no match for the legal defense of deception employed by Nutrilite. As reported triumphantly in Rehnborg's biography published by Amway, "During the settlement talks, Charlie (Rhyne, Nutrilite's attorney) , took the vitamins and minerals, one by one, and wrung allowable claims out of the FDA. The consent decree listed 54 claims that anyone could make about vitamins and minerals."[150] Nutrilite then proceeded to use the approved words "wrung" out of the FDA, to make the same dangerous and false claims. Nutrilite called it a "new language." This linguistic distortion in a successful defense of a strategy of deception laid the foundation for an extensive and sophisticated use of words to control thoughts. "War is peace," as Orwell might have phrased it.

To achieve what the FDA termed a "subterfuge," Mytinger and Casselberry hired the prominent attorney, Charles Rhyne, who would later became world famous for his involvement in one of America's greatest deceptions: the Watergate scandal and cover-up by President Richard Nixon."[151]

While Rhyne's legal maneuvers and skills as a wordsmith mostly protected Nutrilite from the FDA's medical fraud charges, the fake identity of "direct selling" and the deft and devious use of sales vocabulary successfully disguised "the plan" from commercial fraud charges. Only in the late 1960s did state and federal regulators finally begin to see through the schemes modeled on Nutrilite as product-based pyramid schemes disguised as "direct selling."

MLM was threatened with the revelation that its impossible income promise was the driver and false lure behind millions of buy-sell transactions of products, exposing the purchases as a money-transfer mechanism. A specialized language, a form of commercial *doublespeak* was adopted to obscure the entrapping endless chain incentive and to make the purchases appear as ordinary consumer purchases, unrelated to the income scheme.

- Fixed-priced transactions with contract-wholesalers were renamed "retail."
- Recruiters were called "distributors."
- Recruiting rewards became "performance bonuses" and "sales commissions."
- Paying to join the recruiting chain was disguised as signing a "sales contract" and receiving a "sales kit."
- Those who failed to enroll a recruit were renamed "discount buyers."

Though nearly all MLM participants immediately stopped buying MLM products after quitting the income scheme, their purchases made while involved were said to have been based on "love" of the "brand," this also despite the products not being advertised and few MLMs having a recognizable brand. The products never entered the open market. They did not compete on price or quality. The entire system was closed.

The entire model was given an official-sounding term, "multi-level marketing," when in fact, the structure was "infinite." The "levels" were actually just markers of recruiting activity, not management responsibility and nothing was actually marketed other than the income plan itself. In fact, there is no external "market." The recruits and recruiters are their own market.

Since the MLM scheme relied on an economic promise, the greatest linguistic challenge was the false claim of an "average income" gained by "direct sellers." Special methods of deception were needed for creating the false impression that most direct sellers made some money "on average," and that a viable opportunity was available for every new recruit to gain "extraordinary" income. This feat of falsehood had to overcome the verifiable reality that 99% of all people who joined MLMs gained no net income. The "median average" income is zero. Worse, the success of 1% — those at the peak of the pyramid — relied totally on the losses of all the others. They had not out-performed the other 99%. They had plundered them.

Legitimate income in business is a metric involving hard numbers, not vague promises to "feel better," "boost immunity," or gain "inspiration." To show "average" income data when the median average is *zero* requires trickery beyond the linguistic tactics of Charles Rhyne. The adept misuse of statistics was needed.

Lie with Statistics

How to Lie with Statistics, the most popular book ever written in the field of statistics is, arguably, about the most common way that statistics are actually used.[152] Author Darrell Huff acknowledged the book could be "a manual for swindlers" but concluded, "crooks already know these tricks."

The "crooks" and the examples of statistical deceptions referenced by Huff are not sleazy underworld types. They are professionals in the fields of advertising, marketing, public relations, partisan politics, opinion polling, and market research. After World War II, these professions gained enormous power and authority over popular views and behavior. Huff explained how the use of statistics could add "a spurious air of scientific precision" to absurd claims or erroneous conclusions that a common-sense observation or a more careful examination would quickly reveal as nonsense or dangerously false. He gave special attention to the misleading but visually powerful charts, graphs and other data-based representations, the so-called "info-graphics" that can serve as "fluent, devious, and successful liars."

Written in 1954, Huff's book, with illustrations by collaborator Irving Geis, maintained a humorous tone but took the power and misuse of statistics very seriously. He noted, "A well-wrapped statistic is better than Hitler's 'big lie.' It misleads, yet it cannot be pinned on you."

No area of commerce had greater need for a propaganda tool "better than Hitler's big lie" than the newly invented "multi-level marketing." It would need numbers and data in order to charge real money in exchange for something that is non-existent — opportunity for "unlimited income" from an "infinitely expanding" recruiting chain. As Arthur Leff explained, pyramid sellers hawk a mystical commodity on par with the salvation and "prosperity" promised by unscrupulous evangelists or the "dispensations" and "indulgences" sold by corrupt medieval clerics. Such "products" are said to be infinite in quantity, but obtainable only through divinely licensed practitioners and deliverable only to those who pay the going price.

Two intertwining cons were concocted by the founders and early developers of "multi-level marketing" to disguise the core pyramid scam. The first: the new sales model is true "direct selling," heir apparent to the Yankee Peddler. The second: millions of people were actually gaining income. Casting themselves in the roles of patriotic dispensers of wealth, two leaders of the emerging MLM industry, Richard DeVos and Jay Van Andel, gained key leadership positions in the Republican Party and U.S. Chamber of Commerce.

Much credit for the MLM's triumph is attributable to its "fluent and devious" misuse of statistics to support these revered but utterly false identities of "sales" and creator of wealth, now frequently called "job-creator." Promotion was assigned to spin masters at the Direct Selling Association (DSA), the Washington, D.C.-based organization taken over by multi-level marketing companies in the 80s and 90s, and which now serves as its chief propagandist.

Surveys were soon published by the DSA that seemed to show most people in MLM were making modest to extraordinary incomes. "Research" produced data that the median average income (half make more, half less) of all "direct sellers" was more than $2,400 per year.[153] This particular statistic, though fictitious, in fact mathematically impossible, appears to have been carefully chosen to evoke a complex response.

Some journalists, regulators, and consumer protection activists cite this DSA-sourced figure to show a reality of little or no income in MLM. The MLM promoters, however, understand the number produces the opposite effect on the public at large. As a "median" figure, it means that half make *more*. It is an "average" and most people believe they are "above average." Even as a baseline, it validates MLM's most important claim that *most people* do make *some* income. On average, the data seem to prove, it is about $200 a month but could be much, much more. In the real world of work and livelihood, an "extra" $200 a month (or more) is significant. It could be an insurance premium, a credit card bill, even a car payment.

At an October 2016 presentation to the DSA, Edith Ramirez, the FTC chairperson, quoted this famous DSA "statistic" to its own members to make the case that, contrary to the ubiquitous and extravagant income claims by some MLM recruiters, few people gain income from MLM. She scolded the MLM promoters, "The low incomes received by most MLM participants is something that the DSA itself acknowledged more than a decade ago. … DSA cited a 2002 National Salesforce Survey showing that the majority of direct sellers made less than $10,000 per year … with a median annual gross income of about $2,400 or only $200 per month."

Ramirez perfectly demonstrated the spurious air of scientific precision that author Darrel Huff described. She apparently did not examine the DSA's data or citation. The DSA stated to the FTC, "*Over 13.6 million individuals sold for direct selling companies as independent contractors with estimated retail sales of $29 billion in 2004 … Fifty-nine percent of direct salespeople make less than $10,000 per year from direct selling.*"

Thus, the DSA had claimed that 41% earned *more than* $10,000. Forty-one percent of 13.6 million is 5,576,000 "direct" salespeople. Using the absolute minimum of $10,000 would produce $55.7 billion in *earnings* just for the upper portion! This is nearly double the industry's total "sales." *Total* earnings from all 13.6 million would have to be even more multiples of the amount the DSA claimed was the industry's entire "retail sales."[154] She had cited a statistic that seemed to have "precision" but was economically and mathematically impossible.

Knowing full well that 99% of all consumers actually make no net profit at all, and the true "median" income is zero, one can only imagine the reactions of DSA officials when they saw their concocted number repeated by the FTC itself. The reverse psychology it was designed to evoke had produced its intended effect, perhaps beyond their expectations. While $2,400 is only literally a low number as an annual income, when presented as "extra" and as an "average," a subtext promise of high income is imbedded. Knowing that the real figure was $10, DSA officials must have struggled to maintain straight faces when they heard Ramirez repeat data about the majority of direct sellers earning "less than $10,000."[155]

On top of all this mathematical chicanery, the industry's annual revenue figure contains one other gross deception. It is based on "estimated retail." *Actual* retail sales are unverified and, like the "median income," are mathematically contradicted by other DSA data. In 2017, the DSA website informed consumers and regulators that 13 million of a total of 18.6 million "direct sellers" bought products at wholesale that were never resold.[156] So, who produced $34.9 billion in "retail" sales if 70% of the salespeople never sold anything?

Recently, the DSA tried a new subterfuge. The absence of retail customers, a red flag of pyramid schemes, had been getting attention in the media and was highlighted during the controversies over Herbalife. In 2018, the DSA announced it used a new method of counting and determined that actually only 6.2 million people in America were "direct sellers." Twelve million others who had been counted in the total the year before and nearly that many in earlier years were actually "customers," though they had signed contracts as "resellers." Finally, multi-level marketing had found people who buy the products besides the "salespeople" themselves. It was the same people as before, but now they had a new name, "customer."

But, then, to give this new statistic what Darrell Huff might have described as "precision," the DSA added that its new method of counting further revealed that one million of the 6.2 million work "full time." A million people in America able to support their families "full time" from MLM would surely be impressive, *if it were true*. But, like the "median income," it cannot be. If a modest $40,000 gross income, *before all expenses*, were used as the minimum gross income for "full time" status, then one million full-time direct sellers multiplied by $40,000 would total $40 billion in *income*. But the DSA reported that total annual retail *sales in 2018* were just $35.4 billion. The full-timers can't be *earning* more income than the entire industry generates in total revenue. To make matters worse, the number does not account for the incomes of another 5.2 million the DSA said work "part-time." Now the "income" total would be multiples of the whole industry's "sales."

These DSA figures produce only frustration, confusion, bafflement and, eventually, abandonment of analysis. The numbers make no sense. They contradict each other.

Unprintable

Nevertheless, the impossible "median average income" of $2,400 was widely reprinted by the news media for years. In the past, colleagues and I attempted corrections but soon concluded it is futile. We realized that the news media would never report that millions of Americans are being lured into an "endless chain" income proposition, in which purchasing products is just the price to participate. Journalists would not write that millions are trapped in a recruiting scheme that promises to pay cash rewards, but in fact virtually no one who signs up each year ever gains any net income at all or that the promised fountain of "un-limited" income is just the investors' own funds, transferred inside a fixed system. It is unprintable. A Big Lie, it bears repeating, is one so "colossal" that no one would believe that someone "could have the impudence to distort the truth so infamously."

One of my personal experiences with the media is typical of the experiences of my colleagues.[157] An independent journalist at The New York Times wrote a piece for the Sunday edition on March 14, 2009, entitled, "Direct Sales as a Recession Fallback."[158] It reported that in a time of long unemployment lines, ruined saving accounts, and plummeting real estate values, there was, happily, a "fallback" for the average person in "direct selling." DSA spokeswoman Amy Robinson was given the space to inform millions of readers that the direct selling industry is "growing" at more than 4% a year, without noting the quitting rate. Robinson also touted the $2,400 median income number.

In this uplifting and reassuring article, I am quoted sourly and confusingly, warning about pay plans that transfer most of the rewards to the top recruiters.[i] The article notes that "some" multi-level marketing companies might be pyramid schemes and one MLM that is a member of the Direct Selling Association is being "investigated."

I followed up with the journalist to point out the errors in her article, which would likely mislead many people to invest time and money in "multi-level marketing." I quoted her sentence, *"The median income from direct selling is $2,400 annually, according to the association,"* and wrote to her asking for a correction based on what I knew.

---

[i] Deep into the piece, it states, "'Most of the commission should go to the salesperson, not the recruiters above her,' said Robert L. FitzPatrick, founder of PyramidSchemeAlert.org, a nonprofit consumer education Web site. He advised asking a company how sellers are compensated."

Real data, not just claims based on surveys but available in disclosures and court documents from the MLM companies, I explained, show that, *on average*, people *make no profit* from "direct selling," the opposite of what the *Times* article led readers to think.

The *Times* didn't make a correction, though the "median income" statistic is nowhere to be found now on the Direct Selling Association's website.

The Retail Ruse

There is one element at the very core of the "direct selling" myth where statistics are not exaggerated or concocted. Rather, hard data are avoided altogether. While the DSA issues an unverified and economically impossible "estimated retail" volume for the whole industry, each and every company in the industry shrinks in terror from a direct question of how much of its own products are "retailed?"

No other data on the "retail" question — the amount purchased by consumers who are not also "distributors" — can be found among the all the charts, graphs, and numbers on the impressive-looking website of the "Direct Selling" Association. This blackout on retail data, other than the mythical "estimate" for the whole industry, began in the mid-1990s when "level of retailing" emerged as a *sine qua non* for legality.[159]

The percentage of retail sales versus internal purchases and transfers by the distributors themselves inside the "endless chain" does not lend itself to fake numbers like the mathematically mysterious "median income" or the falsified "estimated retail sales" of the whole "industry." A precise number offered by an individual company can put that company into a legal trap. The discovery that virtually no one "sold" a particular MLM's products or virtually none of its participants were making a profit from "retailing" could become the de facto red flag of pyramid fraud.

What mostly drove the MLM industry to ban statistics altogether from the retailing fable was a 1996 federal court decision against the multi-level marketing company, Omnitrition International, a spin-off of the older and larger MLM, Herbalife, and founded by former Herbalife recruiters.[160] Omnitrition became the target of a landmark class action lawsuit brought by distributors that led to a federal court ruling, famous for clarifying what "retailing" means under the law and when applied to "multi-level marketing."

As a legal determinant for multi-level marketing, the retail factor as was planted in the law by the landmark Koscot decision four years before the Amway ruling. That decision permitted MLMs to compensate upline distributors but only on "consummated sales" by downline distributors to persons who were not participants in the scheme. The Amway decision cited Koscot but ignored the critical "consummated" requirement. Instead, it introduced the "Amway rules," for which there was no precedent, as a substitute. Amway convinced Judge Timony and FTC Commissioner, Robert Pitofsky that its business was all about retailing, not recruiting, despite its endless-chain structure, sign-up fees, purchase quotas, "bonuses" paid to recruiters and its claim that sales between people inside the chain were "retail."

Reality was soon replaced with the myth of millions of Fuller Brush-type salespeople and the miraculous resurrection of "direct selling" thought by marketing experts to have quietly died of obsolescence. The myth of "direct selling" and the political protection enjoyed by MLM were already so entrenched that Amway blatantly included in its 1991 "disclosure" that only 18% of its goods were ever retailed to the consuming public. Sixty-four percent (64%) were sold inside the chain to "other distributors" and, according to the disclosure, about as much was "personally consumed" on average as was retailed.[161] Such revealing disclosures about the "level of retailing" soon disappeared after the Omnitrition court ruling.

The potentially disastrous threat — legal and financial — that a true "retail" data point posed for "MLMs" was revealed in 2012 when a hedge fund manager publicly asked Herbalife managers the terrifying question of "how much?" It caused a panic among shareholders. Herbalife's stock instantly plunged 20%.[162] As it turned out, Herbalife would not answer the question because it knew perfectly well that almost no Herbalife products are ever "retailed."[163] The FTC verified this after two years of study. Herbalife paid restituion of $200 million.

Rather than address the "retail" question, which is actually about the claim to be "direct selling," by using faked statistics as is done with the "income opportunity" claim, MLMs now argue that *all* purchase transactions, inside or out of the chain, including those made at wholesale price, yielding no retail profit margin, are "retail." In a February 29, 2012, video interview with Dennis Berman of the *Wall Street Journal*, Amway's Doug DeVos, grandson of one of the founders, made the incredible assessment that there is no commercial distinction between "retail" and "wholesale" or just buying and never selling the goods at all. When asked what percentage of products are sold to the general public, DeVos replied, "… ultimately all of its goes to an end-user. Even if somebody happens to be a distributor, they are their own best customer. So I would say … a hundred percent."[164]

Amway and other MLMs could possibly get away with telling reporters, few of whom had any sales or business experience, that there is no difference between non-negotiable wholesale transactions inside a sales channel and retail sales to the public driven by demand, pricing, quality, and brand appeal. The retail issue could not be so easily dismissed or covered up by government regulators. There are court rulings that defined retail — the Omnitrition ruling as one — and previous prosecutions based on the retail factor, which the FTC had to enforce.

It is at this point where the collusion of government becomes an indispensable element of *Ponzinomics*.[i] The burden of carrying

---

[i] The definition of *Ponzinomics* adopted for this book includes, "*The societal spread of Ponzinomics is necessarily accompanied by governmental collusion.*" On their own, unsustainable and harmful systems, such as MLM, collapse quickly, are exposed and prosecuted, or they are driven out by citizen protest. When backed by government, however, they can persist many years and be normalized by propaganda and the inaction of law enforcement.

the Big Lie now shifts to those who hold the public trust. It requires the invention of a fable not unlike the myth of magical Unicorns, a creature never seen, yet widely believed to exist and even spawned businesses that purposed to sell part of Unicorn horns, said to bring happiness and health.[165]

Legalize Unicorns

With news media and regulators frequently citing a "focus on recruiting" as the "red flag" of a pyramid scheme, the MLM industry needed more than *doublespeak* or fake statistics and diversion to maintain the retail ruse. Into this confusing and treacherous space where millions of people are lured into "direct selling" with their money and hopes, the U. S. Federal Trade Commission brought its power and authority to bear — *to uphold the retail myth.*

Under the thumb of political forces supported by MLM money, the FTC's role is hopelessly conflicted, leading to its own Big Lie. Decades of futile and frustrating effort by consumer activists and MLM victims to get the FTC to investigate MLM recalls Upton Sinclair's famous insight into systemic corruption, "It is difficult to get a man to understand something, when his salary depends on his not understanding it."[166]

In a perfectly ironic circumstance, the interests of both parties, FTC and MLMs, have merged around a common narrative, the legalization of something that does not exist, like a Unicorn. Protective coloring for the FTC has been achieved with a *mythical* definition of MLM, not found in the real world. If this definition were true, it would technically meet the test of legality, as outlined in various court decisions.

> *Multi-level marketing is one form of direct selling, and refers to a business model in which a company distributes products through a network of distributors who earn income from their own retail sales of the product and from retail sales made by the distributors' direct and indirect recruits. Because they earn a commission from the sales their recruits make, each member in the MLM network has an incentive to continue recruiting additional sales representatives into their "down lines."*
>
> *— Definition used by FTC[167]*

Metaphorically, the FTC legalized Unicorns (MLMs that met the retail-based definition) to roam the forests and enchant humans. However, under this policy, if a real creature happened to be found to be impersonating Unicorns by not having the mythical power to enchant (virtually no retail revenue and a main focus on recruiting), it could be removed from the forest (shut down). Since, *officially*, these Unicorn-MLMs do exist, and MLM prosecutions are extremely infrequent, it may be assumed by the public that Unicorn impersonators, (illegal MLMs that are pyramid schemes) are rare.

Political suppression of the FTC — covered in ugly detail in the next section — is matched by absurdly limited resources. The FTC's 2020 budget is just over $300 million with just 1,140 full-time positions. For perspective, the Herbalife settlement of a $200 million fine paid to the FTC and disbursed to 350,000 victims represented an amount equivalent to 65% of the FTC's entire annual operating budget.

The FTC protection policy, like MLM's recruiting scheme, appears on the surface to be its opposite — a "consumer protection" agency to prosecute "illegal" MLMs. It has a record of more than 30 successful MLM prosecutions. A closer look and a study of the FTC's regulatory history reveal only the clamor of gongs and cymbals.

Though MLM presents a new and unprecedented threat to the public — an entire "industry" based upon "endless chain" deception — the FTC has never requested definitive legislation to enable enforcement. To combat MLM pyramids, the FTC interprets the general language of Section 5(a) of the FTC Act to include pyramid schemes as "unfair or deceptive acts or practices in or affecting commerce." Violation of this provision is only a *civil offense*. The Department of Justice, in collaboration with the FBI, the SEC and the Postal Inspection Service, could prosecute pyramid schemes *criminally* for fraud. This rarely happens. Some state

Appearance of Action
20-Year Prosecutions

1. (*2016*) FTC vs. Herbalife,
2. (*2015*) FTC vs. Vemma,
3. (*2013*) FTC vs. Fortune High Tech Marketing,
4. (*2006*) FTC v. BurnLounge,
5. (*2004*) FTC v. Mall Ventures, Inc.,
6. (*2003*)FTC v. NexGen3000.com,
7. (*2002*) FTC v. Linda Jean Lightfoot
8. (*2002*) FTC v. Trek Alliance, Inc.,
9. (*2001*) FTC v. Skybiz.Com, Inc.
10. (*2001*) FTC v. Streamline Int'l, Inc.,
11. (*2001*) FTC v. Bigsmart.com,
12. (*2000*) FTC v. Netforce Seminars, Inc.,
13. (*1999*) FTC v. 2Xtreme Performance Int'l,
14. (*1999*) FTC v. Equinox Int'l, Corp
15. (*1999*) FTC v. David Martinelli, Jr.,
16. (*1999*) FTC v. Five Star Auto Club, Inc.,
17. (*1998*) FTC v. Affordable Media, LLC,
18. (*1998*)FTC v. Kalvin P. Schmidt,
19. (*1998*) FTC v. FutureNet, Inc.,
20. (*1997*) FTC v. Cano,
21. (*1997*) FTC v. JewelWay,
22. (*1997*) FTC v. Rocky Mountain International Silver and Gold, Inc.
23. (*1997*) FTC v. World Class Network, Inc.,
24. (*1996*) FTC v. Mentor Network, Inc.,
25. (*1996*) FTC v. Global Assistance Network for Charities,
26. (*1996*) FTC v. Fortuna Alliance, LLC,

statutes define pyramids or "endless chains" as *felony* violations but those local laws, especially without FTC or SEC support, are almost never enforced.

When the FTC does, on occasion, prosecute MLMs it implicitly treats the companies as outliers, which prevents triggering a wider investigation to see if the mythical entity the FTC calls "legitimate MLM." really exists. No discovery of MLM-fraud triggers an inquiry to assess whether the fabled model that is based on retail sales and provides a viable income opportunity for all recruits exists in the real world.

Further upholding the mythical "legitimate MLM," the FTC has never named or identified a single MLM that serves as a living specimen, an exemplar of a law-abiding, retail-based MLM.[168] In this manner, the FTC could prosecute a few MLM schemes from time to time (less than one a year, on average since 1980) that were found not to meet its definition, that is, were impersonating "legitimate MLM." With a deftness George Orwell would appreciate, with each pyramid scheme prosecution of an MLM, the FTC affirmed that "MLM is legitimate" and, by implication, all the other MLMs uphold the retail-based model and are safe for consumers to invest their money and time in.[169]

It logically follows that anyone who points to the massive loss and dropout rates among recruits or who questions if MLM really is "retail-based," is "anti-MLM." If Unicorns were "legally" defined as real, a person that questioned whether Unicorns really did exist would be treated as a non-believer, a cynic, and "anti-Unicorn."

This unfounded, presumptive, retail-based definition is maintained even as the largest MLMs such as Amway and Nu Skin have paid out millions in class action lawsuits to settle claims brought by consumers that they are not retail-based. When Herbalife was found *by the FTC itself* to be non-retail based, no investigation was made by the FTC to see whether or not Herbalife's practices typified the entire field of MLM.

The FTC uses retail sales a measurable factor in determining MLM legality. With millions of people investing money in the belief that MLMs are retail-based, it would seem that all MLMs would be *required* to verify their retail sales levels. No requirement to disclose retail sales levels has ever been asked for or imposed by the FTC. Instead, when the FTC prosecutes an MLM, the FTC places responsibility *upon itself* to *prove* that adequate retail sales don't exist, a classic challenge of having to prove a negative. Consumer reports of widespread deception or independent analyses of multiple MLMs that show no significant retail sales have been dismissed by the FTC as "anecdotal" or rejected as not "evidence."[170]

The classic tools of propaganda employed by MLM leaders — Big Lie, alternative facts, cultivated myths, *doublespeak*, faked statistics, and discrediting critics — have successfully confused and mesmerized millions of consumers and diverted news media. The control and collusion of the FTC and other sectors of law enforcement, however, required direct action: political influence-buying involving state legislatures, attorneys general, Congress, and the U.S. presidency. Behind MLM's license to fraudulently claim perpetual expansion, falsely promise unlimited income, and openly run money-transfer recruiting schemes disguised as "direct selling," is old fashioned political corruption, boodling and bribing. Public officials have to be "influenced" to protect MLM over the public interest. The story of *Ponzinomics* now enters the dark world of K-Street lobbying, revolving doors between consumer protection agencies and pyramid schemes, and political fixes.

INTERLUDE:
CALCULATORS FOR LOSERS

"Ask him a question," she whispered and urged with a nudge. Equipped with two hidden cameras, one in her hat, the TV producer wanted me to engage the hyperactive promoter on the stage. As famous expert on multi-level marketing and pyramid schemes, I was invited to come all the way to Toronto to help explain how MLM scams work and why Canada's regulators were ignoring them. Part of the investigative report included undercover footage of an actual MLM recruitment meeting held at a local hotel. I thought I was just there to observe and comment later, but the producer wanted some live interaction.[171]

Ok. I rose from my seat ready to put him on the spot. He had just finished drawing on a flip chart an amazing projection for gaining income. All that an attendee had to do, after paying $3,200 was enroll just eight other people, he had explained. They repeated that process, 16, 32 ... Math did the rest, leading to extraordinary wealth. Each enrollee not only gained an income position but also membership in an amazing travel club with great discounts. With the money that people could earn in the program, they would be taking a lot of vacations, he noted. Each level multiplied in size, and the profits from all the levels flowed back to you. Think about it, he taunted us. What's the future in whatever little jobs we were in now? And the cost to take advantage of this was only a few thousand Canadian dollars. Pointing to his calculations on the board, like the blueprint for a perpetual motion machine, he asked triumphantly, "How could you lose?"

But I had my own machine, which I wielded in my hand, a small calculator. I said, "Sir, I entered your recruiting plan of eight recruiting eight into my calculator here," which I now proudly brandished. "It shows that after I got my eight and they did the same, like you said they could, the process could only go just seven more cycles and we would run out of people in Canada. I mean every living soul, including the infants and the elderly. So how could the plan work?"

The giggling and clapping he had been evoking with his good news stopped. The room went quiet. The little calculator remained in my hand like a deadly weapon. Eyes turned to the speaker. But he did not say anything. He let the silence hold the room. Finally, he turned not to me to reply but to everyone else in the room. I became invisible.

"You see," he said, "that's a perfect example of what I was just saying about success and failure, winners and losers. There are those who *see* success, who *believe* in success, who can envision their lives as *total* successes. They will be *winners!* And then there are ... the others. They have *reasons* and *excuses*," he said in a whiney voice, "and," with a pause, "cal-cu-la-tors." Laugher erupted. The room brightened. Freedom and opportunity returned. No one looked at me or my useless, malevolent little calculator. All eyes went back to the stage.

"This is the opportunity of a lifetime. It works. Others have done it. I can swear to that myself. But, you have to reach out and grab that opportunity. If you hear about it but then what you reach for is ... *a calculator*? Well, what can I say?"

PONZINOMICS — POLITICS

Ponzinomics: noun / pän-zē-ˈnä-miks / a pseudo-economic, all-encompassing, delusional belief system that promotes the swindle of a Ponzi or pyramid scheme as a valid economic model that promises believers a fulfilling and financially rewarding way of life, complete with mission, values, leadership and worldview. *The societal spread of Ponzinomics is necessarily accompanied by governmental collusion.*

The Fix

"If what you are saying is true," I am so often asked, "why hasn't the government prosecuted the MLM industry? You think you know more than the FTC and SEC or Congress? Wait … (with a derisive laugh) are you saying the government is in on it too?"

My answer to that question is seldom well received. For calling out and protesting conflicts of interest and revolving-door payoffs from MLM, especially at the FTC, and linking regulatory inaction to political influence-peddling, I am rebuked by colleagues for "crossing a line," attacking allies, impugning the character of honest civil servants or, in seeming contradiction, for holding unrealistically high expectations for integrity from government. The nation's political leaders know the facts of MLM and its dire financial and social consequences but allow it — profit from it. This is too much to point out, bordering on conspiracy theory or anti-government nihilism.

Yet, just as dissection of MLM's defining elements reveals a calculated swindle, the record of government toward MLM lays bare the nasty reality of a political fix. MLM is sustained not by law or markets but by *Ponzinomics*, a delusional belief system that relies upon and requires government complicity. President Trump's direct and personal role as MLM's namesake endorser, and his ceremonial anointment of Betsy DeVos from the Amway family to the Presidential Cabinet, only made official what has been going on for 40 years under Democrats and Republicans.

In 1982, just after Wisconsin's prosecution of Amway for deceptive income claims and false solicitations, Amway was prosecuted for massive criminal tax evasion by Canada. Amway pled guilty and paid the largest fine ever levied by that country at the time.[172] Wisconsin and Canada's findings provoked no interest at the FTC or Congress.

Tell-all books were courageously published in the mid 1980s by former MLM adherents, Stephen Butterfield and Phil Kerns, which revealed not only pervasive deception but also an enormous and secretive business in tandem with Amway to induce recruits to buy books, audiotapes, and to attend costly seminars, all additional costs for the elusive "success."

Four more books were published in the late 1990s about a pervasive culture of deception within multi-level marketing, destruction of relationships, violations of trust and ethics and the relationship of the "model" to pyramid fraud. Curiosity at the FTC was not piqued by any of the books.[173]

A series of FTC and SEC prosecutions of smaller MLMs revealing remarkably similar patterns of deception and consumer losses were conducted in the late 1990s and a new consumer organization, *Pyramid Scheme Alert*, was created in 2001 to address documented deception and consumer losses in all MLMs. Regulators paid little attention.

A national exposé aired in 2004 on *NBC Dateline* that used hidden cameras and testimonials from victims to document the false income claims made at Amway's ubiquitous recruiting meetings.[174] No inquiry from the government followed.

In the mid-2000s, two more remarkable books were published, offering first-person accounts of the deception and mind control employed to lure people into pursuing the Amway promises of income. The writers were dismissed by Amway as disgruntled and were never consulted by authorities.[175]

In 2007, the government of England sought to have Amway shut down as "inherently objectionable." Among the findings of UK regulators: 71% of Amway's U.K. salespeople earned no commissions at all; of the 30% that earned some commission, two-third of them earned on average just $27 a year. U.K. authorities discovered that 75% of all commissions paid by U.K. Amway were transferred to just 101 salespeople positioned at the top. Even so, United States regulatory authorities showed no interest. American news media never reported the prosecution.[176]

In India, Amway's CEO was arrested for violating state laws against pyramid schemes.[177] American media ignored it. No U.S. law enforcement followed up with Indian authorities.

Despite events and increasing documentation available on losses and lies at an industrial scale, the FTC, SEC, or the FBI were not moved to reconsider the premises of the 1979 decision or take any further look into MLM. Allowed to make occultic claims of "unlimited" rewards based on an "infinite," non-diminishing market for all who believe (and pay), Amway devolved from a pyramid selling scheme, the progeny of Nutrilite, into what author Steven Butterfield called a mind-controlling "cult."

Scores of new MLM's spun off from Amway. All enjoyed the broad political protection that Amway gained for "direct selling" and developed powerful tools of persuasion. The Commissioner who wrote the FTC's acceptance of Judge Timony's pyramid scheme ruling in 1979, Robert Pitofsky, became FTC chair in 1995 under President Bill Clinton. His handpicked director of the Consumer Protection Bureau, Jodie Bernstein, later became a lobbyist for Amway.[178]

Like the comforting legends of "direct selling" and "income opportunity" that shroud the MLM business, regulators and lawmakers are swathed in their own protective myth of good government valiantly battling evil pyramid schemes. Government often fails, the tale ruefully admits, not due to corruption or neglect, but devilish maneuverings of highly paid pyramid lawyers, inadequate statutes, uninformed legislators, and insufficient budgets. Pyramid fraud endures *despite* government's good faith effort. To mention a "fix," — political payoffs and revolving doors between regulators and those regulated — is insulting, impertinent, wrong-headed, and irresponsible. The public is expected to be grateful at least for the work of regulators, however inadequate.

Legend and Myth

MLM's mythic promises of "income opportunity" began pouring out across the country as legendary "Reaganomics" promised "Morning in America." Millions of households signed up for an increasing array of MLMs. Optimism, always with the smiling face of MLM since the days of Dale Carnegie, was national policy. This held true even as factory jobs went overseas, wages declined, corporations "downsized," and small town economies collapsed. The experience of losing money in the new MLMs and the conflicted personal experiences in the recruiting schemes were swept into the powerful national messaging that now mimicked MLM's story line. "Jobs" were demeaned, entrepreneurs and wealth exalted, the poor reviled as losers, social services were diminished, deception or pollution in the cause of commerce was rationalized, and violation of social bonds for financial gain was justified.[i] Communities and even families were deconstructed into isolated individuals[ii] in a winner-take-all "free market."

In the emergence of MLM at this time, a new business model was born, nurtured by official FTC assurances it was not a pyramid scheme but "direct selling" and that its income promises were, if not fulfilled, still "legitimate." The *inherent* deception of

---

[i] The film, *Wall Street*, opened in theaters in 1987, in which ruthless corporate raider Gordon Gekko, played by Michael Douglas, captured the national mood, proclaiming, "Greed is good."

[ii] The deconstruction of modern social life into only private, personal or family affairs was famously asserted by Reagan counterpart, Margaret Thatcher, Prime Minister of the UK, " ... you know, there's no such thing as society. There are individual men and women and there are families."

an endless chain, the foundation of all previous prosecutions of pyramid and Ponzi schemes, was re-interpreted:

All pyramid schemes are inherently illegal. Some are more inherent than others.

In the new ideology of *Ponzinomics*, the American Dream was franchised as a pursuit of wealth at the end of an "endless" recruiting chain. All future MLMs would enjoy legal status and claim the same miraculous economic powers, beyond all other businesses, jobs, or profession. As the self-proclaimed standard bearer of the American Dream, MLM pledged a safe haven from global market and government forces to restrict it. It claimed to deliver what the American Dream promised.

Suppressing the terrible truth of MLM that it is the antithesis of this Dream, a social and financial nightmare, would require a political fix of global proportions.

Breaking the Spell

That "MLM" is permitted to operate with impunity due to political collusion and influence-buying is a view many find unthinkable, unbearably negative. Individual corruption is comprehensible. Systemic, enduring and bi-partisan protection of an insidious global scam is beyond the purview of "news." It would require a new vocabulary for reporting regulatory actions. To acknowledge the reality is to erode confidence in all governmental agencies. Institutional corruption will not be examined or acknowledged by the implicated institutions. As a perspective, it borders on conspiracy and provokes confusion and despair for many people.

To break the spell of disinformation and to venture into this culturally unspeakable territory requires adopting, at least briefly, a perspective from another era. The adopted way of looking harkens to a time before government corruption was normalized as "lobbying," "special" interests, and "soft" money, to an era when these were called boodle, graft, bribe, fix, and kickback. These plain and understandable terms have largely disappeared in modern coverage of campaign or electoral politics, concealing their effects. There is little investigation to explain exactly how the money affects the views, behavior or fortunes of those in Congress who receive it and there is no public discussion of standards of integrity or ethics of office holders. The role of money in politics is now treated like capital and revenue in business, a sort of fuel necessary for the process to function. Terminology that contrasts "interests" against the needs of the entire nation has been altered today to where virtually everyone is reduced to private membership in a respective and competitive "interest group," pensioners and school teachers on par with pharmaceutical giants.

The era and the perspective to be adopted for examining how MLM escapes law enforcement is that of muckraking journalism, reform, and good government movements at the beginning of the

1900s. The courage, perspective, and the factual revelations of two crusading authors of that time, David Graham Phillips and Lincoln Steffens, offer guidance through today's baffling phenomenon of pyramid scams preying upon the public as legitimate income opportunities in full view of consumer protection agencies.

To investigate and analyze corruption in the U.S. Senate in that seemingly long ago era, *Cosmopolitan Magazine* in 1904 dispatched famed writer, David Graham Phillips. His findings of more than 100 years ago eerily mirror our modern times. It turns out that many important things bearing on protection of the public interest have changed little. The Senate at that time was sometimes referred to as the "the rich man's club."

Phillips was a published novelist and well-known investigative journalist. His work is often credited with the passage of the 17th Amendment to the U.S. Constitution, which changed the method for choosing members of the U.S. Senate from smoke-filled state legislature selection to the statewide popular vote enjoyed today. Many of the targets of his Senate inquiries later resigned or were not re-elected. His provocative work resulted indirectly in his early death when a deranged person who believed a character in a Phillips's novel was based on a member of his family murdered him at age 44.

"The rich man's club" is still with us, despite the passage of 100 years' time and the 17th Amendment. In a February 2018 article, "The Wealth of Congress" published in the politically influential *Roll Call* newspaper, writer David Hawkings, cited data showing the median net worth of Congress (half have more, half less) is 500% greater than the median net worth of the voters.

In the introduction to Phillips's book, a collection of his investigative articles called *The Treason of the Senate*, the publisher offered some context for Phillips's work that is hauntingly current. It referenced data showing that "one percent of the families living in the United States held more property than the remaining 99 percent." Based on its policies, attitude and actions, it concluded the Senate represented only the one percent. It asked, rhetorically, who did not already know that a petition signed by a million of the common people would not have even half as much influence in the Senate as "a mere nod of a Havermeyer, an Armour, or a Morgan" (the rich and powerful of that day).

Phillips examined how the corruption of the Senate related to this upside-down economic structure of America. How could it be — in a democracy — that the interests of the "Amours and Morgans" were put ahead of the public and to what effect? Perhaps most relevant to understanding MLM influence-buying, he probed the character and psychology of elected office-holders and the many lower level officials who facilitated the betrayal of public trust. In that era, taking money from "special interests" that harm the public was viewed as "treasonous." Phillips observed that the elected official representing "interests" while taking an oath to serve the public, "chooses to be comfortable, placed and honored, and a traitor to the oath and the people rather than to be true to his oath and poor and ejected into private life."

Phillips began his series of articles, with a profile of the most famous New York lobbyist at the time, Chauncey Depew. In a "revolving door" pattern that is routine today, Depew moved from government office holder to paid lobbyist, working for Commodore Vanderbilt's railroad and financial empire, and then into public office as a U.S. Senator. As a senator, he was infamous as the protector and promoter of the interests of the Vanderbilts and Henry Hyde, founder of Equitable Life Insurance, the largest insurance company at that time. Phillips asserted that in an economy of "concentration," with 99% having less than 1%, politics "does not determine prosperity" but it does determine the "distribution of prosperity." The Senate, he said, is the "final arbiter of the sharing of prosperity."

From that perspective, how would *decriminalizing* or *legalizing* pyramid schemes, which systematically transfer the wealth of millions of people to a tiny handful, be seen? By U.S. law and under the prevailing regulatory policy since 1980, perpetrating a "pyramid scheme" is — effectively — not a crime, just an unfair and deceptive "business practice." By placing "pyramid schemes" under the FTC's jurisdiction, which cannot bring criminal cases, rather than the Department of Justice or the FBI, which can, Congress created a safe haven for MLM-style pyramids.[179]

In 1973, Walter Mondale, U.S. senator from Minnesota and later vice president to Jimmy Carter, put forth Senate Bill 1939. It defined the universal characteristics of MLM — payments to join, recruiting for rewards, and the promise of "endless" payments gained from purchases of recruits. It clearly distinguished pyramid purchasing from retail selling.

Senator Mondale cited a letter from Minnesota's attorney general that referred to "evils" of "pyramid sales distribution" and cited the need for a national law that would criminally outlaw them. In particular, he cited the recent FTC prosecution of the MLM, Holiday Magic, which consumed three years of legal maneuverings by the FTC, leading only toward a civil settlement or actions.

Mondale's bill stated,

> *Whoever, in connection with the sale or distribution of goods, services ... knowingly sells or offers or attempts to sell a participation or the right to participate in a pyramid sales scheme shall be fined not more than $10,000 or imprisoned for not more than five years, or both.*[180]

The bill was never made into law[i] and, from that point forward, the FTC took charge of almost all pyramid scheme law

---

[i] Walter Mondale introduced a similar bill in the next Congress, S.1509 (94th), which, like S.1939 (93rd), passed in the Senate but was killed in the House.

enforcement. Wrongdoing and financial harm of pyramid schemes were downgraded to mere civil complaints involving fines and promises to change, without admission of guilt.[181]

Phillips presciently observed the early formation of an insular, amoral world of Washington politicians and lobbyists. That world is familiar to us today and has grown to include think tanks, politically connected law firms, and some universities and law schools. The members of these DC-based professions regularly switch roles like actors in a play. He noted their cynicism about corruption and how their sense of shame atrophied. In this mindset, he observed, these lobbyists and politicians viewed their service to special interests as a "sort of patriotism."

By adopting, at least temporarily, the sensibility and ideals reflected in Phillips' 1904 analysis, the influence of "multi-level marketing" on government in which protecting MLMs from law enforcement is treated as a "sort of patriotism" may be better understood. MLM's existential need from government is not in land, franchises, tax advantages, or government contracts, as the targets of Phillips' investigation notoriously were. To run its predatory and deceptive operations would require the organization of the world's first Pyramid Lobby with its own offices in proximity to other large lobbies for banks, firearms, and casinos on infamous K Street in Washington, D.C. Its mission was clear: protection from fraud prosecution in the United States and, by political extension, the world.

Its methods would be the same as those of other lobbies that seek undue favor from politicians and government officials, mainly by purchasing insider-influence with campaign money, jobs, speaking fees, and lucrative connections to law firms and trade associations. Conversely, any officials that opposed the Pyramid Lobby would become targets of negative ads, adverse publicity and labeled "anti-business" and enemies of the American Dream.

Rise of the Pyramid Lobby

While many people are somewhat aware of large lobbying forces in Washington such as Big Tobacco, the Gun Lobby, and Big Pharma, few know of the existence of the Pyramid Lobby, a spectacularly successful influence-buying and propaganda machine that has been able to extend to over 100 countries, including in its sphere a president of United States, former MLM spokesman and namesake promoter, Donald Trump.

Historical insight into the formation of the Pyramid Lobby begins more than 40 years ago with the dubious honor that Amway owners were given at the highest level of government even while the company was being prosecuted by the FTC."[182] The incident shows that well before the FTC strangely capitulated to Judge Timony's exoneration of Amway in 1979, the foundation of the Pyramid Lobby had already been laid and was exerting its formidable power over law enforcement.

Even while the FTC prosecution was underway, Amway's founders were invited guests to the White House.[183] As Amway was engaged in continuous procedural delays against the FTC staff attorneys, it was simultaneously in direct communication with President Gerald Ford, a personal friend, political patron, funding recipient, and former congressional representative of the district where Amway is based. Amway heavily funded Ford's "museum" and presidential library. Ford was even the keynote speaker at the opening of the "Amway" Hotel in Grand Rapids.

In 1975, the time of the filing of the prosecution, it was the last days of the scandal-plagued Nixon presidency. Amway founders already had a powerful political base in Michigan, strong ties to Congress, and equally strong ties to the presidency. Amway was capable of influencing large numbers of votes in Michigan and beyond. The *Washington Post* reported DeVos's and Van Andel's rise to prominence in Washington after Ford became president.

This was between 1974 and 1976, while FTC staff attorneys were vainly pursuing a pyramid scheme case against Amway after Nixon resigned.

The *Washington Post* further reported the extraordinary connections Amway had inside the White House, "In 1975, when Amway came under a Federal Trade Commission investigation as an alleged pyramid scheme ... Van Andel and DeVos had a 43-minute Oval Office visit with Ford ... A month later, after the private meeting with President Ford, Van Andel was quoted in a Michigan newspaper as saying that Ford was aware of Amway's troubles with the FTC. Later, Warren Rustand, director of Ford's scheduling office, and William Nicholson, his assistant, were listed as stockholders in a Nebraska insurance company being formed by Van Andel and DeVos ... Nicholson was later hired in Amway's government affairs office."

It cannot be proven that Amway's political power base improperly influenced the FTC's decision to accept Judge Timony's ruling. However, the reality of Amway's politically protected status cannot be denied in the years immediately after the FTC ruling as Ronald Reagan took office. The Pyramid Lobby was growing in size to protect Amway from any review by the FTC and the protection would expand to cover the growing number of new MLMs, including Herbalife that launched in 1981.

The *Washington Post* reported that Amway's DeVos and Van Andel were "regulars" at Reagan White House events, noting one formal event they were invited to attend to honor a head of state, even while Canada was trying to extradite them for tax fraud.[184]

In 1981, just after the FTC dropped its charges of pyramid fraud against Amway, Washington's elite assembled in Grand Rapids, Michigan, at the gala for the opening of the $7.1 million Gerald R. Ford Museum. Guests included President and Mrs. Reagan, Chairman of the FTC Casper Weinberger, Vice President

George H.W. Bush, former Secretary of State Henry A. Kissinger, and top leaders of Canada, France, and Mexico.

Quietly seated among these political powerhouses were the event's underwriters, Amway's founders, DeVos and Van Andel. The *Washington Post* reported, the two were at the same table with Alexander Haig, who was the U.S. Secretary of State to president Ronald Reagan. Previously, Haig served as Nixon's Chief of Staff during the tumultuous Watergate period and retained the job when Ford took office. About a year after the formal dinner for dignitaries in Grand Rapids, Haig joined Amway as paid consultant to aid its international expansion.[185]

The amazing feat of Amway's moving, in less than three years, from the prosecution for pyramid fraud and Canadian arrest warrants for massive tax evasion to the pinnacle of American politics can be understood only by a closer look at the events and politics around that famous FTC case, a pivotal event in the untold story of multi-level marketing. The forces that shaped that event reveal how and why MLM is with us now.

Escape from Prosecution

The odor of a political fix around Amway's escape from prosecution and immediate rise in political status is difficult to avoid when one examines the facts of the FTC cases against Amway's peers and competitors in the early 1970s. FTC attorneys argued the Amway pyramid scheme prosecution on essentially the same bases as the cases it had brought against at least two other MLM schemes, Holiday Magic and Koscot, which were both successfully shut down. Only Amway was allowed to stay in business. With its two main rivals shut down by government, Amway was left predominant in the new field of "multi-level marketing," a position it holds still today.[186]

The FTC's lead attorney in the Amway case, Joseph Brownman, successfully prosecuted Holiday Magic. But after the perplexing Amway defeat, he made no public comment on the case for 40 years. Only after retiring from the FTC, Joseph Brownman broke his silence in 2018.

On "The Dream" podcast, an 11-part documentary on multi-level marketing, Brownman said he took no direct part or even sought to stay informed about the subsequent FTC actions toward MLMs. "Maybe I was so disappointed, I didn't care anymore," he said. He acknowledged that, to this day, he is confused by Judge Timony's ruling. Most puzzling to him was how the FTC staff's carefully gathered data from five states that documented market saturation for Amway recruits was, as he put it, "not rejected, but ignored."[187]

There were no essential differences between Amway and the other two large MLM companies the FTC prosecuted and no significant difference in the approach used in the respective FTC prosecutions. There was, however, an *extra-judicial* difference between the public profile of Amway's owners and the owners of those other two and their respective *political* status. As earlier noted, Amway's two founders held top positions with the National Republican Party and the U.S. Chamber of Commerce. Rich DeVos was a key fundraiser in the Ronald Reagan candidacy for president. They also presented themselves in conservative dress, as traditional business executives, pious Christians, patriots and philanthropists. They cultivated relationships among conservative politicians, hired mainstream lawyers, employed government officials as consultants and associated Amway with heartland images. Amway's advertising spokesman was conservative comedian, Bob Hope, known for entertaining American soldiers in foreign or combat locations.

In jolting contrast, William Penn Patrick, the owner and CEO of MLM Holiday Magic, reportedly the fastest-expanding MLM of that era, was a member of the extremist right wing John Birch Society. In 1966, he ran against Ronald Reagan for the Republican nomination for Governor of California on a platform far to the right of Reagan. A year later, Patrick was nominated for Vice President of the United States by the outlying California Theocratic Party. In addition to his political quests, Patrick unsuccessfully fought against the adoption of one of the country's first state statutes against pyramid selling schemes, California's "Endless chain" statute.

A 1967 profile by *Los Angeles Times* columnist Paul Coates described Patrick as "the strangest politician." It reported that when running for governor against Ronald Reagan, Patrick called Reagan a "jackass," a harsh epithet to say publicly in that era. He launched a recall vote against Senator Frank Church of Idaho for this opposition to the Vietnam war. In a speech to the United Republicans of California, a conservative wing of the party, Patrick said, "I disagree with those who want to impeach Earl Warren (chief justice of the U.S. Supreme Court). I think they should hang him." Former Assistant Attorney General of Wisconsin Bruce Craig recalls personally delivering a subpoena to Patrick in his office and noticing a pistol sitting on his desk. He did not know if it was loaded.

Patrick produced an LP record in which he presented his prescription for living, "Happiness and Success through Principle." In the recording, he defends "selfishness." Patrick exalted personal wealth as a reflection of how much good a person has done (the corollary being lack of wealth indicates a deficiency in virtue).

Glenn Turner, the owner of other large MLMs the FTC prosecuted, was a clownish and controversial figure from South Carolina with a cleft palate and a background of extreme poverty. He used his background to brand his "unlimited" income schemes, claiming that if a "poor boy with a hare lip" could succeed, anyone could. In a 2018 feature article on the unfinished "castle" Turner was building in the Orlando area before law enforcement closed down his pyramid scheme, Turner is described by the real estate agent as attention-seeking and money obsessed. "He wore red suits and was flashy and drove Cadillacs and was all about himself ... He would hold these seminars and run in front of everyone and yell, 'Money! Money!'"[188]

Turner's attorney was the publicity-crazed F. Lee Bailey who was eventually indicted on mail fraud charges in connection with his ties to Turner. Turner unsuccessfully ran for a Congressional seat in Florida as a Democrat in 1974 when the Republican incumbent was indicted for taking bribes in return for his influence with the Federal Housing Administration.

Turner learned about "multi-level marketing" as a top recruiter in William Penn Patrick's Holiday Magic scheme. He defected from Holiday Magic and launched his own scheme, different only in name and line of products offered. The constant increase in the number of "MLMs" is officially reported as company start-ups. In reality, each of them — from DeVos and Van Andel's defection from Nutrilite to form Amway, and Turner's defection from Holiday Magic to form Koscot, to now, perhaps more than a thousand others — is actually just the broadening of one gigantic "endless chain" with many tentacles. In structure, policies, practices and consequences, all MLMs are essentially identical.

Holiday Magic and Koscot were shut down and Turner went to prison. Amway, to the amazement of the FTC's own staff attorneys who brought the case, was exonerated and its founders showered with honors by America's political and business establishment. In the emerging ideology politics of *Ponzinomics*, all MLMs are equal but some MLMs are more equal than others.

Ponzinomics Joins Reaganomics

Following its escape from FTC pyramid prosecution, and gaining further advantage with its main competitors being shut down by federal regulators, Amway also slipped out of the grasp of Canadian authorities. *The New York Times* reported that the Royal Canadian Mounted Police had made an investigation that led to criminal charges against DeVos and Van Andel who were subject to arrest if they crossed into Canada. They were charged with using "false or fictitious invoices and price lists" since 1965 to lower the duty on merchandise shipped into Canada. DeVos and Van Andel could have been sentenced to up to 10 years in prison. [189]

Amway at first denied all charges, vowed to fight the case, and threatened to sue a newspaper that had published details of the massive tax scheme. Then, it was suddenly revealed that a deal had been struck in which Canada dropped criminal charges. Amway admitted guilt and paid the largest fine ever assessed for a fraud conviction in Canada.

While the Canadian tax fraud case against Amway developed, Amway solidified its influence-buying power base as a major contributor to the National Republican Party. The *Washington Post* reported that Van Andel and DeVos moved into conservative business circles and political fund-raising activities. They were listed in *Fortune's* list of the four richest Americans, estimated to be worth between $300 million and $500 million apiece, and held the title of "Eagle" in the Republican National Committee for their fundraising and personal contributions.[190]

Over the next few years, under the Reagan presidency, the Amway "eagles" merged their "business model" with the prevailing political philosophy of the Republican Party, which was making *Ponzinomics* national public policy. This merger can be officially dated as January 26, 1984. On this day, which was just two months after Amway paid its enormous fine to Canada and criminal fraud charges were suddenly dropped against the owners, the Reagan administration publicly endorsed Amway's message and model. This powerful endorsement publicly downplayed or erased the Canadian criminal case and the earlier charges of price fixing, deception and pyramid scheme fraud brought by the FTC and the state of Wisconsin. Amway's claim to provide "income opportunity" to millions of recruits, which Amway called "Independent Business Owners" (IBOs), was seen by Reagan's handlers as a perfect fit for the Republican narrative of individualism and small business while also reducing government supports for public health, education, and retirement, and eliminating consumer protection regulations. The realities that few Amway "IBOs" actually sold anything at all, did not own any business, gained almost no profit, and most quit within a year, were buried in the hype.

A *Washington Post* story at the time reported that, in 1983, an Amway lobbyist came to "his friend" who worked as an official scheduler for President Reagan's government trips. He had a plan for Reagan to speak to a huge Amway rally in Atlanta, Georgia, in January the following year. The two men, the Amway lobbyist and the Reagan administration official, had worked together in the Nixon administration. They discussed how there was a way to publicize and acclaim a direct connection between Reagan's politics and Amway's "income opportunity" scheme.[191]

In the end, Amway's corporate support for Reagan — and Reagan's support for Amway's "income opportunity" scheme — were recast from political *quid pro quo* to a mutual celebration of treasured American values. The values to justify the "endless chain" were melding with the values considered mainstream business ideals. The scheduled Amway event the Amway lobbyist wanted Reagan to speak at was renamed a "Spirit of America-Salute to Free Enterprise" rally. The event's sponsor officially changed from Amway to the established voice of American business, the Chamber of Commerce. Amway paid the costs and most of the thousands of attendees were Amway recruits.

The entire event was held the day after Reagan delivered his state of the union message to Congress, taking President Reagan directly from Congress to Amway. The affair was officially called "non-partisan," but it revealed that the new boundaries between Republican politics and Amway's pyramid recruiting were now barely discernible. Like the Amway-funded President Gerald Ford museum dedication, which became a NBC television show starring Amway-endorser Bob Hope as MC, the "Free Enterprise" rally, starring Ronald Reagan, was filmed with Amway leaders on stage with the President. Videotapes of the production were sold to Amway distributors for $90 (in today's currency) to motivate them. As pyramid economics became national political policy, pyramid politics became profitable business.

Gaining influential-positions in national business organizations and the Republican Party, staging events with celebrities and presidents for apparent endorsements worked only so far. To smoke and mirrors would be added smoke-filled rooms, old-fashioned boodling and bribing. For the Pyramid Lobby, whose insatiable need for more territory and whose schemes were multiplying in number and size, this would mean buying favors in every state, in Congress, among state Attorneys General, with U.S. Presidents and then with governments across the globe. It would continue with bribery charges against MLMs in China, where MLM-legend held that Carl Rehnborg's dream was born.

Boodling and Bribing

Pyramid Lobby Goes Public

Through the years of presidents Ronald Reagan and George H. W. Bush, 1980–1992, the FTC was silent and idle regarding pyramid schemes. What had been identified just seven years earlier by Senator Walter Mondale and by state attorneys general as an "immediate need for uniform Federal legislation, which will protect all consumers from the evils of pyramid sales distribution," was seemingly forgotten when Reagan took office. Media coverage declined even as MLMs were mushrooming across the country. The Pyramid Lobby had little to worry about.

But, after the Bill Clinton administration and a Democratic Party majority in Congress came into power in 1993, fear and loathing erupted in the MLM "industry." The Pyramid Lobby rapidly ramped up against the possibility that MLM's pyramid recruiting and false income claims, resulting in huge consumer losses, might be exposed and prosecuted under a Democratic Party-directed FTC.

To combat this, the Pyramid Lobby first adopted a more professional facade as the "Direct Selling" Association. In 1990, MLM enterprises began to take over the DSA as MLM schemes were multiplying and authentic direct selling companies disappeared. Already 25% of members were "MLM" with the remainder using the traditional and legitimate door-to-door model. Today, the DSA membership is almost 100% "MLM" as true direct selling has all but vanished due to obsolescence.[192] Outwardly the DSA was the official "lobby" of "multi-level marketing." It even located its headquarters on the infamous K Street in Washington, D.C. with others of that notorious business. Yet, the Lobby's foundation was still its deep ties to the National Republican Party and its mainstay was still the Amway Corporation. Support was also, quietly, being purchased across the aisle, as *Ponzinomics* itself pervaded both parties' economic and social agendas with strong emphasis on the financial side — banks, debt, Wall Street — of the economy. Under Reagan this was called "supply-side" or "trickle-down," and later *Reaganomics*. Under Clinton this came to be called the "Third Way."[i]

In a 1997 op-ed in the political journal, *Roll Call*, Amway-spouse, Betsy DeVos made it plain that MLM would play an important role in getting George W. Bush elected in 2000. Referring to Amway's enormous funding of political campaigns, she admitted the money was to "buy influence," stating bluntly, *"We do expect some things in return."*[193] Her husband, Dick DeVos, heir to one of the Amway founders, individually donated $48.8 million to 514 different candidates and causes over 21 years, including his own failed 2006 gubernatorial campaign.[194] During hearings for her appointment by President Trump as head of the U.S. Department of Education, Betsy DeVos acknowledged to a Congressional committee that her family may have contributed as much as $200 million to the Republican party and Republican candidates.[195]

While purchasing bi-partisan influence was now a priority goal, the most immediate perceived threat to address was the Clinton presidency and his Democratically controlled FTC. The lobby had effectively prevented "MLM-type" pyramids from criminal fraud prosecutions led by the Department of Justice and investigated by local police or the F.B.I. They would be treated only as a type of "unfair business practice" with cases handled by the FTC. Yet, even these types of cases had the potential to secure cease-and-desist orders, seizures of records, and individual company collapses. They also had the potential to spur class action suits that could lead to federal court rulings and interpretations affecting MLM. The lobby therefore concentrated on getting a Republican elected President in 2000 and to gain Republican control

---

[i] Like the term, "Multi-Level Marketing" itself, the "Third Way," is indefinable.

of Congress, which would, in turn, suppress the FTC and other law enforcement. How the Pyramid Lobby gained the support of the Democratic president, Bill Clinton, and controlled a Democratic-led FTC would only become apparent much later.

Between January 1, 1991, and June 30, 1997, according to the consumer watchdog group *Common Cause*, Amway and affiliated donors made soft money contributions to the Republican National Committee totaling $4,147,000. In April 1997, the co-founder of Amway Corporation gave $1 million to the Republican Party, one of the largest single donations on record from an individual at that time. Federal Election Commission records show that Richard DeVos and his wife, Helen, wrote two $500,000 checks on April 2, 1997 from their personal accounts.

In a 1997 article, nationally syndicated columnist Molly Ivins reported that the budget package passed by Congress that year provided a tax break "worth $283 million to one corporation: Amway."[196] Amway at that time employed as its tax lobbyist Roger Mentz who was Assistant Secretary for Tax Policy in the Reagan administration.[197] According to Ivins, "(Republican) House Speaker Newt Gingrich intervened at the last minute to help get the special tax break inserted in the bill." Besides its close ties with Newt Gingrich, Ivins reported, "House Majority Whip Tom DeLay, a onetime Amway salesman, also remains close to the company." In the same year, *Mother Jones* magazine reported that Republican Congresswoman Sue Myrick of Charlotte, North Carolina, owed her election to Amway, with almost half of her total campaign funds coming from Amway people. Myrick's congressional district was home to the largest Amway distributor in the world, Dexter Yager.

Describing Amway's formidable political lobbying power in Congress, Ivins revealed, that Amway actually had its own "caucus" of members of Congress. They were representatives who were given significant campaign contributions and they met "several times a year" with Amway officials to promote or defend Amway. Among key topics for discussion was "China's trade status." As will be documented later in the book, getting Congress to open China to Amway recruiting was a critical need of Amway at this time, as saturation in other markets was encroaching on "growth."

In 1999, the Republican Majority Issues Committee (RMIC) founded by Representative Tom DeLay (R-Texas) held its inaugural fundraising event. The RMIC declared its intention to "identify, educate, and mobilize conservative voters in key House races."[198] The private event was held aboard the DeVos family yacht. DeLay, a former Amway distributor, was later indicted on criminal charges of conspiracy to violate election law in 2002 by a Texas county grand jury. He resigned his position in Congress in 2006, was convicted, and sentenced to three years in prison but an appeals court later overturned the conviction.

In the 2000 election cycle, Amway is listed by OpenSecrets.org as among the top eleven contributors to the Republican Party, just below another corporate luminary that also had extraordinarily close ties to top officials in the Republican Party, Enron.[199] Enron was named "America's Most Innovative Company" by Fortune magazine for six consecutive years, from 1996 to 2001. In 2001, it was revealed that Enron's remarkable "profits" were non-existent, the fabricated result of fraud.[200]

Describing the events at the 2000 Republican Convention in Philadelphia where George W. Bush was nominated, *The New York Times* wrote, "For the party's top underwriters, there will be an array of gold-plated events in Philadelphia, including cocktails with General Colin L. Powell and an evening cruise on the Delaware River aboard the 'Enterprise,' the yacht owned by Richard M. DeVos, the Amway founder, who is a Bush supporter."[201]

At this point, the mid to late 1990s, these enormous campaign payments and intense lobbying activities by Amway were chiefly aimed at electing a Republican as the next president and getting Republican majorities in Congress. This was believed critical to stopping FTC or other possible regulatory actions against pyramid selling schemes. Prosecutions of MLMs had markedly increased between 1996 and 1999 though no large or significant MLMs were yet targeted. Evading or interfering with law enforcement was hugely important to maintaining MLM but only as long as an even more important goal was achieved — opening more of the globe to recruiting. Amway was running out of human beings to sell its "unlimited opportunity" to.

Opening China to Pyramids

The Pyramid Lobby was successful in helping to elect George W. Bush and to strengthening its position in Congress. Yet, before that happened, Amway also faced an immediate and existential economic need for geographic expansion. Having penetrated almost every other part of the world, Amway was running out of new markets to penetrate and churn into saturation with its endless chain proposition. Lobbying to both Democrats as well as Republicans would be required to open the largest of all new markets, China.

Creating a kind of ironic circle, Carl Rehnborg's journey to China in search of commercial opportunity was now being repeated. Amway, founded by two Nutrilite recruiters who defected and took thousands of "downliners," acquired Nutrilite in 1972, just a year before Rehnborg's death. Mytinger and Casselberry's "plan" that Mytinger jokingly predicted would sign up "everyone on earth" had indeed spread worldwide, but China, the most populous of all nations, had been out of reach due to politically imposed trade restrictions. This had to change for Amway's survival. Quitting rates always threatened to outpace recruiting. Reaching China's massive population could not wait for the 2000 presidential election.

Amway and a few other "MLMs" entered China in the mid-1990s under auspices of the Clinton Administration's Dept. of Commerce. Avon was one of them and was still employing a more traditional "direct selling" model. Predictably to those few who understood the nature of "MLM," introduction of the American-invented endless chain system immediately provoked a recruiting mania in China among hundreds of thousands seeking the legendary "unlimited income." It was followed by their inevitable losses, which only generated more MLMs, each claiming to possess the Holy Grail of "individual opportunity," the explosive promise of capitalism newly introduced to China.

In an intensely compacted time frame, and lacking the cultural and financial background on which MLM had been built in the U.S., China was re-enacting MLM's American trajectory. Large American MLM companies — the *first* ones in — dominated, but many new ones were rapidly forming, each a replica of previous ones while claiming to be "unique." The migration of millions of people from "failure" in one MLM to failure in another was exploding in China as it has in the United States.[202]

The idea that "MLM" was merely a pretense of capitalism was even more unthinkable in China than in the U.S. Undoubtedly, Chinese enthusiasts had been told of what Ronald Reagan had said of Amway and multi-level marketing. "You really are capitalism in America," he said.[i] MLM promised to be not the capitalism of the sweat shop textile mills and electronic device assembly plants, but the heavenly gates of Wall Street, Las Vegas, and Madison Avenue combined — equity, self-employment, compounding returns without more work, and the treasures of "capital gains" — finally coming to the laboring classes.

But, MLMs' hallmark massive and orchestrated rallies and the cultic character of the new business alarmed the Chinese government, a centrally controlled system that imposes a single ideology on the entire country. Claiming the new MLMs were "sects and cults that spread superstition" the Communist government banned MLMs through a national law against pyramid sales schemes. Riots immediately broke out in some provinces among tens of thousands of newly recruited MLM followers frantic to gain the wealth MLM promoters had promised or at least to recoup the investments they had already made. A 1998 *Chicago Tribune* article, "U.S.

---

[i] Delivered at a Reagan campaign rally for Amway distributors, May 1980, and famously quoted in Phil Kerns's *Fake It Til You Make It*, the first book to expose MLM. Reagan spoke at various Amway events. In *Amway, the Cult of Free Enterprise*, Stephen Butterfield wrote, "the (Amway) drive for Reagan had all the histrionics of a Billy Graham Crusade."

Hopes China Will Ease Direct-Sales Ban," quoted a local Chinese newspaper story that in one scheme, "70,000 people surrendered their savings to a selling scheme based on cashmere sweaters. One person committed suicide ... after the company failed to meet its promises of riches, the newspaper said. Other operations seemed to be evolving into virtual cults."[203]

MLM's "endless chain" model was invented in the U.S. It produced similar consumer manias and caused the same scale of losses in America. Several books had already been written about Amway as a "cult," depicting MLM owners as cult leaders. Yet, the *Chicago Tribune* article quoted an Amway official claiming the chaos, losses, frauds, and personal tragedies taking place in China were connected only to foreign or China-based MLM companies, not to U.S.-based Amway. Amway, it noted, is "... by far the largest U.S. company operating in the direct-selling market (of China). It has 80,000 distributors."[204]

U.S. Trade Representative, Charlene Barshefsky, who was appointed by Democrat Bill Clinton, appeared to agree with Amway. She intervened on behalf of the U.S. MLM industry to have the ban lifted at least on American companies that were the prototypes of all others. "U.S. companies have $120 million invested in the direct-selling market and provide incomes to 2 million Chinese," she stated. The *Tribune* article did not explain and Barshefsky did not cite data or evidence, as to how MLMs were providing "incomes" to 2 million people. It did note, however, the vast majority of that total "investment" in the new business was made by only one company, Amway, with $100 million invested including a $30 million plant in Shanghai planned.[205]

Acknowledging the direct assistance from the Clinton Administration in an April 9, 1999, press release, Steve Van Andel, son of one of the founders, welcomed reports of U.S. and Chinese Governments cooperation and expressed gratitude specifically to Clinton's Trade Representative, Charlene Barshefsky.

China Leverage

Amway's, and by extension MLM's, *de facto* immunity from prosecution in the U.S. from 1980 forward was ensured by key influence within the Republican Party, pivotal support for the election of Ronald Reagan, and a top level positions in the U.S. Chamber of Commerce. This transition to "Reaganomics," the decline of labor unions, and the end of the "New Deal" social service role of government, were momentous historical developments that have reshaped American politics and economy and in which Amway played a key role.

Similarly, Amway's *de facto* exemption from the sweeping ban on "direct selling" and its subsequent and rapid growth in China were ensured by political leverage at a historically momentous point in *China's* development. Amway's pivotal leverage over China was tied to China's efforts to gain access to the World Trade Organization (WTO). Once again, Amway played a key role in promoting that goal on China's behalf, and all the consequences that unfolded in the U.S.

The opening of China to "normal" trade relations and WTO membership, leading to a gigantic transfer of American manufacturing to China was a development of such a scale that it transcended partisan politics. Top officials of both the Democrats and Republicans facilitated this extraordinary change. It resulted in the de-industrialization of America, the production of goods with far cheaper labor in China, and was associated also with the virtual elimination of American labor unions. The main advocate for this massive change was the American business establishment, Wall Street, and the largest corporations in the country, represented by the U.S. Chamber of Commerce.

Amway's central role in this epic development is revealed in a June 8, 1999, Congressional Committee Hearing on "United States-China Trade Relations and the Possible Accession of China to the World Trade Organization." The hearing was part of a decade-long effort to "normalize" trade with China, eliminate tariffs and facilitate more transfers of production and greater sales to that country. China did in fact gain WTO membership just two years after this Hearing.

Phillip Crane, an Illinois Republican, prominent conservative, and a recipient of Amway campaign contributions, chaired the Committee. Addressing the Congressional Committee in support of China, the spokesman for the United States Chamber of Commerce was none other than Steve Van Andel of the Amway Corporation, son of Amway co-founder Jay Van Andel. At the 1999 hearing, Steve Van Andel was identified on the list of scheduled testimonies as "Amway Corporation, and U.S. Chamber of Commerce." Reflecting Amway's insider influence and lofty status with the Republican Party, Van Andel was warmly introduced. Crane noted that he personally knew Van Andel's father and repeated the myth that Amway was started from nothing "in a basement" and built up into a billion-dollar enterprise.

Other speakers opposed or expressed extreme reluctance to support normal trade relations. They cited China's violations of labor law, banning of unions, slave-like wages, suppression of human rights, lack of environmental protections, theft of intellectual properties, and restrictions on sales of American-made goods in China. They expressed concern that good paying jobs would leave the U.S.

Treading the fine line between acknowledging these unfair and harmful realities and claiming China's entry to the WTO would somehow correct them, Van Andel lauded the Chinese government for working with Amway during the ban on direct selling imposed several years earlier. He said China met demands of "foreign investors" and applied laws "in fair and responsive manner."

The enormous — and enduring — benefit Amway gained in protection from law enforcement in China, which began under Clinton, was recently documented in a January 2018 article in *The New York Times* on current tensions in China about, once again, an outbreak of national hysteria over MLM pyramid schemes. Filed from China, and citing government sources and direct interviews with Chinese MLM participants, authors and officials, *The New York Times* article quotes government data in China showing that Amway is now "the largest of the multilevel marketing companies (in China), with 1.5 million distributors, more than all the others combined." The article also noted that 30% of all Amway revenues are now coming from Chinese recruits.[206]

Following the 1998 crackdown on all "direct selling," China eventually passed a strict anti-pyramid scheme law in 2005 — the most direct and clearly worded anti-MLM law in the world. Yet, almost immediately, the law was mysteriously not applied to U.S.-based MLMs. Soon, MLMs enterprises began explosively multiplying in size and number in China. A Chinese critic who wrote a memoir about his experiences stated, "This industry is absolute chaos for China" … and added, "The root problem is that the government is riddled with corruption and not doing its job."[207]

The fears of Communist party security officials of MLM "cultism" that had prompted the clampdown in the late 90s, leading to the Clinton Administration rescue, materialized. Participants and others accused Amway of running a pyramid scheme in China as it is in the USA and other countries. Ex-distributors organized online forums to warn the uninformed. Amway's name in Chinese, *an li*, also means to "promote heavily" or to "be brainwashed."

Amway was, strangely, enjoying immunity from law enforcement in China, just as it does in the USA, while its main MLM competitors such as Avon, Usana, Nu Skin and Herbalife, were harassed by regulators.

Harvard's Help

Amway was able to spread its influence in China and remain unphased by law enforcement not only with U.S. government help but also with the support of prestigious American institutions such as Harvard University in an Amway-Harvard "partnership." The financial ties between Harvard and Amway were revealed in a September 24, 2013, story in *Bloomberg News* by Dune Lawrence, entitled "Amway Embraces China Using Harvard Guanxi." Lawrence reported that Amway was underwriting a program in which Harvard received payments to provide a public policy training program for provincial leaders of the Chinese government. The Chinese participants were called "Amway Fellows" and the Amway-paid program included tours and meetings at Amway headquarters. The article revealed how Amway leveraged Harvard's influence and its respected university status, a form of affiliate marketing called *Guanxi* in China, to protect its commercial scheme in China from fraud investigations.

In response to an inquiry from former Assistant Attorney General of Wisconsin, Bruce Craig, about the propriety of Harvard's endorsement of Amway, David Elwood, Dean of Harvard Kennedy School, wrote in November 2013, "Our funding arrangement with Amway (China) is animated by that mission and the belief that we are contributing to the public good in China." As more negative revelations about "MLM" surfaced during the FTC prosecution of Herbalife, and following persistent further inquiries, Bruce Craig received a one-sentence email in 2017, from Douglas Elmendorf, the current Dean of the Harvard Kennedy School, that cryptically stated, "We do not currently have a program involving Amway, and we have no plans to reinstitute such a program."

A *New York Times* article, which referred to this Harvard scheme[208] after Harvard withdrew, offered one telling example of how Harvard aided Amway in evading law enforcement, while other MLMs, Avon, Usana, Nu Skin, and Herbalife were pursued. In one city with more than 3 million people where Amway was aggressively recruiting, dozens of former (Amway) distributors accused the company of abetting extortionate practices that left them in debt. They accused their "upline" recruiters of "conning them into buying products they could not realistically sell." One recruit ran up debt of hundreds of thousands of dollars, telling the *Times* reporter, "I was brainwashed."

In May 2016, the Chinese government initiated an investigation. Then, it inexplicably stalled. The official in charge was transferred. Ex-Amway recruits believed regional officials involved with Amway had suppressed their testimonies and complaints and a local television station was instructed not to report their case. The local TV journalist said the suppression directive came from high up in the government's "propaganda department" which was headed by an official who participated in the Amway-Harvard promotional scheme.

Related to bribing Chinese officials to maintain "direct selling" licenses, the MLM Nu Skin paid an SEC fine of more than $700 thousand; Avon was fined $135 million; federal investigation of Usana on bribery claims is ongoing; Herbalife set aside $125 million for potential fine payments. The scale of all MLM bribery to evade China's strict anti-MLM law can be glimpsed in the 2019 federal indictment of Herbalife. It describes cash payments, vacation, travel expenses, and other gifts by Herbalife officials of more than $25 million followed by accounting fraud to coverup the payments.[ii] In September 2019, Herbalife agreed to pay a civil penalty of $20 million. In the settlement statement, the

---

[ii] The revealing Herbalife-China-bribery indictment is preserved on the Pyramid Scheme Alert website at https://pyramidschemealert.org/wp-content/uploads/2020/05/HerbalifeSECBriberyChinaIndictment.pdf

SEC used the FTC's definition of MLM in which "sales" are referenced as the basis of compensation, acknowledged that the MLM model is illegal in China, and affirmed Herbalife "made false and misleading public statements in numerous U.S. regulatory filings regarding its China business model." It also detailed how Herbalife concocted an hourly wage system to effectively camouflage the recruiting payments in China. None of this led to the FTC investigating Herbalife or other MLMs further.[209]

Amway itself, by far the largest of all MLMs operating in China, has escaped any formal investigation or prosecution, and its scheme with Harvard to provide all-expense paid trips for Chinese government officials in America is not classified as "bribery."

The Clinton Boodle

How could it be that, in the late 1990s, Democrat Bill Clinton's representative in China "went to bat" for Amway and Mary Kay? Amway was leading a national effort to elect Republican George W. Bush, and coordinating campaigns to establish Republican dominance in Congress. It was seeking to stop FTC prosecutions. The FTC and the state of Wisconsin had prosecuted Amway for deception and price fixing. Amway had pled guilty to a massive tax evasion scheme in Canada. Clinton's aid to Amway to forestall global saturation would not only lead to more harm to more people, it would also feed the money machine working against Clinton's own party and consumer protection efforts.[210] Helping Amway was therefore contrary to the public interest but also to Clinton's own political interests. Or so it would seem.

In 1995, Clinton brought back into the FTC, this time as chairman, Robert Pitofsky, the person who had written the FTC acceptance of Judge Timony's ruling on Amway, exonerating it of pyramid scheme charges.

When he returned as FTC chairman, Pitofsky carried out a policy of prosecuting a few smaller MLMs, upstart competitors to Amway, giving an appearance of "anti-pyramid" consumer protection. This policy's actual message was to certify the legitimacy of the MLM industry and to protect the larger MLMs such as Amway. None of the prosecutions led to any wider inquiry into the MLM industry. He appointed Jodie Bernstein as Chief of the Consumer Protection Bureau, who later worked as an Amway lobbyist. Pitofsky's policy galvanized the official policy of the FTC that, while a few MLMs may cross the line into pyramid fraud — using a Unicorn-like definition of "MLM" — MLM is legitimate.

The rare and selective Clinton/Pitofsky prosecutions became the FTC prosecution pattern for Democratic administrations, with virtually no pyramid prosecutions at all occurring under Republican presidents. Of 26 cases in the years following the Amway decision, 18 were brought or prepared in the final few years of the Clinton administration; another five of the 26 in the waning days of the Obama term.[211]

The contradiction and ineffectiveness of this policy was brought directly to Chairman Pitofsky's attention in February 2000 by former Assistant Attorney General of Wisconsin (now retired) Bruce Craig. He wrote to Chairman Pitofsky, that he observed the "rules" cited by Pitofsky in 1979 to protect against MLM deception and consumer harm were given only token recognition and were not enforced. This led millions of victims to believe their losses were their own fault. He cited some that lost life savings, stable jobs and their marriages. He petitioned for an enforcement review.

Chairman Pitofsky ignored Bruce Craig's request. The Clinton-Pitofsky-led FTC did not make any effort to determine the efficacy or enforcement of "rules" by Amway. It did not examine whether purchase-quotas imposed on distributors and reward payments based on recruits' purchases, not sales, served to stimulate pyramid recruiting over personal and profitable retailing. It did not examine whether the massive loss and churn rates were consequences of an income proposition that could only be profitable to the top level recruiters dooming all others by the money-transfer design.

At that time and through early 2000s, whatever influence-buying the Pyramid Lobby was conducting, which could account for the Clinton administration's failure to act and for Robert Pitofsky to ignore a person of the experience and stature of Bruce Craig, was unknown. The Clinton administration's gentle treatment of the MLM epidemic seemed inexplicable. In more recent years the rewards to Democratic leaders for MLM protection and for aiding MLM in China have been revealed. The theorem of boodling and bribing as the driving force behind such actions, expounded by journalists such as David Graham Phillips almost a hundred years earlier, was once again validated.

In 1996, Clinton taped a two-and-a-half-minute video presentation on behalf of the "Direct Selling" Association, now representing MLMs that had taken over the group. The video begins with the visual image of the famous Presidential Seal. He recites "growth" statistics provided by the DSA, omitting quitting rates. Echoing Ronald Reagan 20 years earlier, Clinton calls "direct selling" the "heart of the American Dream." He claims there are 21 million direct sellers in the world (based on the earth's population in 1996, this would leave only 271 humans, including infants, elderly and desperately poor, for each of the "direct sellers" to sell to).[i] He applauds the expansion of MLM (called direct selling) into China and Russia, (three years later, MLM-style direct selling would be banned in China as a cult engaging in criminal activity) and urges more recruiting, noting, "we need even more of the kind of opportunity direct selling represents." This video is often linked and cited by MLM promoters as "proof" of the legality and legitimacy of the MLM system and is posted on Direct Selling411, the YouTube channel of the Direct Selling Association.[212]

In February 2013, Amway reportedly paid Bill Clinton the astounding "speaking fee" of $700,000 for a speech delivered at an Amway event in Japan.[213] Clinton's aid to MLM in China and inaction at home against any major MLMs hinted that a political fix was in force during his terms of office. If that were not enough evidence, the payment of this magnitude from MLM, and the im-

---

[i] As of 2018, the World Federation of Direct Selling Associations claims there are 118.4 million "independent representatives" worldwide. This would mean each one has only 64 other human beings to sell to, including infants, elderly and abjectly poor. (https://wfdsa.org/wp-content/uploads/2019/06/Sales-Seller-Report-FINAL.pdf)

age of Clinton sharing the podium at that speaking event with Amway CEO, Dick DeVos — an arch-foe and ideological antagonist of supposed Democratic Party values and policies — should make the case for old-fashioned boodle.

A second top official from the Clinton administration also emerged as a champion of MLM: Madeleine Albright, Secretary of State, served as a business consultant and a brand ambassador for the multilevel marketing company, Herbalife. In 2014, *The New York Post* reported that Albright's "lucrative gig" promoting Herbalife earned her an estimated $10 million. Albright's firm, the Albright Stonebridge Group, leveraged her diplomatic credibility gained as a public official under Clinton to expand Herbalife recruiting in other countries. She was particularly effective in getting "Herbalife licenses in China."[214] Albright was the second U.S. Secretary of State to become an MLM "ambassador." Amway hired Alexander Haig shortly after he left that same Cabinet position for Ronald Reagan.

In recent years, the revelations of other prominent Democrats joining the cause of pyramid protection for fees and jobs have corrected earlier thinking that Republicans hold a monopoly in this lucrative protection program. Formerly known as the "Amway Caucus" in the 1990s and composed only of Republicans, today forty-one members of the House of Representatives have joined the newly re-branded "direct selling caucus." Eighteen members are Democrats.[215]

State-by-State Influence-Buying

Without FTC or SEC support, few states would ever prosecute a large MLM, yet the mere presence of state anti-pyramid statutes or regulations posed a constant threat in the view of the Pyramid Lobby. The DSA, over time, has lobbied states to repeal or reword their laws so that retailing requirements were eliminated. Among the states to change or adopt the DSA-worded laws are Georgia, Louisiana, Maryland, Montana, Wyoming, Texas, Utah, and Tennessee. The influence-buying and selling extends into every state legislature.

I have been consulted by various state Attorneys General offices who acknowledged being blocked from MLM prosecutions by legislators in their states with MLM ties. Some were told MLM prosecution would lead to cuts in their annual agency budgets. Others acknowledged the limits of their staffs and resources against large MLM defense funds.

Beyond getting state laws changed, the Pyramid Lobby also focused on state Attorneys General to become MLM allies. The "industry" has claimed as one of its great promoters the former Attorney General of Utah, Mark Shurtleff. While still serving as a public official, Shurtleff appeared to have publicly and officially endorsed the MLM, Usana.[216] He was also instrumental in protecting MLM pyramids by supporting a new law in Utah that effectively exempted MLMs from the statute's narrowed definition of a "pyramid scheme." Examining contributor records of Shurtleff's 2012 election, the *Salt Lake City Tribune* reported, that just two MLMs, Usana Health Sciences and Nu Skin International, accounted for about 10% of Shurtleff's total and half of what he gained from all MLM companies that year. It also noted that Shurtleff "backed a 2005 bill that some contended safeguarded their business."[217]

In 2014 Shurtleff was arrested in Utah on bribery charges, along with another former Attorney General of Utah, John Swallow, who was also a major MLM backer.[218] According to a 2012 investigative article in *Harper's Magazine* by Jeff Ernsthausen entitled "Pyramid Insurance," Shurtleff received campaign contributions totaling more than $475,000 from members of the Direct Selling Association (DSA) since 1999, accounting for 14% of his donations from sources other than the state Republican Party.[219] Regarding Shurtleff's successor, John Swallow's ties to MLM, the *Harper's* investigation reported that $114,000 of funds raised for his election campaign to date (June 2012) was traceable to MLM-related sources.

North Carolina was also specifically cited in the *Harper's* investigation. North Carolina was once noted for active prosecutions of MLM pyramids under its clearly worded anti-pyramid scheme statute, but no longer. According to Jordan Maglich who operates a national data based called "Ponzi Tracker," North Carolina is now within the top 20 percent of states where Ponzi schemes operate.[220] The state has not initiated a MLM prosecution in many years, despite a major increase in MLM recruitment and in number of MLM companies in the state.[221] Even the notorious North Carolina-based Zeek Rewards scheme, which was classified as an illegal multi-level marketing company and the largest Ponzi on record in terms of numbers of victims, was not prosecuted by the state. Federal agencies closed the company and later brought criminal charges against the CEO who went to prison.

During the attorney general administration of Democrat Roy Cooper (elected governor in 2017), North Carolina became home to the headquarters of ACN, the MLM famously associated with and promoted by President Donald Trump. North Carolina is also the site of a major new distribution center for Herbalife, the

MLM that was fined $200 million by the FTC and ordered to stop "unfair and deceptive trade practices."[i]

Executives from ACN, according to the *Harper's* investigation, gave $84,550 to North Carolina Attorney General Roy Cooper, "since the run-up to the company's relocation there in 2008 — nearly 85 percent of their total campaign contributions during that period." ACN even got $600,000 in tax subsidies to move to Concord, North Carolina.[222] ACN paid Donald Trump more than $8 million to speak at its meetings and endorse the scheme.[223]

Seeing the special value of their public offices to MLM lobbying needs at the state level , two former state attorneys general — Chris Gorman, Kentucky Attorney General from 1992–1996, and Robert Stephan, Kansas Attorney General from 1979–1995 — became "legal advisors" to the multi-level marketing company Fortune High Tech Marketing. In 2013, the Federal Trade Commission and three states filed charges against the company for operating a pyramid scheme. The company was shut down. At the time it had more than 160,000 signed up as "distributors."[224] Gorman of Kentucky and Stephan of Kansas, along with Grant Woods, former attorney general of Arizona, also sold the same "advisory services" to the MLM, ACN, which also hired Donald Trump as its main endorser and motivation speaker.

The Pyramid Lobby's multi-pronged lobbying with state legislatures, governors and state Attorneys General, along with this local efforts aimed at members of Congress may be seen as spade

---

[i] As a native and current resident of North Carolina, and as president of *Pyramid Scheme Alert*, I wrote Mr. Cooper in 2014 asking him to investigate Herbalife. He did not respond. He has not taken action against Herbalife, despite the FTC prosecution and FTC findings related to lack of "retail" sales that could put Herbalife outside the legal bounds of the NC anti-pyramid statute. The letter is preserved at https://pyramidschemealert.org/wp-content/uploads/2014/08/LettertoNCAGReHerbalife.pdf

work at the foundation of America's political establishment. Yet the entire coordinated campaign still depended on securing a sympathetic U.S. president, at the very top of that establishment. Powerful influence was needed over the U.S. president to reign in the FTC and facilitate MLM expansion and protection with governments around the world.

Buying into the White House

Even under a Democratic President and Congress, the Pyramid Lobby prevented FTC prosecution of any large MLMs. During that time, it weakened state anti-pyramid statutes and leveraged the Departments of Commerce and State to open the largest market in the world, China, overcoming Chinese government efforts to outlaw MLM.

But it was with the election of George W. Bush, the first candidate the newly branded and greatly enlarged Pyramid Lobby played a major role in bringing to office, that MLM could publicly claim part ownership of the White House.

With its now openly recognized political influence, MLM could now collect what Betsy DeVos called "some things in return." They were quickly delivered. George W. Bush appointed attorney Timothy Muris to head the FTC as chairman. Muris's last job before chairing the federal agency that regulates multi-level marketing was as an attorney with the antitrust division of the firm Howrey, Simon, Arnold and White, LLP. The antitrust division of Howrey counted the Amway Corporation among its largest clients.

As the new chairman of the FTC, Timothy Muris appointed David Scheffman as the FTC's new chief economist. Only a year earlier, Scheffman worked as an expert for the multi-level marketing company, Equinox International, a member of the Direct Selling Association that had been prosecuted by the Clinton-FTC for operating a pyramid scheme. Scheffman testified *against the FTC* and on behalf of the scheme, arguing that the Equinox business model was legitimate, operated just like Amway, and was not a pyramid scheme. The FTC ultimately succeeded in shutting down Equinox and recovering about $50 million for consumers. However, the FTC estimated that consumer losses at the hands of Equinox exceeded $330 million.

During the tenure of FTC Chairman Timothy Muris, the FTC issued a highly publicized pro-MLM letter, which the MLM "industry" dispersed widely to its recruiters to claim that the FTC had reversed and repudiated its longstanding interpretation of Section 5 of the FTC Act. Entitled a "Staff Advisory Opinion — Pyramid Scheme Analysis," it was signed on January 14, 2004, by James A. Kohm, acting Director of Marketing Practices, Federal Trade Commission. The letter was addressed to Neil H. Offen, President, Direct Selling Association.[225]

After leaving the FTC in 2004, Muris joined the Washington, D.C. law firm, O'Melveny & Myers. The website of O'Melveny & Myers listed Mr. Muris as "representing Primerica Financial Services ... in the Federal Trade Commission's Business Opportunity Rulemaking proceeding." Primerica is a member of the Direct Selling Association and a multi-level marketing company. A 2006 letter sent to the FTC on behalf of Primerica argued against the proposed FTC disclosure rule. Muris and former FTC Director of Consumer Protection, J. Howard Beales, who Muris also appointed, signed the letter.[226] Beales was also known for his consulting work for Reynolds Tobacco and his public defense of the youth-targeting *Joe Camel* advertising campaign, including testifying against the FTC.[227]

Another alumna of the FTC, Jodie Bernstein, joined the law firm Bryan Cave after serving as Director of Consumer Protection at the FTC from 1997 to 2002. In that capacity, Ms. Bernstein lobbied the FTC on behalf of the Amway Corporation, arguing against regulation.[228] Her law firm, Bryan Cave, defended the notorious Ponzi operator Reed Slatkin, and previously represented Michael C. Cooper, president and chief executive officer of the MLM company, Renaissance the Tax People, which was shut down by the state of Kansas as a pyramid scheme.[229]

Serving as George W. Bush's "spiritual advisor" at this time was a former high ranking (Diamond) distributor with Amway and regular Amway convention speaker, evangelist Doug Wead. Wead was President George H. W. Bush's liaison to the Christian Right. *Time* magazine referred to him as "the man who coined the phrase the 'compassionate conservative.'"

Yet, for all this activity and insider influence during the Bush years, the Pyramid Lobby remained largely unnoticed by the American media. It was not until the 2012 presidential election involving Republican candidate Mitt Romney that the media finally identified the Lobby as a significant force in American presidential politics. At this point the Lobby was much larger than the influence of Amway and its founding families. In fact, the center of power of the Pyramid Lobby itself was beginning to shift from Michigan to Utah. Clans of avowedly devout Mormons were taking up the *Ponzinomics* banner that the Calvinist Amway families had held for 30 years.

A report in the investigative magazine, *Mother Jones* entitled, "Get-Rich-Quick Profiteers Love Mitt Romney, and He Loves Them Back," documented the long and deep connections between Romney and multi-level marketing.[230] The article documented two secret $1 million donations made to Romney, traced to two executives of the MLM, Nu Skin. Author Stephanie Mencimer additionally revealed the co-founder of MLM, Xango, was Romney's 2008 campaign finance director; another MLM founder donated $500,000; and the founder of MLM, Melaleuca, was his current finance chair and a million-dollar contributor to Romney's SuperPAC.[231]

The *Mother Jones* exposé of the imbedding of MLM into Mitt Romney's 2008 and 2016 presidential campaigns showed how the base of Pyramid Lobby had widened beyond Amway and its powerful grips over the Reagan, Clinton, and Bush presidencies. The MLM power base now included Nu Skin and other Utah-headquartered and Mormon-affiliated MLMs, still maintaining the façade of religious piety of leaders and a doctrine that sanctified pursuit of wealth.

This expansive pattern further extended in the Obama presidency and the Democratic Party side of Congress. In this phase under Obama, the MLM scheme, Herbalife, is shown as yet another wing of political influence-buying, capable of silencing Democratic leaders, pulling the strings of Wall Street and controlling FTC prosecution.

What distinguished the Obama era is that, in 10 years leading to his election, awareness of MLM fraud had also increased along with the expansion of the Pyramid Lobby's disinformation and influence-buying. Whistle-blowing websites appeared. A small but skilled group had launched an anti-pyramid scheme non-profit organization for consumer education and advocacy focused directly on MLM. A popular Yahoo chat group, *MLM Survivor*, was operating and there had been several successful class action lawsuits against MLM. For the first time since MLM propaganda and FTC policy about the normalcy and legitimacy of endless chain schemes had dominated public forums, hope for change and uncorrupted law enforcement was in the air.

To understand how the confluence of a hope-inspiring Obama presidency and Democratic Party control of Congress and the FTC failure to confront the Pyramid Lobby, once again the perspective and moral compass of the muckraking era at the start of the 20th century must be visited.

Hope and Boodle Under Obama

As a regular contributor to the popular *McClure's* "muckraking" magazine at the beginning of the 20th century, investigative journalist Lincoln Steffens wondered about the root causes of pervasive corruption, not just in Washington, D.C., but locally in cities where bosses and machine politics dominated. It was in cities, he believed, where democracy should more directly reflect the values of the average American. Long before the federal government developed social services, a national pension, health insurance, or consumer protection laws, people's basic needs were met locally. Corruption at the local level, therefore, was a direct assault on the needs and rights of one's neighbors. Like others of his time, Steffens viewed the selling of public office for private gain to be a form of treason.

In 1904, Steffens was assigned to visit America's cities notorious for their political machines that delivered votes to hand-picked politicians who then dispensed public franchises, favorable zoning, lucrative utilities, and vital commodities to the highest payers of graft. What he discovered, later compiled in his most famous book of the time, *The Shame of the Cities*, did not give comfort to readers. Steffens concluded that bedrock values of America, in which wealth is automatically accorded exalted status and the pursuit of wealth is equated with the pursuit of happiness, led good people into serving "interests" over public good. He found that the primary drivers of political machines — the corrupters and bribers — were cities' respectable businesspeople, members of the Chamber of Commerce.

Steffens's discomforting message was that corruption was less an alien feature of city life than it was native and systemic, American Pie. The inclination to sell out the public for private gain was done for a higher cause, a cause that a city's leaders and ordinary citizens reflexively, unquestioningly honored, even when vital needs and the public's interest were harmed. He wrote,

> The commercial spirit is the spirit of profit, not patriotism; 'My business is sacred,' says the businessman in his heart. Whatever prospers my business, is good; it must be. Whatever hinders it, is wrong; it must be. A bribe is bad ... but it is not so bad to give one, not if it is necessary to my business.

Steffens's perspective is needed to understand how and why MLM has been protected for the last 40 years — by top leaders of both political parties and other entities — who could somehow claim that Amway's pyramid recruiting scheme was representative of their own economic policies. Steffens' keen insight is better applied to the behavior of Democrats, whose economic policies are supposedly driven more by Main Street USA needs and whose candidates have received far less cash from the Pyramid Lobby. Steffens helps to explain how it is that MLM remained safe and unexamined even during the times when the Democratic Party had the most influence over the FTC, SEC, and Department of Justice. When both parties honor protecting pyramid schemes, *Ponzinomics* has moved beyond a Main Street delusion. It is an official national belief.

The Foreword of *Ponzinomics* stated the harsh fact that all who have sought to oppose the phenomenal spread of "MLM" have lost. What was achieved from these foiled campaigns were troves of credible testimony, verified facts and hard data on precisely how the MLM scam operates and the scale of harm MLM causes. The truth has become readily available. To understand why the scam persists, we are left, finally, to move past the forces of propaganda and influence-buying to unexamined or avoided factors within our own communities and our own culture.

To understand our current dilemma, Steffens would likely guide us to look at the Obama years. The Pyramid Lobby's favored party was out of power; more information was made public about MLM than at any other time. There was seemingly good reason for hope.

Obama's chair of the FTC, Jon Leibowitz, had no known history with MLM. The head of Consumer Protection, David Vladeck, whom Leibowitz had appointed, also had no apparent connections. In fact, Vladeck was associated with the Ralph Nader-founded *Public Citizen*. During Obama's second term, for the first time in MLM history, the business media finally took an interest in MLM as a major part of the U.S. economy and a significant sector of Wall Street securities. This was prompted by hedge fund manager, William Ackman's campaign to expose the MLM, Herbalife. It would seem that, if at any time since 1979 the *public's* interest could be represented and the reality of MLM investigated, this was the period.

Hope of consumer activists was bolstered in the propitious year of the Obama election when a federal court ruled that a class action lawsuit against Amway, the largest case ever mounted against an MLM for operating an illegal pyramid scheme, could go forward. On that ruling, Amway quickly moved to out-of-court settlement and paid out millions to the plaintiff's attorneys and clients.[232] *Si, se puede!*

Adding to the heightened expectations, just before Obama was sworn in, Bernard Madoff came forward to confess running one of the largest Ponzi schemes in American history. It had been operating as a presumed legitimate business for a dozen years in the heart of Wall Street and led by one of the financial community's trusted representatives. This shocking revelation along with the national collapse of what was called the mortgage "bubble", put the terms, Ponzi, robbing Peter to Pay Paul, unsustainable, last ones in, collapse, and pyramid scheme, on front pages and in news stories day after day, including explanations of how pyramids and Ponzis work and the inevitable harm they cause.

Despite this historic backdrop, dismayingly, the revelations and the settlement payment in the Amway lawsuit provoked no inquiry, statements or actions from the Obama FTC related to MLM pyramids. Direct inquiries to the FTC or to Obama from victims and consumer activists were, distressingly, ignored. With a seeming political firewall around MLM, the American news media did not investigate the MLM phenomenon, despite clues pointing to MLM's disguise as "direct selling", just as Madoff was dressed up to appear as a "hedge fund," both operating in plain sight.[233]

In 2010, I wrote, published and sent to Obama and various members of Congress a 25-page report, entitled *"The Main Street Bubble, a Whistle-Blower's Guide to Business Opportunity Fraud; How the FTC Ignored and Now Protects It."* On the cover, it was subtitled, "Memorandum to President Barack Obama and Members of Congress Overseeing the Federal Trade Commission and the newly created Consumer Financial Protection Bureau." The "memorandum" not only documented the known facts about massive consumer losses and decades of outrageously false claims but also addressed the special harm MLM was inflicting with its false "opportunity." MLMs were accelerating their harm during the Great Recession as millions more people were unemployed, faced foreclosure, and were in desperate need of income.

The Main Street Bubble also revealed the pattern of FTC staff and officials moving through a "revolving door" of jobs and positions with the "MLM industry." My report was cited in the nationally televised 2013 *CNBC* documentary, "Selling the American Dream," produced by Herb Greenberg. It included an interview with me in the segment, entitled, "Multi-Level Marketing Critic: Beware 'Main Street Bubble.'"[234]

I received no reply. Still, I maintained hope that change was forthcoming.

This tenuous hope was violently shaken when Obama's FTC Chief of Consumer Protection, David Vladeck, now a professor at Georgetown Law, publicly challenged the reality that the billions in *annual* losses suffered by millions of people who invested in the Herbalife "income opportunity" were due to "misrepresentation." He also defiantly challenged the assertion that the losses even constituted an "injury" to consumers.[235]

Business journalist Herb Greenberg asked Vladeck on camera about MLM-related consumer losses. It was the first time since Obama took office that anyone in his administration had made any statement at all about the spread of MLMs. Vladeck, the appointee of FTC Chair, Jon Leibowitz, who was appointed by Obama, not only rebuffed the record of losses, he also implied that if they occurred, it was the responsibility of the losers, exactly the claim of MLM companies. Consumer activists and MLM victims were stunned and baffled.[236]

Vladeck's abrupt and visibly angry retort to Greenberg and his lack of interest in the findings about Herbalife's false income claims caused some to suspect a powerful political "fix" was at work and that the Obama administration was either a part of it or Obama-FTC officials saw which way the political wind was blowing and simply didn't care.

These dark suspicions slashed hope but did not answer the baffling question — how could it be that a fix would exist between the Pyramid Lobby and the Obama administration?

Preventing Disclosures

More evidence surfaced that a fix or an extraordinary indifference was operating at the Obama-FTC. In the first term of the Obama administration, besides maintaining the previous administration's eight-year virtual lockdown of the FTC regarding prosecution, the Obama-FTC under Chairman Leibowitz took the extraordinary action of exempting MLMs from its own newly enacted "Business Opportunity Rules" (BOR) disclosure requirements. The action enabled MLM to solicit investment funds from millions of people without disclosing loss, failure, or risk levels.

The bureaucratic processing of the Business Opportunity Rule (BOR) dates to 1978 when a comprehensive disclosure rule was enacted to regulate franchising. The franchise disclosure rule also covered other non-franchise "business opportunities," but exempted opportunities whose initial costs were less than $500. This provision opened the door for MLM firms to evade the disclosure rule through the simple expedient of keeping the initial fee at $499 or less.

After that enactment to ensure fair franchising solicitations, the brand new "industry" of multi-level marketing exploded into hundreds of enterprises that annually solicited money for "home-based business opportunities" from tens of millions of American households. MLMs offered, "distributorships," not franchises. Recruits could subsequently be charged thousands more than initial fees to obtain higher "ranks" where greater rewards were promised and even more fees could be extracted for "training," "sales leads," or "motivation" seminars.

Beginning in 1995, the FTC began developing a rule that would include business opportunities. The "Business Opportunity Rule" (BOR) moved through the bureaucracy at glacier speed and was finally presented for public comment in 2006. The language plainly showed the FTC staff's intention to extend disclosure requirements to the vast new field of "MLM." The FTC explained that:

> Two important types of fraudulent or deceptive opportunities that would fall within the proposed Rule's coverage are work-at-home schemes and pyramid marketing schemes.[237]

Supporting the rule's intent to address "pyramid marketing schemes," aka "multi-level marketing," the FTC reported that in 2005, it had received 17,858 complaints related to these types of "business opportunity" solicitations, placing it among the leading categories of complaints. It also noted that many business opportunity scams escaped disclosure rules on franchising with startup charges just below $500, the franchise rule's trigger point.

In response, the DSA orchestrated a letter writing and congressional lobbying campaign calling for the *exemption* of MLM from a proposed rule that was specifically aimed at MLM. After a closed meeting of DSA leaders with the FTC staff, the 2006 version of the proposed rule was revised to prevent MLM solicitations from being effectively included. The full FTC Commission signed off on the new rule, with MLM exempted, in 2012. In ratifying the exemption, the Obama-administration FTC Commissioners directly contradicted the original statement of purpose for the Rule, arguing that disclosures, which were considered critical for consumers to make sound investment decisions in franchising, were not needed or useful in MLM.

In a 2014 article, "How Lobbying Dollars Prop Up Pyramid Schemes," *The Verge's* Matt Stroud provided a detailed report on how the Pyramid Lobby achieved this total reversal, exposing tens of millions of U.S. citizens to "unlimited income" propositions, without recourse to needed facts or disclosures.[238]

Stroud described a ... "decades-old political strategy" by the multi-level marketing (MLM) industry giving "handsome donations" to dozens of members of Congress who, in turn, "pushed federal regulators away" from prosecuting MLM. Importantly, he explained how it also resulted in federal regulators not defining the difference between what the FTC defined as a legal and an illegal pyramid scheme.

Stroud noted that when the "business opportunity rule" was proposed, Herbalife, one of the largest MLMs and with publicly traded stock, went on a political "spending spree." Among the financial beneficiaries, he noted Wisconsin Congressman Paul Ryan and Pennsylvania Senator Rick Santorum. Democrats included New York Congressmen Edolphus Towns, Eliot L. Engel, and Gary Ackerman. Through 2008, Herbalife spent more than $800,000. *Open Secrets.org*, the website of the non-profit Center for Responsive Politics, documented that Amway, the largest MLM political influence-buyer, tripled its expenditures between 2006 and 2007. Over the next decade, *Open Secrets* reported that Amway spent about $400,000 each year on lobbying. This does not include the millions paid by family members of Amway's founders.

Under intense political pressure from members of Congress, who were receiving millions in donations from MLM companies, the FTC engaged in puzzling and contradictory reasoning to justify its reversal of policy. When the "business opportunity" rule was officially adopted in Dec. 2011, with MLM "exempted," the FTC stated that it decided to narrow the scope of the rule to avoid including "sellers of MLM opportunities." This was exactly the opposite of the rule's original intent. It claimed that the exemption was supported by a majority of the "approximately 17,000 comments that argued that the initial rule Opportunity Rule "failed to differentiate between unlawful pyramid schemes and legitimate companies using an MLM model."

This was an amazing claim. The FTC itself had *never* offered a usable way for consumers to make such a distinction. Its silence on clarifying how to recognize MLM pyramid frauds and its unfounded references to the existence of such a distinction to justify the MLM exemptions led *New York Times* op-ed columnist Joe Nocera to write, "The F.T.C.'s refusal to define a pyramid scheme — and to act aggressively on that definition — is a dereliction of duty."

Nocera revealed the naked political muzzling of the FTC in reporting his interview with FTC officials:

> *"'I have nothing for you,' said Frank Dorman, a spokesman for the Federal Trade Commission. 'Lots of reporters have asked that question. Our final response is, We're not going to answer it.'"*
>
> *Nocera explained, "What had I asked that was so sensitive that the F.T.C. wouldn't respond? I had requested that the agency explain what distinguished an illegal 'pyramid scheme' from a legal multilevel marketing company."[239]*

For those willing to look directly at FTC actions and words, it became difficult to avoid the conclusion that the FTC refused to explain the distinction between "MLM" and a pyramid scheme because there is none, and the FTC knows it.

Even more to the point of using the distinction for eviscerating the "Business Opportunity" rule, the rule was never intended to detect or prevent pyramid schemes in the first place. It was only to ensure that consumers would be able to do "due diligence" when being solicited to invest in a "business opportunity" legal or otherwise. Exempting MLMs left the BOR with almost nothing to cover and no purpose.[240]

The response the FTC received from those arguing for MLM exemption, which the FTC used to justify its reversal, was sometimes as bogus as the reasoning used by the FTC. FTC officials knew the cookie-cutter letters were orchestrated by MLM lobbyists. All the letters were recorded on the FTC website as public comments on the proposed rule. Those it received from MLM officials and owners were even less credible than the harvested and mailed bulk from adherents. In the case of one DSA member company, Pre-Paid Legal, later renamed LegalShield, the company argued that nearly 500,000 North American consumers "depended" on it for "income." In fact, as the company's own SEC filings revealed, 80% of its "salespeople" never achieved even one sale and only 2% made 10 sales. The mean average "income" of all the salespeople was about $5 a week, *before costs.*

As part of the recorded comments sent to the FTC, Brett Chapman, General Counsel of Herbalife wrote, "Within the United States, HLF has approximately 250,000 Independent Distributors, each of whom is a small business owner, and each of whom would be adversely affected by the new requirements contained in the Proposed Rule."[242]

In 2016, the FTC prosecuted Herbalife for illegal practices associated with a pyramid scheme after FTC field research showed that virtually no Herbalife "small business owners" earned a profit and some suffered crushing losses.

Other letters predicted the MLM business would be "devastated" or that "self-regulation" or the DSA's "ethics" rules were adequate. In the end, the FTC staff accepted the MLM arguments and recommended that MLMs be exempted and the full Commission agreed to the exemption.

Punishing Wall Street Short-Sellers

The FTC's investigation of Herbalife, which occurred under the Obama administration, was the most important development and historic opportunity at the FTC since 1979. However, it was prompted not by Obama policy or regulator vigilance or even by consumer complaints or class action lawsuits. Short-sellers on Wall Street did it.

The investigation happened only after two years of intense public pressure and media attention on Herbalife caused by a $1 billion short position taken against Herbalife's stock value by the hedge fund, Pershing Square Capital Management, led by William Ackman. This was not the first time that "MLM" was challenged by short-sellers. Convicted felon turned consumer crusader and Christian minister, Barry Minkow, had mounted a publicity-driven attack on Nu Skin, Usana, Herbalife and Medifast. His campaigns were fact-based and led to brief stock market plunges, followed by settlements and restoration of earlier price points. Minkow revealed the vulnerability MLM incurred by taking their schemes to Wall Street. Court challenges by MLMs to his exposure campaigns failed, establishing both the financial and legal foundation for exposing MLM on Wall Street.

As a short-seller Ackman was in another class altogether. He put hundreds of millions on the line. He was able to spend millions to support his campaign, and, unlike Minkow, who later went to prison, again, on activities unrelated to his MLM short-selling campaigns, Ackman was credible. Indeed, he was famous for making big bets on market realities that few others detected.

The 2014 FTC announcement that it would officially investigate the practices of Herbalife renewed lost hope among many victims, activists and observers that the Obama-FTC — following the departure of Leibowitz and Vladeck— might finally act.

The FTC action against Herbalife marked the first FTC public examination of any large or publicly traded MLM since 1979. That glaring fact raised troubling questions and provided ominous clues as to an eventual bad outcome for Ackman. With 35 years of experience with the "MLM industry," what would the FTC expect to find that would be new or unknown? If the FTC did choose, at long last, to enforce the law on Herbalife, how could it explain the previous long absence of consumer protection? How could it argue that Herbalife, one of the oldest MLMs and a ranking member of the Direct Selling Association, was "rogue?"

Herbalife was sued by the state of California and by distributors in two class actions lawsuits alleging pyramid fraud. Yet, it was only after unprecedented publicity generated by the hedge fund campaign that the FTC undertook an investigation. Then, inexplicably, the "investigation" ran on for *two more years*. During this crucial period as negative revelations poured out and the specter of a possible FTC prosecution loomed, Herbalife's stock price was upheld and tremendously increased by Carl Icahn and other Wall Street figures.[243]

With the stretched-out FTC deliberations and the Wall Street maneuvers to orchestrate a "short-squeeze" in which Ackman would be forced to buy shares to cover his "short" and thereby drive the price upward, many analysts expected the short-selling hedge fund, Pershing Capital, to abandon its position. This conceivably would have taken pressure off the FTC to take any significant action. Pershing, however, held. The negative publicity and revelations continued. Media interest escalated. The FTC was pressured into doing *something*. The whole world was watching.

In the end, the FTC did not "discover" anything different from or contradictory to what it had been told repeatedly by class action attorneys, whistle-blowers, writers, and consumer advocates, the so-called and much-maligned "anti-MLM" groups and individuals. The facts were 30 years old. Herbalife's practices and business model had not changed since its founding. The short-seller was proved correct in his fraud thesis about Herbalife.

California Boodle

One of the most astounding facts that revealed the old age of the known but ignored facts about Herbalife is that Herbalife was (and still is) already under a permanent injunction in the state of California against the very marketing practices that the hedge fund and previous lawsuits alleged.[244] The "permanent" injunction was imposed in 1986, yet mysteriously never enforced by California's attorneys general. The California injunction stated:

5. A. Defendants shall not establish, maintain or operate a marketing program in which:

(1) A participant pays a valuable consideration for the chance in whole or in part, to receive, either directly or indirectly, compensation, which is based on other than retail sales for introducing one or more additional persons into participation in defendants' marketing program or for the chance to receive compensation, either directly -or- indirectly, when the newly introduced participant introduces a new participant into defendants' marketing program;

(2) Any compensation, however denominated (including but not limited to "commissions," "overrides," "achievement bonuses," or any term of similar import), defendants pay or participants receive is based upon anything other than the retail sale of defendants' products; and

(3) A participant can obtain any specific level in defendants' Marketing program based upon criteria other than the amount of retail sales made by the participant or person(s) introduced into defendants' marketing program by the participant.[245]

In the brightness of media interest, Pershing Square and consumer activists called upon the current attorney general of California at the time, Kamala Harris (now a U.S. senator from California and Vice-Presidential candidate) to ask why the injunction was not being enforced.[246] Their inquiries did not prompt law enforcement but revealed yet another manifestation of financial entanglements between MLM and regulators.

Herbalife's corporate office is based in California (its actual legal headquarters are in the Cayman Islands), which partially explains the political lockdown of law enforcement in the state. Herbalife could spread money to California charities, vendors, and politicians, and it employed a lot of Californians. But perhaps more important to law enforcement at that moment in time was that the California Attorney General, Kamala Harris, it turned out, had recently married Douglas Emhoff, a partner in the law firm, Venable LLP, which represented Herbalife. Venable was Harris's third largest contributor in her Senatorial race in 2016 and she was Venable's second largest recipient of contribution.[247] For Harris to enforce the injunction against Herbalife, one of her largest contributors and her very own husband's employer could have been Herbalife's defense attorney!

The *New York Post* reported that court records showed Emhoff's firm had represented Herbalife as recently as 2013. The article raised the questions of why Kamala Harris had not enforced the permanent injunction against Herbalife for making false income claims, and whether Harris was in violation of the state's conflict of interest regulations. She refused to disclose if her office was investigating Herbalife.[248]

To make matters even more conflicted and jeopardizing to the public interest, Venable later made a bid to oversee Herbalife's compliance with the FTC settlement terms that required restructuring and reform of marketing practices.[249] When Harris was elected to the U.S. Senate from California, Emhoff went to work directly for the law firm, DLA Piper, which was acquiring his firm, Venable LLP. DLA Piper represented Amway in the largest class action suit ever filed against the company. The suit charged that Amway was a pyramid scheme. Amway settled the suit by paying approximately $50 million without admitting guilt.

In the end, Kamala Harris, the state's top law enforcement officer, never did enforce the injunction. Her successor, the newly elected California Attorney General Xavier Becerra, has also not acted. It is unlikely that he ever will. Before his election as the new California AG, Becerra served as a U.S. congressman and former chair of the Hispanic Caucus. *Open Secrets* reported that Herbalife had recently contributed to the Hispanic Caucus for the first time and wrote, *"Herbalife already has one friend in the Congressional Hispanic Caucus. Rep. Xavier Becerra (D-Cal.) represents the Los Angeles district where Herbalife has its corporate headquarters and he has cautioned his caucus colleagues not to rush to any conclusions about (Herbalife)."* It further reported that Herbalife gave Becerra more than $20,000 in 2011–2012. *Herbalife was Becerra's third largest contributor and the top money recipient from Herbalife in the 2012 cycle."*[250]

FTC Boodle

In July 2016, in a detailed Complaint,[251] the FTC finally announced government findings of pervasive deception and a fraudulent business model in which Herbalife participants did not — and could not — earn profits from retailing (direct selling) but only from recruiting. It showed how the Herbalife model *required* participants to *buy the products* in order to gain access to the falsely promised recruiting rewards, giving a lie to Herbalife's claim that the products were being purchased based on brand preference.

The Herbalife income scheme, the FTC revealed, resulted in the vast majority of everyone who ever participated failing to gain a profit. The Complaint also documented how Herbalife targeted vulnerable immigrants and others lured into investing. It presented evidence of misleading and false claims of high incomes. The victims hardest hit, according to the FTC, were those that had bought into what Herbalife called "Nutrition Clubs," most of whom were immigrants. The "clubs" it revealed, were actually high cost recruiting centers, just another form of "pay to play" in the endless chain.[252]

In its settlement, announced the same day the devastating findings were presented, the FTC famously and perplexingly did not label the company a "pyramid scheme," while detailing the precise characteristics of and the scale of damage caused by a pyramid scheme.[253] After more than three years, in which the business media speculated and debated about Herbalife as a pyramid scheme, the word "pyramid" did not appear in the FTC Complaint or the Settlement even as a reference point. Nor did the FTC immediately enjoin the company from practices it had determined to be illegal and harmful. Instead, the FTC announced that under an agreement in which Herbalife admitted no wrongdoing, it would allow the illegal practices to continue, while gradually requiring changes through a complex compliance process. Herbalife agreed to pay $200 million to be distributed to victims by the FTC.

Six months later, on January 10, 2017, the FTC mailed out 350,000 checks, totaling $200 million in restitution to victims of Herbalife. It described the payments as

> *providing partial refunds to people who ran an Herbalife business in the United States between 2009 and 2015, and who paid at least $1,000 to Herbalife but got little or nothing back from the company. Most checks are between $100 and $500; the largest checks exceed $9,000.*[254]

Most victims of Herbalife paid in something less than $1,000 to Herbalife, yet still a substantial loss for them. *They got nothing back.* The payments were only to *U.S. citizens* during a six-year period. Herbalife had been inflicting losses on millions of people since its inception in 1981. The order allows Herbalife to continue these same practices in the rest of the world that it deemed illegal and harmful in the U.S. More than 80% of Herbalife business is outside the U.S.

At first, surprisingly impressed that the FTC had acted at all, most observers soon experienced a wrenching *déjà vu* realization. The FTC actually *protected* Herbalife and once again insulated the "MLM industry" from investigation. The conspicuous avoidance of the term "pyramid scheme" undercut all other statements and the facts of the investigation. The $200 million restitution payment imposed on Herbalife, large in terms of MLM enforcement history, had no significant impact on Herbalife's $4 billion finances. Similarly, it offered no economic justice to the millions of consumers left out of the "settlement."

And then, the most shocking revelation: the entire FTC negotiation with Herbalife that led up to the simultaneous release of the FTC Complaint and the Settlement was hatched out with the consultation of the FTC's own former Obama-appointed chairman, Jon Leibowitz. He was now working for Herbalife, against the FTC. While Chair of the FTC, Leibowitz oversaw the exemption of MLM from FTC's Business Opportunity disclosure rules. He also maintained the pattern of selective MLM prosecutions that are always "fenced in" to ensure the "industry" was not affected. Leibowitz's Consumer Protection chief, David Vladeck, who had rudely rebuffed consumer complaints about Herbalife, appeared to have no financial ties to the Pyramid Lobby. But his immediate boss and the person who gave him his job did indeed have ties.

Leibowitz, a Democrat and married to the *Washington Post* op-ed writer, Ruth Marcus, known in her field as a liberal Democrat,[255] was first appointed to the FTC by Republican George W.

Bush in 2004.[256] Immediately prior to his appointment to the FTC, Leibowitz worked for four years as the top lobbyist for Hollywood, the Motion Picture Industry. During the Herbalife investigation, prosecution and simultaneous settlement which occurred after his departure from the FTC (2014–2016), it was revealed that Leibowitz *"Advised Herbalife in connection with its $200 million settlement with the FTC relating to allegations that it engaged in unfair and deceptive acts and practices."*[257] Then, when the ink was barely dry, on the day of the "settlement," Herbalife announced in a press release, "The Board also appointed Jonathan Leibowitz, partner in the law firm of Davis, Polk and Wardell, and former Chairman of the Federal Trade Commission, as a Senior Advisor to the Board."[258]

Fortune magazine quoted Herbalife management's letter to shareholders that revealed a pre-planned dis-information campaign when the Settlement would be announced. The FTC claimed the settlement required fundamental restructuring of Herbalife's U.S. business model, but Herbalife reported to its investors, "Today we announced a settlement with the FTC that *does not change our direct selling business model.*" Adding to the letter's theme of triumph and defiance, it reported that the Board appointed former FTC Chair, Jon Leibowitz, as Senior Advisor.[259]

Wall Street Believers

By agreeing (with Herbalife) not to use the term "pyramid scheme" in the FTC Complaint and allowing Herbalife to admit no wrongdoing while continuing its illegal practices, the FTC put a knife into the back of the hedge fund and other short sellers that had called Herbalife a pyramid scheme and even a "criminal enterprise." Most of Wall Street, led by Carl Icahn, embraced MLM's endless chain as a real business. In the carefully worded FTC Complaint the wrongdoing became only excesses in the praiseworthy pursuit of profit by one member of a legitimate "direct selling" industry. The Ponzi model was protected. Wall Street now *believed* in it too.

The FTC denied the heretical short-sellers their rightful market compensation, even as it confirmed their documented research of deception and harm at Herbalife. In an article entitled, "Here's Why Herbalife's Shares Are Soaring Today," *Fortune* magazine reported the net result of the Settlement terms, "The news sent shares of Herbalife up sharply by 18% in early trading."[260]

Publicized on the same day as the FTC settlement was announced, Herbalife's proclamations that its "business model" was exonerated were widely adopted by the business media. The story line drove the continued rise in Herbalife's stock price and further punished the short-sellers, leading to eventual capitulation.

Acknowledging the stabbing, *Fortune* reported that Herbalife's press release "stuck it to Ackman" by recommending that he show "humility" and recognize he is "wrong." The release was penned by the Herbalife spokesman, a particular public figure that made it a political and financial *coup de grâce*: Alan Hoffman, former Chief of Staff for Joseph Biden, Obama's Vice President and Democratic nominee for President in the 2016 election. A July 2014 news article in *Time Magazine* aptly explained the significance of Hoffman's high profile role. It reported that in his new job with Herbalife Hoffman would be in charge of "government affairs." It noted that it's a "big job," as Herbalife was under investigation by the FTC, DOJ, and the FBI, over allegations that Herbalife is "a predatory pyramid scheme."[261]

Mainstream Ponzinomics

Taking notice of self-dealing among some members of the George W. Bush Administration about a decade ago, *New York Times* editorial board member, Adam Cohen, found the muckraking journalist of an earlier era, Lincoln Steffens, still prescient and relevant. Cohen quoted Steffens, "In all cities, the better classes – the business men – are the sources of corruption, but they are so rarely pursued and caught that we do not fully realize whence the trouble comes."

Herbalife's CEO Michael Johnson, formerly the CEO of Disney, a member of what Steffens ironically called the "better classes," handed out money and jobs to a long list of government officials to protect Herbalife from law enforcement.

Among public officials who took money from Herbalife under Johnson's direction and sought to protect it is the former mayor of Los Angeles, Antonio Villaraigosa. His paid support was especially significant since most of Herbalife's victims when the FTC began investigating in 2014 were Latinos. The Los Angeles Times reported, "Since leaving the Los Angeles mayor's office in 2013, Antonio Villaraigosa has made more than $4 million by advising companies such as Herbalife..."[263]

Former FTC Commissioner, Pamela Jones Harbour, who was also a Commissioner during the "Business Opportunity Rule" disclosure controversy through 2009, became Herbalife's "Senior Vice President and Legal Officer, Global Member Compliance and Privacy." She is now also a member of the Board of Directors of the Direct Selling Association, the lobbying arm of multi-level marketing companies with Herbalife as one of its largest members.[264]

Added to the list of Herbalife recipients are the earlier-mentioned former chief of staff to the Vice President of the United States, Alan Hoffman, and former FTC official, Eileen Harrington, who publicly boasted of leveraging her public service position into paid work for a MLM company. In 2016, she described herself as "former Acting Director of the FTC's Bureau of Consumer Protection ... with direct responsibility for the FTC's enforcement and regulatory oversight of business opportunities like Herbalife," and now a "consultant to Herbalife."[265]

The Herbalife controversy, 2013–2017, ceremonially raised the banner of *Ponzinomics* over Wall Street. Government officials openly joined the movement and avowed their faith in the "endless chain." Selling influence to protect such schemes was now called "consulting." FTC officials openly, boastfully sold their public-trust positions for lucrative jobs defending the protecting MLM. The brazenness of the MLM revolving door to the FTC, and other federal, state and city agencies fulfilled what journalist David Phillips predicted in an earlier era. The shamelessness and zeal of the boodler and grafter was now exalted in elite corporate, financial and government circles as *"a sort of patriotism."*

The collusion of government enables *Ponzinomics* to endure despite disclosures, class action lawsuits, whistle-blowers and even Wall Street short-selling. Government power and authority holds back the forces of the market and civic action. Yet, to complete the story of how MLM has endured and spread, the other defining element of *Ponzinomics* must now be confronted: its identity as a "delusional belief system" capable of convincing millions of people it can provide not just wealth but a fulfilling "way of life." We must now look at how MLM can take over people's minds and entire lives with its claims to provide values, life-mission and a total worldview. We must be willing to see MLM as a cult movement, unique in character and enormous in scale, a cult of capitalism.

A CULT OF
CAPITALISM

Taken, Body and Soul

In 2001, I co-launched *Pyramid Scheme Alert* (PSA), the first international association to expose and prevent pyramid scheme fraud. I produce and curate content on the PSA website and have replied to innumerable consumer inquiries from many countries. The site receives thousands of visits a month and is regularly referenced in the news media.

From this unique vantage point, I've heard countless questions and stories from confused, deluded, and damaged individuals or, friends and family of individuals, about their experiences with MLM. It is gratifying to bring clarity to some, but mostly this is a lonely and frustrating experience. The escape and cries-for-help questions are depressingly similar, whether from India, Mexico or Cleveland. Sample correspondence I received, directly quoted:

> *From a 28-year-old woman in Houston, Texas: One of my family members has repeatedly been burned by these schemes. He had to sell his car to buy food, and went $5000 into debt to buy inventory. He will never repay that amount. It also helped destroy his marriage, and was a major factor in a disruption of our relationship with him ... I attended a meeting with another family member, and it was pure cult mind control.*

> *From Japan: My precious friend of my life as she was introduced "MLM" products ... One day, she said to me that she'll become a distributor to advertise excellent products for people's health and her dream. She is now working at a company who sell jewelry but wants to resign the company and go to overseas for her study and joys. Then, I said as "well, it must be a good system ... and I also became a member as an user ... I really regret to my easy words of then ... Of course, she asked me to "help" her but I do not understand how I could do ... I researched about MLM ... visited many-many website of*

Japanese and reached to your website of which must be most understandabl ... to explain "What is MLM??" In order to rescue her from the current nightmare, I want to have your comment and precious words how I can make her normal. I know I have to explain about differences of MLM and Re-al-World but do not have "KEY WORDS" to wake her up!! ... I do not want to lose her.

I am a family member of a daughter/husband who are addicted to an MLM! Now affecting their new son cause they have him with different babysitters all the time so they can attend MLM meetings! I am a very concerned mother/grandmother!

I suspect that my son has become deeply involved with the Amway cult. His behavior has become BIZZARE ... He has become very secretive about his life ... changed his name and has adopted a cult mentality. How can I help him without alienating him as a "non-believer?"

From Europe: I would like to share my story. I have been to-gether with my spouse 9 years, we have three children togeth-er. A year and a half ago, he joined an MLM company. He started reading all the books required, was wandering around with his headset on, listening to motivational files, was writ-ing papers to manifest goals and dreams, pages and pages. After some time, I noticed that he didn't earn as much as he told me he was going to. Bills were unpaid ... His personality changed. He started to look down on ... me, on everyone ... They tell him, don't stop. Keep on! I have heard from many of our friends. Some of them joined and have lost a lot of money. He also put himself up as customer, with my credit card, in order to gain the Diamond title ... Breaking up families. It is tragic. Warn others.

Our daughter is caught up in a MLM company. They have 64,000 followers, 30,000 already with the new APP and plan a million users in a couple of weeks ... just launched their new recruiting tool with a FREE APP to saving money from consumers which includes their introduction to Cryptocurrency.

I recently told my husband he was going to have to choose between me and "The Business"... He held meetings at our home where his sponsor repeatedly told his down line that retail customers were little more than an afterthought. He also encouraged these people to commit tax fraud and bragged about his own illegal tax write offs. The final straw for me was a few weeks ago when he asked me to attend a "Dream" event. I felt like I was trapped in a nightmare I couldn't wake from ... He has sunk no less than $20,000 into "building his business" and has not made one red cent in profit ... when I confronted him ... I discovered how completely brainwashed he was ... not only (about) his own financial situation but the fact that in order to succeed himself would require his conning other good, decent, trusting people ... it was like talking to a brick wall ... I'm praying we survive this. This sinister corruption has got to stop!

Often, I am profusely thanked just for listening and validating their experiences. These tragic "losers" are told *they* are the crazy ones. MLM is "direct selling," they are reminded in every news story on the subject. The FTC, members of Congress, the Chamber of Commerce, and courts around the world tell them, "MLM is legitimate." The media regularly publish stories of "success," to verify the "opportunity" of multi-level marketing. MLMs are even endorsed by famous politicians, clergy, and sports stars. After all, MLM victims are asked, were they *guaranteed* a profit? Aren't their losses their own responsibility, as in any business?

In the face of this official legitimization, there is little I can say or do that will make a difference. As their stories verify, financial losses are not the only or even the most significant cause of disruption and harm. The MLM victims seem no longer connected to objective reality, to family, or to their own personal history, but rather they are bound to MLM leaders and captured by a delusion. Critical thinking is recast as nihilism. Facts are rejected as attacks.

Officially, what is happening — experienced by millions around the world — has no name. When it is named, it dare not be said. What these families are dealing with is far more than a business scam. MLM participants have been taken, body and soul.

Whose Name Dare Not Be Said

Accompanied by colleagues, I met with hedge fund manager Bill Ackman at his skyscraper offices in Manhattan at the beginning and throughout his ill-fated 2013–2018 campaign against Herbalife. Among our little group were attorneys that had sued MLMs, a former regulator and family members of MLM victims. None of us had previous knowledge of his pyramid-fraud-thesis campaign, nor had we been consulted by Ackman's office prior to the famous announcement of his billion-dollar "short" position. We were strangers and provincials in Ackman's financial tower, but we had deep knowledge and long experience with the deviant world of Herbalife and the MLM phenomenon he had entered.

In various meetings and in correspondence after his announcement, my colleagues and I sought to offer this Wall Street maven, respectfully, information and advice that perhaps seemed to him bizarre, conspiratorial, and irrelevant. Ackman had ventured into a financial Twilight Zone, despite his long experience as stock trader. We tried to explain that in this unnamed dimension, truth is stranger than fiction. Belief, not facts, rule. The financial failures of millions of people, not consumer products, are the tradable commodities produced for profit. The laws of economics are reversed. Like Alice, he had climbed through the mirror.

We told him about MLM's deeply imbedded K-Street lobby and its linkage to another powerful lobby for vitamins and food supplements, which enabled it to legally hawk miracle potions and fountain of youth lotions. We provided a list of revolving-door connections between FTC officials and the MLM industry. We told him of our own history of having presented most of the same facts he now publicized to the FTC, evoking only silence, dismissal, or insult. We documented the highly paid support MLM has gained from powerful public figures such as Madeleine Albright and Bill Clinton, and we warned of MLM's record of ferocious legal attacks upon critics and whistle-blowers.[266]

There was one defining element of MLM, however, that our group refrained from speaking about. We withheld it perhaps sensing it would only take us into an even deeper realm of absurdity beyond the one we were already in as a small band of citizen activists. Sharing and explaining this element with Ackman would marginalize us even further than our current status as zealous "anti-MLM" crackpots, dream-stealers, and targets for hate mail and MLM SLAPP lawsuits.

We saw little point in arguing that he should not treat Herbalife as a business at all. He should address the entire industry of MLM, Herbalife being only one face of it, as a cult, *a cult of capitalism*.[267]

To grasp why those of us who met at Ackman's office did not have the "cult" conversation, first imagine the preposterousness of our band of protestors seated in a luxurious sky-scraper office above Manhattan. Sandwiches and cookies are on the side table with iced drinks and hot coffee. At a richly inlaid, large conference table, we are speaking to one of Wall Street's masters of the universe. His dashing good looks and globe-trotting are grist for lifestyle articles. He graduated *magna cum laude* from Harvard. With Warren Buffett and Bill Gates, he had publicly committed to give at least half of his fortune to charity. He reportedly threw frequent parties at his swanky upper eastside apartment. He has a YouTube video, entitled, "Everything You Need to Know About Finance and Investing in Under an Hour" that attracted more than 2.5 million views. His hedge fund at the time was worth in excess of $11 billion.

At our meeting, imagine that we would proceed to inform him that the enormous investment he had just made, the largest in his career, was based on a fundamental misreading of the targeted company. It is not a real business or even a fraudulently operated business, *as he mistakenly thought*. Though he had a staff of Ph.D. researchers, we would attempt to teach him *Marketing and Economics 101* of MLM. MLM represents less than 1% of retail sales, the supposed market space it has been developing for more than 60 years. It does not take market shares from actual retail companies. Its products are not unique. There is no demand for MLM goods. Many are exorbitantly priced. Few people could name even one MLM product brand name. MLM does not invent or introduce new technology. As a channel, it does not reach any specialized market or provide any service not already generally available. Its overall economic impact is to impoverish its users. As an "industry," it is a chimera, serving no market need, we would say.

About its true identity as purveyor of deceptive and harmful money-transfer, underneath its *business disguise*, we would explain its insular and totalistic belief system that extends beyond work to a participant's entire life. In this belief system, money is a *moral* measurement. The reward of "unlimited income" that the leaders promise is not mere dollars. It is a portal to happiness and fulfillment, a utopian paradise. Wealth is infused with righteousness, exalted status, spiritual meaning and purpose.

Gaining the promised wealth occurs without value-added activity. It is obtained from new members endlessly joining the financial structure, with portions of their investment capital transferred to existing members. The structure is believed to be capable of *perpetual* expansion, producing a continuous flow of money to all members no matter when they join, as long as they keep buying, recruiting and believing. Though ultimately all revenues are the *members' own money collectively*, they are led to believe that capital gains can be delivered to each and all, forever.

According to dogma, any losses suffered among members are only due to those members' individual failure of judgment or lack of effort or *loss of faith*. To ward off negative thinking or doubts that might *cause* losses, the believers are trained to maintain a perpetual temperament of blue-sky optimism and to repeat nonsensical aphorisms that short-circuit logic. The faces of the believers are always smiling.

There was some precedent we could have cited that he had challenged something more akin to Scientology than an Enron or a Worldcom or even a Madoff. One of the very first books ever written (there are only a few) by an MLM participant that shed light on its realities had the term "cult" right in the title. Stephen Butterfield's exposé, *Amway, the Cult of Free Enterprise*, would presumably have been used by Ackman's researchers during due diligence.[268] My own book, *False Profits*, which they might also have seen during their MLM deep dive, described how MLM grew out of treasured and psychologically defended American values, twisted into a national swindle.

Butterfield recounted the extraordinary and ultimately very negative effect Amway's program of "mind training" had on his own life as one of hundreds of thousands of Amway's "Independent Business Owners." He concluded Amway was less a "business" than a belief system.

Despite books[269] and many online testimonies from baffled family members about loved ones undergoing radical conversions affecting personality, speech patterns, and basic outlook on life, we did not raise the cult factor with Ackman. The business media was fixated on a titanic battle between hedge fund managers, Ackman and Carl Icahn. It treated Herbalife's stock price as the only issue of consequence and showed no curiosity about the cult reality. The strange behaviors of MLM adherents were treated as positive responses to "marketing" and "charisma."

Organizationally, we would have explained, the MLM cult is elaborately ranked. The wealthiest hold the status of gurus and prophets. Those that lose deserve and caused their plight, in that fantasy world. Information is dispensed on a "need to know" basis. Those above see the entire operation. Those below see only what is presented to them, allowing no overview, insight or foresight. Actual workings of the scam are closely held secrets.

We would explain to Bill Ackman how MLM uses an invented arcane vocabulary that is unintelligible to others. Employing an epistemology of the advertising industry *in extreme form*, truth is whatever facilitates expansion. Facts themselves are irrelevant. Deception is celebrated if it sustains hope and increases revenue. Any statements that question the system or threaten loss or inhibit expansion are false, heretical or malevolent, according to its ideology.

Farcical Realization

Apart from our tale sounding fantastical, conspiratorial, or paranoid, it is likely that Bill Ackman would have made a farcical and disturbing realization. While comprehending that our description of the secretive culture and delusionary beliefs of "multi-level marketing," he might also recognize an eerie portrait of his own insular milieu of Wall Street. He might have perceived his own role of famous "upline" guru, emulated by other "downline" investors, all believing in the illusion of an ever-expanding securities market, on a finite planet. He might have seen MLM's "endless chain" as a mirror of Wall Street's belief in perpetual capital gains, with unlimited money infused into securities trading. No one on Wall Street admits to an ultimate limit to market growth. What threatens the market is only loss of "faith." Bears and short-sellers are infidels.

The leaders of Ackman's sect speak the proprietary gibberish made famous by Allan Greenspan to explain the vicissitudes of "the market." Like the MLM "plan," in his Wall Street world, the mysterious "market" is infallible. Its Invisible Hand governs all life. Resistance to it is futile and self-destructive. Individuals or political leaders who challenge or attempt to circumvent the market are misguided, blasphemous and dangerous.

So, in the end, we evaded the deepest truth. During our meetings we never got to that reality whose name we dared not say, and which Ackman could never discover in his Torah-like studies of SEC filings or other financial data. The more he plumbed and exposed Herbalife abuses *as a business*, the more he obscured reality.

My colleagues and I only spoke about MLM as an extremist cult of capitalism promoted by economic alchemists who cast a thought-reform spell over recruits amongst ourselves.

The C-Word

In the closing days of 2014, the media were awash in stories of the battles between Bill Ackman and Carl Icahn over Herbalife's stock price. Interest occasionally spilled over to the wider subject of "multi-level marketing" and other companies of this type. During this time, two young journalists with the radio/online documentary show, *This American Life*, began an investigation of a multi-level marketing company called "Wake Up Now."[270]

This American Life, an NPR show produced by Ira Glass, is broadcast on more than 500 stations to about 2.2 million listeners. The journalists took a line of inquiry never seen in the news media coverage of "MLM." They asked, "What is it?" They interviewed me for insight into what they felt were inexplicable aspects of Wake Up Now, making its self-definition as "direct selling" invalid on its face.

Back in September 2013, the Direct Selling Association issued a press release announcing that Wake Up Now applied for membership.[271] Wake Up Now was also a Wall Street stock traded on the Over-The-Counter (OTC) market. Revenue had grown from $1 million in 2011 to $12 million in 2013. Just for the first half of 2014, the company reported revenue of $26 million and a "customer" base, i.e., distributors, numbering 100,000. Its stock price had risen from pennies to $6 a share by April 2014.[i]

What attracted *This American Life's* interest was not its financial profile or even the typical MLM pyramid questions. Rather it was that Wake Up Now was all the rage among millennials. Like all MLMs it promised a utopia of security and income. This

---

[i] Within a year of its peak growth and its exposé on *This American Life*, Wake Up Now collapsed and closed down. The company blamed its CEO for siphoning funds and misuse of revenue.

message, tragically, now resonates with young people even as they just begin their work careers. Already, this generation faces a limited market for decently paying work. Career stability is already obsolete. Many face "gig" work and carry significant debt from school. Many cannot imagine buying a home. Wake Up Now promoted a tailored solution, extraordinary income, and lifetime security gained not from Dilbert-style labor in cubicles, but from fun socializing with other younger people, "networking," just as many already do online.

Journalists Brian Reed and Bianca Giaever observed the behavior of Wake Up Now's promoters and followers sufficiently to know — without need of experts — that its claims to be "direct selling" were absurd. More remarkably, they were also not particularly interested in the legalistic matter of whether Wake Up Now was a pyramid scheme. They explored what other journalists averted their eyes from. They probed into this MLM's apparent identity as a cult movement.

Before *This American Life's* inquiry, and for much of the media still today, the disturbing characteristics repeatedly observed in multi-level marketing, well known as cult hallmarks, were ignored or, if acknowledged, couched in vague terms, such as "cult-like" and "quasi-religious." This was also despite that the largest MLM, Amway, had publicly acknowledged cultism within its operation. In a 1985 profile, *Forbes* magazine reported that Amway's founders hired a trusted aid of former President Gerald Ford to "cleanse" the sales force and downplay "cultism."[272]

The commonly used euphemisms for cults seem to reference nothing more serious than exaggerated claims or inappropriate appeals to emotion. Only on rare occasions would a greater danger be suggested. In May 2013, for example, the *New York Post* ran a story headlined, "Herbalife Suspends Cult Distributor." The article described Herbalife recruiting in Israel where one top recruiter was using "humiliation, threats and sexual abuse" to enforce obedience among his Herbalife recruits.[273]

In the report on Wake Up Now the C-Word (cult), without qualification or euphemism, broke through on National Public Radio. The show's two correspondents observed a syndrome of characteristics having nothing to do with "business," and leading them to open other possible explanations, such as ritual social club like the Masons or even a form of religion.

Journalists Reed and Giaever were baffled how tens of thousands of people, mostly young, and many African-American and Latino, would buy the scheme's commodity products and dubious services at $80 to $150 per month. They pondered how the scheme convinced so many to work at no profit and what led them to believe they would be successful when virtually none before them had been? They asked how it could be that the followers believed so fervently in a company, founded only a few years before, that offered no new technology and not even advertising support. Its products were mundane and uninteresting — paid access to discounts available for free in the open market on ordinary goods and services, and an "energy drink" laced with caffeine.

Non-businesslike behavior included a god-like status accorded to Wake Up Now's leaders; rank-and-file distributors unable to describe the company's business model or the pay plan; absence of sales training; 5-hour promotional events with repetitive messages that the attendees later mimicked word for word; near ecstasy displayed by recruits over commonplace product announcements; unquestioning faith they would become wealthy from the scheme, in the face of a *disclosed* report of 96% loss rates. The journalists wondered how to describe the attendees at a large Wake Up Now event — Members (of what)? Customers (buying what)? Prospects (for what)? Salespeople (selling what, exactly)? Believers (in what)?

When they arrived at the show's premise, these journalists of *This American Life* had recognized the tactics of the leaders and the behavior of the followers to be quite terrifying. Wake Up Now was a cult, an "economic cult." The participants in Wake Up Now behaved as if they were brainwashed.

Mind Control

From its earliest days, multi-level marketing included pseudo-psychological self-improvement programs that claimed powers to drastically alter an individual's outlook and attitude and to instantly facilitate effectiveness, especially financial success. The three largest and fastest growing MLMs that the FTC targeted in the 1970s — Holiday Magic, Koscot Interplanetary, and Amway — each had indoctrination programs, euphemistically termed "mind training," "transformational," or "motivation" courses.

Dare to be Great, the Koscot-related program owned by Glenn Turner, operated in 13 countries. *Mind Dynamics,* the Holiday Magic program by its founder William Penn Patrick, was the subject of a best-selling book in 1972 that exposed "military-like tactics." The book, *The Pit,* was made into an award winning film, *Circle of Power,* co-produced by Anthony Quinn. In 1983, the authors, Gene Church and Conrad D. Carnes, wrote a follow up book, *Brainwash.*

Amway became prominently identified with "motivation" groups with its associated "tools" scheme, called Amway Motivational Organizations (AMO). These were technically owned and run by "black hat" distributors with enormous downlines of recruits. They were "exalted" by these followers as near deities. The "tools" were books, audios, and videos produced by the leaders and sold at enormous profit margin. The followers were instructed to listen, read, and watch the materials constantly, day after day, and to purchase new materials weekly. The indoctrination also included elaborately staged, large-scale spectacles on weekends, attracting tens of thousands of adherents, often extending into the early hours of the morning and featuring nationally famous speakers like Newt Gingrich, Oliver North, and O. J. Simpson.

Three books about Amway's mind control program by former distributors, *Amway, the Cult of Free Enterprise* by Steven

Butterfield; *Amway Motivation Organizations, Behind the Smoke and Mirrors* by Ruth Carter; and *Merchants of Deception* by Eric Scheibeler; all describe coercive persuasion, manipulation, and immersion into cult membership carried out in the AMO programs.

William Penn Patrick's, Glenn Turner's, and Amway's respective indoctrination programs have been described as precursors or in the same category with "large group" training programs, such as Werner Erhard's *est* or *Lifespring,* and are related to "human potential" and "transformational" programs taught at the Esalen Institute in Big Sur California established in 1962.[274]

The human potential movement and all its various groups are traced to the humanistic psychology taught by psychologist Abraham Maslow. They incorporated Freudian psychoanalysis and behaviorism and were viewed as "positive" approaches to mental health, enabling participants to "actualize themselves" and achieve "peak experiences." The term, "human potential" is reportedly from Aldous Huxley, an early teacher at Esalen.[275]

Birth of the "Commercial" Cult

Based on what is known of it, the first MLM, Nutrilite, operated just as an endless chain scam disguised as a vitamin sales company, using false promises of income as its main lure. One of two MLM inventors, William Casselberry, was a psychologist who had published a "self-help" book, *How to Use Psychology in Everyday Living,* that claimed to hold "scientific laws" for living. The "laws" were general principles for getting along that were commonly taught as sales "psychology."

It was not until two of its top recruiters defected to form a copycat scheme, later called Amway, that "MLM" took on it current cultic character. As awareness of the false income promise grew from the sad experience of huge numbers of "quitters," the need arose for more powerful recruiting and persuasion, domination of thought and behavior and the silencing of ex-re-cruits. In Amway, MLM quickly morphed into a delusional belief system with hierarchy, rules, specialized language, and god-like leaders promising utopia for believers and a wretched future for "quitters, losers" and "negative thinkers." To the illusory and de-structive "endless chain," Amway grafted a façade of piety that sanctified wealth-seeking and portrayed its founders and top re-cruiters as geniuses, heroes and Christian role models.

Amway's metamorphosis into a new form of cult occurred when cults of various types began to proliferate in America, the late 1950s, 60s and early 70s. MLM's identity-altering programs, however, pre-date the burgeoning cult phenomenon of that era. MLM's persuasion systems are rooted in earlier non-academic programs aimed exclusively *at salespeople*, as discussed much earlier in this book, during the dream-journey of Carl Rehnborg and his enrollment in a Dale Carnegie course. In that bygone era, when small farms and towns dominated the American land-scape, before World War II, professional salespeople comprised a small, often vilified, cadre of the American work force. As the solider-ants of the market, before mass advertising and the fields of PR matured, it fell to salespeople to bring commercial messag-es to the public directly and persuade them of needs they didn't know they had so they would buy.

To excel in this less-than-exalted service, salespeople were subjected to a unique form of training most people would not tolerate or would find repugnant. The training for market com-bat required a makeover of personality, an adoption of at least the outward appearance of confidence and the fierce determina-tion to succeed against constant disrespect and rejection. Most important, for a driving motivation, they were taught to *believe* in the ultimate value of gaining wealth.

Long before multi-level marketing shamed its adherent with the specter of "loser," salespeople were mercilessly indoctrinated with the winner-or-loser philosophy of life. Fortified with the spirit and the doctrine of the marketplace, they were then trained in the weaponry of persuasion, manipulation, and domination. Before "sales-and-marketing" became an academic discipline, it was an underground belief system, an ideology, and a philosophy for living, crassly commercial in character. The discipline of sales was presented as more than tools of a trade. It was "self-improvement," a study of human nature, a pathway to success in business and happiness in the rest of life.

To recall, MLM was invented in the period in America when, as historian Richard Huber explained, a profound cultural shift occurred "from character to personality." The new American "personality," suited for a new consumption-based economy, was that of the archetypal salesperson.[276] The most influential promoter of this cultural transformation, according to Huber, was not an academic, preacher or a psychologist, but a would-be actor and successful public speaking teacher, Dale Carnegie. Carnegie's book and companion training course promoted what Carnegie claimed was a "new way of life."

It was at a Dale Carnegie mind-training course that Carl Rehnborg met one of his future partners, William Casselberry, a pop psychologist who would transform Rehnborg's tiny company. Dale Carnegie's wildly popular book, *How to Win Friends and Influence People* was published in 1936 only a few years before and perhaps served as the model for Casselberry's own book, *How To Use Psychology In Everyday Living*.

Casselberry's psychology text was part of the movement of academic credibility being added to what was earlier understood as a commercial belief system, an ideology of the sales world. Character, emotions, values, personal relationships were re-interpreted into commercial, marketing terms for commercial purposes. As Carnegie advised, "You don't feel like smiling? Then what? Two things. First, force yourself to smile. If you are alone, force yourself to whistle or hum a tune or sing."[277]

MLM's "endless chain" proposition, the core of the deceptive money-scheme, was assembled from elements of American heritage including the folkloric Ponzi scheme of 1920s, the money chain letter mania in the 30s, and the manipulative and deceptive door-to-door sales culture including "referral selling" schemes. It included the cruel management manipulations of salespeople made famous in the plays and later films, *Death of a Salesman* and *Glengarry Glen Ross*. Perhaps most important, it was based on pervasively commercialized fantasies promoted by Disney, McDonalds, and constant marketing that were replacing engagement with reality and were reshaping American values, encompassing grief and death, recreation, food and health. MLM expanded the fairy tales into work and livelihood.

MLM's evolution from a business opportunity scam into a national cult movement was similarly founded upon elements readily at hand and current in America. The Calvinist ethic brought over by Puritans, teaching wealth as virtue and poverty as sin; the American-invented religions of Christian Science, Mormonism, New Thought and Prosperity Theology, teaching spiritual and positive-thinking pathways to wealth and perfect health; popular views of "the market" as a supreme and mystical force governing personal and national life; the manipulative new sales "personality"; and the deceptive logic and claims in mass advertising — these cultural fantasies are raw materials for an alternative reality involving new identities.

The Village of 'Everything Is Possible'

Covering up the impossibility of the endless chain proposition at the center of MLM's creed would require that traditional beliefs and values associated with capitalism be exaggerated and distorted into a grotesque version of The American Dream myth. The pyramid proposition itself is an absurd misappropriation of the general tenet of *perpetual* capital market growth. MLM deviously distorts this general concept into a specific business model for every individual's "downline" to expand to "infinity." No company or industry had ever offered such a false income proposition or made it into a business model, until MLM.

To dispel critical thinking and immerse recruits in the fairy tale, extreme persuasion and thought-control were necessary and such methods were also readily available on the American scene. The "transformation" movement and the explosive rise of MLM beginning the 1960s are virtually concurrent. Amway and one of its counterpart schemes at that time, Holiday Magic, were both started within just a few years of the Esalen Institute, the progenitor of many Large Group Awareness Training programs, some with credentials of academic psychology and proclaiming "breakthrough technologies" in "human potential."

In addition to running *Mind Dynamics*, the mind reform training program of Holiday Magic, founder William Penn Patrick produced a booklet in 1967 later made into an LP recording, entitled *Happiness and Success through Principle*. The recording is presented as a moral prescription for life, a righteous and authoritative argument for acquisitiveness and rationale of wealth as a natural outcome of virtue. It has the tone of a stern religious sermon, *economic* dogma as an all-encompassing moral code.[278]

Both William Penn Patrick and Glenn Turner, founder of the rival MLM Koscot, cast themselves as the holders of eternal secrets to happiness and financial success, converting their recruiting schemes into human-potential crusades. Turner's own recorded homily, *The Village of Everything Is Possible*, promotes the magical belief that all life circumstances can be altered by a positive shift in viewpoint and attitude and that optimism and confidence ultimately determine reality.[279] This metaphysical claim made the finite limits to recruiting and the fact of market saturation mere circumstances to be overcome with *belief*.

The refrains, *believing can make it true, everything is possible, and miracles can happen,* are now ubiquitous in the human potential movement, many churches, self-help groups and are taught even in corporate training courses. What is often overlooked in these magical tenets is the corollary: nothing is objectively true.

Viewed generally as a positive, inspiring and uplifting perspective on life, in the hands of pyramid scheme charlatans and cult leaders, the "everything is possible" proclamation becomes a tool to destroy personal identity, subvert critical thinking and to blow up life-long perceptions of what is real and true. When life circumstances, background, direct experience or a lifetime of learning are dismissed only as a limiting perspective that can be reshaped, abolished or "transformed" by merely altering perspective, people are suddenly vulnerable to new and dominating interpretations. Thought control and undue influence are more possible.

Describing the classic conditions where authoritarian rule gained acceptance, Hannah Arendt explained "[people] reached the point where they would ... think that everything was possible and that nothing was true ... [the public] did not particularly object to being deceived because it held every statement to be a lie anyhow."[280]

While less flamboyant than Patrick and Turner, Amway's two founders, Jay Van Andel and Richard DeVos, were no less doctrinaire, and portrayed themselves in similar fairy tale roles as geniuses of startup capitalism, creators of "winners" and "millionaires" and champions of "small business." They added claims of Christian piety and law-abiding rectitude. Their bios depict them as having personally built a financial empire from a tiny "startup" business based on "door-to-door" selling" and "run out of their basement."[281]

This fictional narrative abetted the false claim that Amway's endless chain scheme was a "breakthrough" opportunity for the average person to become successful and wealthy like DeVos and Van Andel and other top Amway recruiters who were similarly portrayed. The storyline was embraced by the Republican Party and the U.S. Chamber of Commerce where they insinuated themselves into top positions. Their bogus bios as iconic American success stories who are now offering everyone else a way (Amway) to replicate their wealth and success meshed with extreme political and economic agendas opposing government safety net programs and promoting individualism. *Ponzinomics* was imbedded into the American Dream mythology as a true pathway to its fulfillment.

In fact, DeVos and Van Andel floundered in failed enterprises after leaving military service and then signed on as door-to-door sales *recruiters* for Nutrilite. The pair spent more than a decade at Nutrilite, groomed and trained by MLM's inventors, William Casselberry and Lee Mytinger. By chance, they got in at the very beginning even before Nutrilite had competitors and when the company explosively spread its recruiting scheme across the entire country. The FDA prosecuted the company because the recruiters (DeVos and Van Andel included) were making dangerously false medical claims to new recruits and the public. Van Andel and DeVos were pushing classic snake oil, according to the FDA. Later, the FTC would claim they were pushing *financial* snake oil too.

The two defected from Nutrilite about 1960 to spin off a virtually identical and competing enterprise they called Amway, precisely copying the Nutrilite structure and pay plan. They even brought over the very same terminology, calling their endless chain scheme mysteriously "the plan." They also persuaded as many as 5,000 of Nutrilite's sales force to defect with them to launch Amway. Leveraging political connections, they escaped subsequent pyramid fraud prosecution, but were found guilty and penalized for income claim deception, price fixing, and tax evasion.

From its own disclosures and court data, it is fully documented that far less than 1% of people enrolled each year in Amway's "income opportunity" made any profit all. Some reported devastating losses in addition to profound social dislocation. Calculating all the people all over the world that have invested time and money in Amway since its inception and factoring the enormous churning of new recruits, the shocking reality is that Amway arguably caused more financial loss to more people than any comparable "business" on earth. It achieved this infamous record while proclaiming itself the "greatest income opportunity in the world." Such is the total disconnection from the real world that people experience when entering MLM's "alternative fact" universe. It is a world as fantastical as any of the exotic and bizarre cults that are known today, while dressed in conventional business attire and other trappings of authentic business. The scale and audacity of the MLM deception, including how the scheme operates, where it came from, who its leaders are and what consequences it produces are literally beyond most people's imagination.

Only in America

With magical beliefs based on *economics* sweeping America, *market* values preached as prescriptions for happiness, schools of psychology and religions equating *wealth* with "personal fulfillment," and the smiling sales "personality" mandated for "success," MLM offered the organizational vehicle to weave these American trends into an extremist and delusional ideology of capitalism. The totalistic belief system developed its own language, mimicking financial and sales jargon, commercially-oriented values based on sales and pop psychology, and a worldview *of extreme and rapacious individualism* resembling that of an amoral corporation. As more MLM's were formed, precisely duplicating existing ones, they coalesced into a large-scale *commercial cult movement*, the first in the world. The fairy tale stories of Carl Rehnborg as father of MLM and the vitamin industry, of Amway as a phenomenal "start-up," of legality for endless chain recruiting, and of Amway's billionaire founders as champions of "small business," these became fables and tenets of the new creed.

The new cult movement was not established structurally as a church, political movement, or a school of philosophy, though it resembles all of these. MLM was organized as the most revered institution in modern America — a chartered business that promised "self-employment" and the exalted status of "owner" to its followers. Officially, it did not convert or persuade or dominate. It *sold* its beliefs and its false promises of wealth-and-happiness, making them appear as voluntary commercial contracts. At a time of rising anomie, it promised guiding truths, a supportive community and financial security. It appropriated the name and assumed the identity of the extinct but still revered field of "direct selling," conjuring the celebrated Yankee Peddler, icon of American enterprise.

Like all cults, MLM proselytizes, but not just as a mission. MLM recruiting, falsely depicted as "direct selling," is an existential mandate, the yellow brick road to its promised utopia for participants, the vital source of funding for the organization. Like all cults, the recruiting solicitation is deceptively disguised as a social invitation, and further disguised by the innocuous activity of buying and selling ordinary products. Success and profit are gained from the purchase-investments of "friends and family" facilitating the viral-spread of the solicitation to the dinner table, into places of work and worship.

To complete the necessary ingredients of a cult movement, MLM's earliest promoters, like so many that followed, assumed playbook roles of holders of ancient secrets to wealth and happiness. MLM did not rely on a single cult leader. It precisely scripted the role for thousands of actors to play the part of prophet and guru in the multitudes of tentacles of new "companies" and the "lines of sponsorship." All would trace back to Nutrilite and its MLM architects, Mytinger and Casselberry, with Amway generating the greatest number of cloned descendants.

Some religions and some political movements claimed similar powers and raised similar levels of hope and loyalty as MLM. Only MLM offered a precise and proprietary "plan" that was measurable in real dollars in the here and now. Its top leaders lavishly and shamelessly displayed the money they said awaited all others who followed them. The movement required signing a legal contract and it charged an advertised price. It promised "total freedom" while requiring strict obedience, unquestioning acceptance and absolute conformity. It characterized every other livelihood as enslavement, making MLM the only option for believers. Those that follow discover it is the narrowest of paths, leading nowhere, while requiring servitude, continuous payment and constant proselytizing.

The new commercial cult, multi-level marketing, would be promoted with methods formerly reserved for fundamentalist religious, political extremists, radical therapies, or authoritarian dictatorships. These propaganda and persuasion methods subvert critical thought, separate believers from all others, and inflame dreams while instilling fear and dread. They empower leaders to exert near total control over adherents.

Hidden in Plain Sight

When MLM began to explode in the U.S. in the early 1960s, corresponding with Amway's debut, the larger phenomenon of religious, political, self-help, and philosophical cults in America was also growing. The new cult phenomenon was not hiding. Solicitations, public displays, and strange costumes made encounters with some cults almost unavoidable in major cities. MLM solicitations were also entering daily life disguised as house "parties," huge "motivation" rallies, home-based "opportunity" presentations, and disguised social invitations.

For all their strange new manifestations, cults were hardly recognized as a significant phenomenon — until some exploded into horrifying violence. Infamous cults that gained public attention only when they self-destructed included the Branch Davidians, a religious sect started in 1959 and ended in fire and death in 1993 in Waco, Texas. The Heaven's Gate cult started in the 70s and ended with mass suicide in 1997. The People's Temple founded by Jim Jones moved to California in the 1960s with thousands of followers. It ended in 1978 with a mass suicide and murder of 900 of its members in Guyana and the murder of a U.S. congressman.

Cult presence was noted occasionally in media reports of strange spectacles, including zombie-like behavior or extreme expressions of loyalty or near-worship of leaders. Whistle-blower reports occasionally made it into public awareness telling of abusive persuasion methods and sexual exploitation of members by the self-appointed leaders. In 1973, the Unification Church (Moonies) claimed several thousand members in America. The Hare Krishna movement, founded in the mid 60s, had 50 centers in the U.S. by the 1990s, the largest with 500 members. Much larger groups that have been popularly described as cults include Scientology, Transcendental Meditation, and followers of Bhagwan Shree Rajneesh.

A 1978 *New York Times* article, "Investigating Cults," described a state of national confusion. Despite tragedies such as the Jonestown murder and suicides, it noted the obstacles to remedial action of First Amendment rights, the puzzle of determining exercise of free will versus coercion, and the outward similarity of cults to some legal organizations, especially some churches or the military.

Obstacles notwithstanding, the article acknowledged the plain reality that if cults can operate unhindered (there is no law against cults), then society "may fear for its safety." The capability of cults to "compromise (an individual's) psychological integrity" leads to "deceptive recruitment, fraudulent fund raising fraud and violence."[282]

Twenty years later, *The Washington Post* provided a special series — "The Cult Controversy, Spiritual Quest or Mind Control?" — reviewing the status of understanding over the previous 50 years, a period coinciding with MLM's development. The series focused on two of the earliest organizations identified in the 1950s as cults, the Unification Church (Moonies) and Scientology. It showed how, by the 1990s, cults had increased in size and manifested terrifying capacity for harm, citing the sarin gas attack by a cult on the Tokyo subway. In that shocking incident in 1995, cult leader Shoko Asahara, an admirer of Adolf Hitler, and members of his Buddhist sect, were accused of releasing a lethal nerve gas on a crowded Tokyo subway. Investigations revealed the cult had secretly developed a global network of front companies to make chemical and biological weapons. Investigators determined the group had as many as 60,000 members in Japan and thousands more in Russia.[283]

Academic study of cults has been based mostly on the work of just two researchers and writers, Robert Jay Lifton and Margaret Singer.[284] Their seminal works on the defining traits of cults are part of studies of "mind control," also referred to as brainwashing or thought reform. The behavior of American POWs during and after the Korean War provided some of the early field research material for harmful persuasion methods.

There is no consensus as to why the cultic organizations in religion, politics, therapies, and other fields — including MLM — emerged in the 1960s and 70s and have grown and proliferated since. Cults defy precise classification; the phenomenon of sudden personality changes among its members, irrational loyalty, and acceptance of delusional claims of cult leaders, remains mysterious.

Two writers, Fran Conway and Joe Siegelman, are among the few dedicated to exploring the phenomenon. They coined the term "snapping" to describe the often sudden and extreme change that comes over otherwise ordinary people who become enmeshed in cultic organizations. In the 2011 update of their 1979 book, *Snapping, America's Epidemic of Sudden Personality Change*, they acknowledge that the cult phenomenon and its dangerous methods of persuasion have spread into most areas of the culture, including "commercial sales," noting that cults in these areas were inconceivable only a few years before.[285]

A frequently quoted 15-point checklist of the defining characteristics of cults was included in the book, *Take Back Your Life: Recovering from Cults and Abusive Relationships* by Janja Lalich and Madeleine Tobias. Among these hallmark characteristics are: "The group is elitist, claiming a special, exalted status for itself, its leader(s) and members ... and the group has a polarized us-versus-them mentality, which may cause conflict with the wider society."[286] These classic traits are ever-present in MLM where founders and upliners are "exalted" for possessing secrets to success and serving as living role models for perfect marriages, higher morality and American patriotism. Adherents are told they hold membership in a special community of "winners;" those who criticize or question the movement are vilified as "pathetic losers."

Academic studies of multi-level marketing cults are virtually non-existent though the cult elements of MLM are frequently referenced in media in recognition of disturbing cultic behavior of MLM recruits and hallmark cult tactics observed at MLM spectacles.

In 2009, British newspaper, *The Guardian*, published an article on cults by cult expert Rick A. Ross who has worked with MLM cult members. Citing the findings of Lifton and Singer, Ross identified three main characteristics of a cult. When these characteristics are understood and applied to MLM, the "business" disguise falls away and MLM's true identity begins to reveal itself. The first is the role of MLM leaders that Ross described as "objects of worship." Unlike real business leaders, the MLM founder or "upliner" is unaccountable, holding sole and total authority. They present themselves as the "source" of the group's power and success, while failures are always shifted to lower level individuals. The so called "education" in MLM is "coercive," presented as dogma beyond question and requires actions, in the case of MLM, that cause social and financial loss to the members while enriching the leaders. Finally, and perhaps as a consequence of the warped power relationships, cults are known for extreme exploitation, including sexual and financial of vulnerable members.[287]

Steve Hassan, an American cult expert and author of *The Cult of Trump*, a book that argues Donald Trump is a cult leader using classic cult persuasion methods, has publicly referenced and discussed MLMs and assisted MLM victims in gaining their freedom.[i] Among the Thought Control evidence he cites is the use by cults of "loaded language and clichés, thought-stopping techniques to prevent critical analysis."[288]

---

[i] Steve Hassan produced in 2010 a 35-minute video discussion of multi-level marketing deception and persuasion methods with attorney Douglas Brooks and Robert FitzPatrick, https://vimeo.com/15649228

Hassan's website, *Freedom of Mind*, has a page dedicated to MLM. "Multi-Level Marketing Groups Defraud Consumers!" He describes MLMs as "commercial cults." Like all cults, initial solicitations by MLM are deceptive and manipulative, disguising the nature of the organization and the recruiter's true purposes. Hassan cites a key feature that further separates MLM from real business, which is based on measurable market facts and data. In MLM, belief, not objective reality, is presented as the basis for success. Total belief is said to result in spectacular rewards and failures are attributed to loss or weakness of faith. "Doubt and critical thinking become faults."[289]

Hassan and Ross are part of a small, sometimes controversial, group called "cult exit counselors." They specialize in helping individuals regain their freedom from cults, including MLMs. The number of people involved in MLMs that have been served by this group is insignificant, relative to the scale of need, but they are the only people addressing this need directly and professionally on an individual basis.

Rick Ross's book, *Cults Inside Out*, includes a chapter entitled "Amway Intervention" that provides useful guidance for anyone seeking reconnection with friends or family members entrapped in a MLM cult. The chapter recounts Ross' experience helping a college student whose life took a downturn after being recruited into Amway and the family saw him as "obsessed." The family hired Ross to help them reach their son as their own efforts had failed. Ross's sessions with the student continued over three days. Reflecting that MLM cult members have been separated from objective reality and their personal histories, he advises connecting in some way with the MLM victim's past. "This may stimulate memories can be recalled and reinforced as a pathway back to reality and core identity."[290]

The only writer to directly and extensively address multi-level marketing as a large-scale cult movement is English activist

David Brear. He is not published, nor is he an academic or psychologist, and he does not provide professional counseling for pay to victims as Ross and Hassan do. Unlike Hassan, Brear was never in a cult. But Brear's work is available online on his remarkable blog that reports more than a million and a half views.[291] He is frequently consulted by the news media. Brear's blog, *MLM, the American Dream Made Nightmare*, was inspired by a profoundly and tragically disruptive experience within his own family involving Amway. This led to years of inquiry and the formulation of a precise understanding of the MLM phenomenon, which he characterizes as a "cultic racket" and a "ritual belief system." Brear's unique contribution is in identifying MLM's actual and true identity, the core reality almost uniformly avoided or missed by the news media that refer to MLM in its disguise as a "direct selling" business.

Using Lifton's defining characteristics of thought reform cults, Brear characterizes MLMs as authoritarian, delusional, and Fascistic in character, and therefore a threat not just to individuals but whole nations. While MLM's goals are seemingly limited to ill-gotten financial gains from victims and MLMs appear disparate and uncoordinated, he reminds readers how National Socialism (the Nazi Party) was similarly dismissed in its formative stages as marginal and unthreatening. Treating MLM as an insidious and disruptive cultural force, Brear's writing often addresses social and national harms, such as Herbalife illegally using at least $25 million to bribe Chinese officials and then covering it up with accounting maneuvers; the dangerously false claims of some MLMs for COVID-19 cures or preventions; or how MLM's can infiltrate and distort other areas of society, citing Amway's Betsy DeVos extraordinary power over American schools.[292]

Brear begins his own list of cult characteristics with "deception."[293] He notes that the very first encounter people have with MLM is deeply deceptive, signaling sinister manipulations and potentially disastrous consequences. MLM recruiters deviously misrepresent the recruiting solicitation as a purely social contact or as a product-oriented demonstration.

Additionally, Brear addresses another hallmark trait of MLM almost universally ignored by the media and academia, the factor of "mystification." He cites the common practice of portraying the MLM as a "breakthrough," making extraordinary financial results possible beyond what any other business could. The "infinite" levels and the myriad of ranks and titles are misrepresented to give the organization a status of an ancient religion or secret society. Mystification separates the recruits from verifiable reality and draws them into MLM-pioneer Glenn Turner's fairy tale world where "everything is possible."[294]

All cult experts agree that virtually everyone is a potential cult member and social forces supporting cult recruiting affect almost everyone. Nevertheless, the enduring popular perception is that cult victims are limited to peculiarly vulnerable individuals facing unusual circumstances. Most people, therefore, believe they themselves would not be cult candidates, or if they were solicited would never succumb. As experts Hassan and Ross attest, even people inside cults believe they would not join one and deny they are in a cult. Cults are therefore protected by the denial and disbelief of people inside them and out. The enslaving power that cult persuasion can have over minds —anyone's mind —remains largely unstudied or ignored, aiding the spread of cults.

The Largest Cult in the World

Most cults that have gained national attention have relatively small followings. They espouse exotic, marginal, and fantastical beliefs involving angels, flying saucers, messiahs, levitation, brain images, or claims to supernatural powers. They may claim to have received absolute truth on tablets or "channeled" into books. Their teachings may include apparent justifications for violence toward non-believers.

The MLM cult is seemingly the opposite. It taps into *national* beliefs and cultural norms generally accepted in virtually every American household. These are embodied in the values, hopes and behaviors associated with the "American Dream," viewed by most people as beneficial and positive. In an impersonal, mass society, MLM claims to address real and immediate needs for livelihood, financial security and community. Its utopian promises of prosperity for all are not generally treated as fantastical or exotic. They are mirrored in advertising, pledged in political campaigns, taught as economic law in some schools, and preached from many pulpits.

MLMs are chartered as legal corporations. The leaders dress in business suits and most profess faith in conventional religions, with Mormonism now accepted as conventional. MLM executives are leaders in political and business organizations, give generously to charities, and appear to have conventional families. They all present the classic salesman's smile and optimism and the enterprises engage in buying and selling ordinary goods. MLMs produce taxable profits and capital gains for shareholders and they are described in the media in the traditional commercial language of production, sales, and distribution. They deliver a message and make promises that all who believe in a version of the "American Dream" would find credible — as long as they do not examine the fraudulent recruiting model, understand its banal origins, know its actual record of devastating losses among adherents and history of law-breaking, and are unaware of its destructive cult methods and character.

Embracing the new persuasion techniques used to indoctrinate salespeople and expanded to "transform" people, MLM has spread nationally and globally, not as a dangerous cult, but viewed by most enrollees when they are recruited as a powerful force for good, reinforcing values that are widely esteemed.[295] MLM has thrived wherever capitalism operates. After China was granted full trade status in the late 1990s, MLM quickly expanded to cover the whole world. In this format, MLM became the largest cult in the world and yet remains unrecognized, hidden in plain sight.

Business Suit Camouflage

The MLM cult movement enjoys one further layer of disguise so effective that it wards off cult accusations even when its global record of losses, deceptions, and abusive persuasion methods are known. This is the nearly universal presumption that a *business*, no matter how deceptive and unfair it might be, could *never* exhibit the defining traits of a cult, as described by Robert Lifton or Margaret Singer.

By definition, business enterprises are finite and measurable. Businesses are based on all sorts of limits — market sizes, number of competitors, brand awareness levels, availability of raw materials, technology, and distribution channels. Businesses can exaggerate products or future profits but they cannot promise utopia. Investors and customers can measure business promises against actual market conditions, competitors and historical performance. The nature of work and business is mundane and measurable in real time and with math. Real businesses are, by definition, not "totalistic." Employees, contactors, and customers maintain private lives, their own beliefs and individual values.

Behind its business disguise, and playing upon popular presumptions of commercial limitations and purpose, MLM is totalistic. It violates boundaries separating private and commercial life; demands 24/7 commitment; and routinely advertises itself as a "way of life." It can elevate its impossible income promise to a *spiritual* pathway to complete happiness, making it impossible to measure, and it can silence its victims, condemning them with a "loser" status. MLM leaders pose as living examples of this state of perfection. The company's "secret" or "unique" system for delivering this happiness — endless chain recruiting, powered by "exponential expansion" — is said to be the *only way* for an individual to achieve this dignity and security.

Failure to recognize MLM's cult identity — in the face of evidence — is reinforced by the official denial of the FTC, most of the news media, and the business community. Just as the simplistic view that because MLM sells products it cannot be a pyramid scheme, its identity as a legal business means, for most people, it could never be a cult.

From my own experience, the greatest barrier to aiding MLM victims is failure to reveal to them what multi-level marketing is and what it is doing: a cultic belief system, seeking undue influence over an individual's mind, gaining full access to their time, resources, especially money, and relationships, and achieving domination over every aspect of their lives. As long as MLM is perceived as a "business," even a dishonest one, its coercive power cannot be effectively combatted.

For those seeking help for a family member, or those seeking to recover from the financial and psychological damage they incurred while in an MLM, the most important realization they can gain is MLM's true nature behind its "business" disguise. When MLM is recognized not as a business at all, but a cultic force, far more people will instinctively avoid it, as they might the Moonies or Scientology, or will more quickly escape its grip. The power of a cult depends on not being recognized as a cult by the victims and civil society.

CRIME, BLAME AND PUNISHMENT

"Criminal" MLMs

Where calculated deception and massive financial harm occur — using cult persuasion to defraud — as occurs in MLM, should there not be accountability, restitution and penalty? Yet, in almost all cases, MLM promoters are not held accountable. When MLMs are prosecuted, the malfeasance is reclassified from criminal fraud to merely an "unfair and deceptive business practice." In these cases, no one goes to jail. No one even has to admit guilt. Penalties, such as they are, are only financial — returning a relatively small amount of the ill-gotten money. Sometimes the businesses close down, but in reality, they continue under new names. Most of the times, they actually multiply into more scams, causing even greater harm. The underlying message to fraudsters is that there is little to fear personally from running MLM pyramid schemes, which are obscenely profitable. The message to citizens is subtler: pyramid schemes are a normal part of business, like being overcharged or getting a "lemon." Responsibility for the harm ultimately belongs with the victims themselves who made "bad business decisions" or failed to recognize the deception, perhaps due to greed, despite fine-print warnings.

On Wall Street, when Bernard "Bernie" Madoff was unable to continue the subterfuge of producing "returns" for his millionaire investor clients, he publicly admitted that all the "profits" in his "hedge fund" came entirely from the clients themselves. The terminology of investment and business was used, but it was just disguise for a Ponzi money transfer. Madoff instantly transformed in the public's view from Wall Street guru, celebrated philanthropist, and man of faith, to scam artist, criminal, and sociopath. His criminal fraud prosecution and 160-year prison term were enthusiastically supported. Some thought punishment should have been harsher.

So why are MLM CEOs that harm, even ruin, far larger numbers of people *on Main Street,* prosecuted merely as civil offenders, punishable only with painless fines and unenforced reprimands, when *Wall Street* Ponzis are treated as criminal enterprises?

Nearing the close of this inquiry and arriving, inescapably, at the question of crime and punishment, it will be helpful to return to the perspective referenced in the Foreword of sociologist Edward A. Ross. In a remarkable little book written in 1906, *Sin and Society, An Inquiry into Latter Day Iniquity,* Ross pondered the impunity of financial wrongdoers in his time:

> *The essence of the wrongs that infest our ... society is betrayal rather than aggression ... we see on all hands monstrous treacheries — boodlers, grafters, violating the trust others have placed in them.*[296]

MLM's primary "sin," indeed its defining characteristic, is the very same hallmark of the new form of crime that Edward Ross identified: *betrayal of trust*. MLM not only betrays the trust of its adherents, but also teaches and incentivizes them to betray their own friends and family. MLM's crimes, if they are to be called that, are without prejudice, absent of aggression, perpetrated by high-minded figures, and are always delivered with a smile. When the victim has been fleeced, the perpetrator can cheerfully say, "Didn't they buy a product?"

Legal Precedent Remembered

To recover a rightful expectation of restitution in the face of colossal deception, government collusion, and cultism, it is not unreasonable to consider or argue for criminal punishment for "MLM" rackets, as Edward A. Ross did in his time. There is historical, legal precedent.

Many people do not know or remember that the prosecution of the MLM, Koscot, often cited for the court's landmark recognition of the *inherent* fraudulence of "pyramid schemes," led to a prison sentence for the CEO, Glenn W. Turner. Few also know that the government also sought prison for Turner's attorney, F. Lee Bailey.[297]

Koscot was closed down, but Turner, in classic MLM fashion, opened another similar MLM that eventually led to his being sentenced to seven years in prison in 1987.[298] He served about four years. Partially retired and living in Florida, Turner died in 2020, age 85. The Koscot.com website redirects to Turner's namesake website, which still offers for sale Turner's videos, seminars, MLM speeches and motivation courses.[299]

In 1998, the SEC charged the MLM, International Heritage, Inc., with operating a pyramid scheme. This led the Department of Justice to bring criminal charges against International Heritage's CEO Stanley Van Etten for fraud, obstruction of justice, subornation of perjury, and false statements. The SEC claimed, "Investors purchased 'business centers' and IHI raised more than $150 million from over 155,000 investors."[300] Van Etten was sentenced to 10 years but was let out after seven in 2012 for informing against his fellow inmates while in prison.[301] Today (2020) Van Etten runs a property management company in Charlotte, NC.

The IHI scheme was featured in a segment of *CBS 60 Minutes*, in which the late Mike Wallace interviewed me to explain the nature of an unsustainable pyramid scheme.[302] According to the *News and Observer* in Raleigh, North Carolina, where the scheme was based, the government determined that Van Etten's scheme was an illegal pyramid scheme because most of its revenue came from money spent by its recruits rather than from each recruit selling goods to the general public. "They were selling hope," said Assistant U.S. Attorney J. Gaston B. Williams."[303]

In 2016, the U.S. Dept. of Justice prosecuted Paul Burks, the CEO of the MLM, Zeek Rewards, for criminal fraud. In its "direct selling" disguise, Zeek claimed to offer a "penny auction" for its members to buy and sell various products. Participants purchased options for participating in the auction and could recruit others and gain rewards as they also participated. An investigation revealed the usual MLM pattern in which most funds used to pay rewards were actually coming from new participants, not generated by the "auction." As stated in the SEC charge:

> *Without new investor (funds from participants) ... revenues would dwindle substantially as less than 10% of daily revenues come from actual retail sales.*

I attended the criminal trial for Zeek CEO, Paul Burks, in Charlotte, North Carolina.[304] The details of his MLM, typical of so many others, were laid out over the course of the two-week proceedings. Zeek ignited the usual MLM mania. In only a year and a half it exploded to $600 million in revenue with one million participants. A jury found Burks, 70, guilty in only a matter of hours. He was sentenced in March 2017 to three concurrent prison sentences of 14 years and eight months.

I asked Assistant U.S. Attorney Jenny Sugar, why she had not called to the stand her retained pyramid expert, Dr. Peter Vandernat. She told me her DOJ team chose not to prove that Zeek is a pyramid or a Ponzi, only that Burks *"used deception to get money from people,"* resulting in harm, the essential elements of criminal fraud. The other DOJ attorney, Corey Ellis, added that there is no federal law against Ponzi or pyramid schemes. However, he noted, the deception deliberately employed by perpetrators in such scams is illegal when it leads to harm, and federal criminal statutes do cover that wrongdoing.

What the U.S. attorneys did not address is why the Justice Department was involved with Zeek, but not in all other prosecutions of multi-level marketing brought by the FTC. Those cases were relegated to the FTC, which cannot bring a criminal case, only a civil one. What made Zeek a criminal fraud and all the others not criminal?

With Herbalife, the FTC took a nearly identical approach and dealt with similar facts as the DOJ did with Zeek. The FTC focused on the deceptive *practices* used by MLM pyramids and documented the subsequent harm, and it chose not to prove a pyramid scheme. But at the FTC, the same wrongs are not "crimes," merely civil offenses.

The MLM CEOs, against whom criminal charges were brought, such as Turner (Koscot and Challenge), Van Etten (International Heritage), and Paul Burks (Zeek), were in the mainstream of MLM. Turner's Koscot reportedly grew to $100 million (in 1970s dollars) in revenue over a three-year period, rivaling Amway in size and influence in the formative years of MLM. IHI was one of hottest MLMs in the mid-90s. More than 140,000 people became sales representatives in just one year and many more joined over the full span of the scheme. IHI's CEO, Van Etten, later acquired and published *Success Magazine*, the MLM industry's flagship publication at that time.[305] Zeek's scheme involved the best-known MLM lawyer in America, Kevin Grimes, not merely as legal counsel but as a conductor of "Compliance Tests" for all Zeek participants. Before that, Grimes was in-house attorney for the MLM, Melaleuca, whose CEO was a finance co-chairperson for Mitt Romney's presidential candidacy. [306] Grimes's other MLM clients included President Trump's now defunct Trump Network. In 2010 the Direct Selling Association awarded Grimes's law firm, Grimes & Reese, a "Partnership Award," stating, "in ... FTC pyramid scheme actions ... (MLM) defendants have sought out their firm for representation."[307]

At Burks's criminal trial, high profile MLM stalwarts testified or were cited for their professional contributions to Zeek. For their industry activities on behalf of Zeek, of the type they provided to many other MLMs, several were sued and fined. Among them

were "leads" generator and trainer Peter Mingils and the ubiquitous MLM promoter, Troy Dooly. The SEC stated that Zeek paid
Dooly $6,000 a month for promotional services, including "re-
sponding to negative press" and promoting Zeek's "founders, officers, products and culture" to bolster Zeek's MLM status. Dooly
didn't disclose the payments to his audience. The SEC issued a
cease and desist order to Dooly and ordered payment of a fine.[308]

MLM marketer Keith Laggos helped craft the Zeek story.
He was later sued by the SEC for this work and fined $79,000.
Gerald Nehra, a famous MLM attorney who previously served
as in-house counsel for Amway, was touted for his legal work
for Zeek. Nehra agreed to pay a settlement of $100,000.[309] Kevin
Grimes was sued by the court-appointed receiver and agreed to
pay $1.175 million as restitution.[310]

In the Herbalife case announced the same year, the FTC took
two years for investigation, which followed *two previous years* of
publicized research and revelations of consumer loss and Herbalife deception, conducted by a major Wall Street company.[311] The
charges against Herbalife — "deceptive acts or practices likely
to cause substantial injury to consumers that consumers cannot
reasonably avoid themselves" — were essentially the same as the
DOJ brought against Zeek and the two businesses were similarly based on endless chain recruiting, with false claims to "direct
selling." Though Herbalife's offenses were on a vastly larger
scale over a far longer period and Herbalife stock is traded on
the New York stock exchange, the prosecution was carried out by
the FTC, not the SEC or the Dept. of Justice. The FTC's civil case
produced only a "settlement" that allowed Herbalife to admit no
guilt and no executives were charged at all. Not one of the consultants, promoters, PR firms, or attorneys, who aided Herbalife
in its deceptive practices, was prosecuted.

The pattern in these and other cases shows that when a Ponzi
or pyramid scheme is classified as "multi-level marketing," the

government treats it differently. This is the legacy of the political "fix" established in the 1980s and upheld by the both political parties. The "MLM" classification has become a *de facto* safe harbor from criminal law. In the rare instances where MLM promoters were treated as criminal perpetrators, such as Zeek Rewards, the schemes were recast more as securities frauds cheating "investors," though the operations were essentially no different from all other MLMs.[312] Fraud is fraud, except when a company is classified as "multi-level marketing." All companies classified as "MLM" are equal under the law, but some are more equal than others.

Theft of the Soul

Is "multi-level marketing" something new in the world of scam, or merely another version of an older, classic con game? In *Swindling and Selling*, Arthur Leff firmly classified pyramid selling in the traditions of grifting, bunco, Spanish Prisoner, and confidence schemes.

More particularly, Leff singled out pyramid selling for its connection to a distinctly American type of fraud that pre-dates MLM, which he termed, "public spectacle" swindles. In this form, the "marks" may number in the millions, all conned at once, unwittingly and repeatedly. Such a fraud always employs the advance-fee deception (pay now, get little or nothing later) but may or may not employ the "endless chain" in which victims are financially induced to enroll other victims.

Yet, despite its virulence, Leff also acknowledged that this strain of fraud is largely immune to criminal prosecution. Leff argued that it operates with impunity mostly due to its close association with institutions that are held sacred or almost universally revered. Using the generic term, "public spectacle," Leff was referencing, with slight tongue in cheek, to fraud operating as religion.

The capacity for charlatans to flourish within religion was dramatically illustrated in the 1927 Sinclair Lewis novel, *Elmer Gantry*.[313] In that tale, the narcissistic, amoral, and predatory character, Elmer Gantry, has a long and successful career as an ordained clergyman. He was handsome, charming, persuasive and seductive. Personally, he held no religious convictions, valued all relationships in terms of money or self-gratification, and cynically ignored and violated the moral principles he preached. Gantry saw religious followers as particularly easy marks for his financial ambitions. He also found the clergy role ideal for perpetrating and concealing his sexual predations.

In the pyramid-selling version of public spectacle fraud, the promoters assume preacher roles on the stage, proclaiming that they personally possess or can channel special power to dispense "success" and fulfillment in the "pursuit of happiness." When the followers lose their money, they are diverted from seeing the trickery of the pyramid scheme and are convinced their "failure" was a moral weakness, a type of sin.

The sale of products, Leff explained, is merely one of the various types of props or devices that "public spectacle" swindles may employ. Other props may include dramatic ceremony, recognition awards, charity work, rousing music, and testimonials of newly discovered happiness. Paid celebrities, politicians, and popular musicians may be used also as props.

Leff's analysis revealed how pyramid selling and religious swindles share the same roots, employ the same tools of deception, are led by similar types of narcissistic individuals, and appeal to the same needs in people. MLMs depict the possession of money as the sign of divine blessing, thereby establishing the commercial enterprise as a church-like dispenser of Grace. Just as Mytinger was trained in his earlier cemetery-plot sales work to present lavish funerals and ornate gravesites as the only proper way to express respect for the dead, MLMs equate profit and wealth with freedom, happiness, and self-worth. And just as Mytinger's sales force cruelly insinuated a simple grave site showed disrespect and insensitivity for "loved ones," MLMs teach that failure to commit totally to "the plan" indicates a "loser" and "quitter" status, perhaps a betrayal of family duty or a lack of self-respect.

The nearly identical trappings of MLM and religion raise the questions, "How do MLMs' teaching of positive ideals cross over into swindle?" and "When do sincere theological beliefs become part of religious fraud?" Like preachers in the pulpits, the MLM stage speakers deliver positive and uplifting messages. How could that be the face of fraud?

To distinguish positive events and inspiration from thefts of the soul requires a restatement of the most basic elements of *all* swindles. Leff's distinction of a religious swindle from honest religious practice is applicable to MLMs' fundamental fraudulence, wrapped in the rhetoric of hope and entrepreneurship. Leff's hallmark traits of fraud are that the perpetrator not only does not deliver the reward promised to his marks, but *knowingly* does so, deliberately and with planning for personal gain and at the cost of the believers.[314]

Multi-level marketing promoters wrap themselves in the trappings of a real business, promising, as all businesses do, the opportunity to gain income. Yet, the MLM plan has been mathematically designed and elaborately formulated so that this promise cannot be fulfilled — and is never intended to be — for recruits. This is equivalent to the swindler who offers "stolen" goods at a steep discount but intentionally never delivers as he does not even have them. MLM promoters do not have the rewards they promise to deliver.

Author Sinclair Lewis revealed the risk of exploring large-scale frauds that are disguised as revered institutions in the way that MLM is camouflaged as "direct selling." *Elmer Gantry* was condemned from pulpits across the country. Lewis received physical threats and calls for his imprisonment.[315] Similar experience has befallen many others who have dared to expose multi-level marketing disguised as entrepreneurship, self-advancement, and personal improvement.

AFTERWORD:
No Hope and None Required

As forewarned, pursuing the untold story of multi-level marketing involves confronting and re-examining long-held assumptions about business, government, American history, and many values and beliefs that MLM corrupted, distorted or used for disguise.

From Carl Rehnborg's sometimes comical dream-quest to Lee Mytinger's and William Casselberry's invention of the first pyramid selling scheme, mysteriously termed "the plan," and since its political protection obtained in the 1980s, MLM advanced an expansive fairy tale version of events, facts and outcomes, as all cons and swindles must.

Enormous ill-gotten resources fund the myth of MLM. The fake identities of "direct selling" and "income opportunity" are spread with classic propaganda methods: Big Lie, utopian promises, dream-vision diversion, repetition, fake statistics and *doublespeak*, which government agencies and news media repeat without inquiry. Against revelations of the enormous consumer losses and the naked deception, MLM promoters and their successors aggressively lobby to stop law-enforcement, corrupting elected representatives and regulators all over the world. As cultism emerged in various forms in America in the mid-1960s and early 1970s, MLM's "plan" rapidly expanded into a totalistic belief system, a pseudo-economic "way of life" that I call *Ponzinomics*. Using cult indoctrination methods, sophisticated PR assisted by government, this delusion is now imbedded in the mainstream culture.

Millions of people welcome the MLM fable as it is deceptively sold to them: *their last best hope for the American Dream.* The bogus offer gains a veneer of credibility in times when jobs are exported and housing and healthcare become unaffordable and while no other voice offers solutions. As so many people see dimming futures and less opportunity for their children, the "market" for MLM continues to increase, including students, military spouses, immigrants, seniors, minorities, and, most important, younger women. Residents of impoverished countries and those adopting market economics are particularly vulnerable.

For some, this epic and tragic true story is more unbelievable than MLM's mystifying claims of "unlimited" income from an eternally expanding recruiting chain. It is harder to accept than MLM's absurd identity of "direct selling" in the era of mass advertising, Wal-Mart and Amazon.com. MLM, in its sheer magnitude, the scale of its victims, its longevity and depth of deceptions, reaching deep into government, is simply beyond imagination or too disturbing. After suffering financial loss and social disruption and glimpsing the truth at least momentarily, millions of MLM victims revert to the fantasy and plunge back into MLM, only to lose more.

For those who are willing to confront MLM's harsh and disturbing realties, there is another challenge beyond deception. As so many have asked me, if not MLM, what is there to place hope in? What hope is there for reform and law enforcement? Journalists who have worked out MLM's delusion and false promises ask me for a sign of hope to include in their stories. Others want a prediction of the end to the losses being inflicted, or for a possibility of MLM transforming into real business.[316]

During the writing of this book, I was repeatedly informed by literary agents and editors that a true account of MLM must end with hope. It must offer a way to move government toward enforcement and oversight. Some urged me to write inspiring stories of breakthroughs and life-changing lessons learned by victims, making failure in MLM a personal pathway to eventual triumph, a rite of passage. Others recommended I recount the experiences of some in MLM who made money contrasted with others who lost, thus a "balanced" tale. This is the theme of so many newspaper articles on MLM that I have been interviewed for. The commercial marketplace is depicted as intrinsically fair, a reliable safeguard against fraud. In the end, these stories conform to MLM's brutal and false narrative that some win, some lose, so what? The Invisible Hand of the market, not the entrapping MLM plan, is the cause of MLM loss rates.

From my own years of experience, I lost hope, and I discovered that none is required to continue providing expert witness and consulting services, to maintain consumer education resources, and to assist news media, authors, researchers, bloggers, victim groups and colleagues in law, academia and non-profits. I no longer refer individuals to complain to the FTC on their own, a futile and frustrating action, given the FTC's history of revolving-door connections to MLM, though an organized large-scale complaint by thousands of victims might awaken law enforcement. I also never suggest contacting the Better Business Bureau. Without knowledge or even efforts at investigation, BBB, like the FTC, routinely and baselessly treats MLM as "legitimate," and it deals mostly just with refund complaints. Some MLMs that have been shut down or sued in class action lawsuits had A ratings.

Currently in 2020, there is no consumer protection organization with dedicated staff or resources that a consumer could turn to for representation against MLM. To my knowledge, there is no current member of Congress speaking up about MLM as a major consumer threat. I am occasionally asked by aggrieved MLM victims for a referral to a class action attorney, which I have done. However, class action lawsuits are rarely filed against MLMs, which typically have enormous legal defense resources and seek to swamp the plaintiff law firms in motions, filings and other costly and delaying maneuvers. If cases are filed, resolution may take years. Victims gain little or nothing in settlements that also produce virtually no positive change by the MLM. Suing MLMs is a risky endeavor for law firms, consuming significant resources, producing high costs and sometimes incurring professional jeopardy.

So what is the basis for my own or anyone else's actions to expose and combat the spread of MLM? It is the innate and unstoppable forces of truth and freedom, the natural enemies of frauds and cults. My work and that of others are not "anti-MLM." Such a term is absurd on its face, like anti-murder, anti-lying, or anti-sex abuse of children. Once MLM's true nature is revealed with its disguise of "business" removed, all that remains is outrageous deception and enormous harm-by-design. No one supports such fraud. Even those who engage in it do not admit to it. No reason is needed to object to MLM and its cultic manipulations or to work to expose it. It is *inherently* objectionable.

It is for this reason that I did not follow the recommendations of various literary agents, publicists and editors to write stories of MLM victims or to construct a "positive" narrative of personal triumphs. The single most important truth and reality I hope readers take from *Ponzinomics* is a practical understanding of what MLM is: a cultic, delusional and fraudulent belief system, using the inherently deceptive pyramid scheme or "endless chain" as a mechanism for swindle. Further, it is my hope that with that understanding, they will see that the primary goal of MLM promoters is to capture minds. The money follows. Their first task in capturing minds, as George Orwell explained, is to control language. Thought follows language, as does behavior. All the business terminology used by MLM — sales, distributors, commissions, bonuses, etc. — is disguise. Using those terms, though it is admittedly difficult to examine MLM without using some of them, obscures the most important truths of the MLM phenomenon.

The banal origins of MLM and transparent con of endless chain sales trickery that went into MLM's invention need to be known in order to pierce the diverting and mystifying language and pretenses of MLM as a "unique business."

Looking ahead, I also hope readers of this book see that, despite the almost total lack of institutional support from government, law and academia, there is growing resistance and exposure of MLM emerging in civil society. More and more people are discovering the truth behind MLM's disguise. The force behind this rise of truth-telling and growing resistance is affirmed in the famous quote associated with the Dutch struggle for independence against the Spanish empire in the 16th century: *One need not hope in order to undertake, nor succeed in order to persevere.*

Just as a truthful account of MLM and its real history must be a tale told by losers, the resistance to MLM fraudulence and government collusion is carried out, as the Dutch perceived their struggle, as a losing fight, until it succeeds. It does not rely on hope. It does not need to. It will continue without evidence of an ultimate vindication. In the face MLM deception, government corruption and efforts to discredit truth-tellers, it cannot be stopped.

For decades, toxic cigarettes were deceptively described by the promoters and mindlessly echoed in the media as cool, sexy, and enjoyable. The U.S. government aided the spread of smoking everywhere around the world and gave cigarettes to U.S. soldiers. Then, suddenly smoking was revealed and condemned for what it actually is and always was — lethal, sickening, and addictive. A similar radical shift in public understanding is occurring for "multi-level marketing."

For the historical moment that the MLM shift took form, I cite November 7, 2016, when the satirist and comedian, John Oliver, dedicated an entire segment of his hugely popular and respected HBO show, *Last Week Tonight with John Oliver*, to say the unspeakable truth — that *all* multi-level marketing enterprises are essentially one and the same scam, and "multi-level marketing" is synonymous with pyramid scheme. The YouTube video of that show, as of 2020, has been viewed more than 25 million times, with a Spanish language version gaining almost 3 million more.

The news narrative shifted the very next day. Reporting on the show, *Newsweek* and *Time* both characterized the MLM model as a pyramid.[317] Even the *Wall Street Journal*, in quoting Oliver, wrote that it's not just that *some* MLMs are pyramids; it's the model itself.[318] A foundation was laid by that show for ground-breaking inquiry into MLM's sordid history of corrupting government in a remarkable 11-part podcast, *The Dream*, produced by Dann Gallucci and Jane Marie in 2018. Millions have listened to it.[319]

It could also be argued that the Netflix documentary, *Betting on Zero*, directed by Ted Braun, was the force that shifted the tide. It provided a narrative and footage that Oliver brilliantly built upon.[320] Before that landmark film, there was the enormous publicity generated by hedge fund manager William Ackman seeking to expose Herbalife. Much of his research he cited was built upon the earlier class action lawsuits against Herbalife and other MLMs, such as Omnitrition and Nu Skin, brought by attorney Douglas Brooks.[321] And before that was the courageous prosecution of Amway led by Bruce Craig, Wisconsin's assistant attorney general at that time. Before then, there were dedicated attorneys within the FTC and other agencies.

The chain of actions, truth-telling and exposures go far back and include many long-forgotten individuals, just as the research and advocacy against cigarettes did before the public-at-large "suddenly" realized its horrific harm and how the tobacco industry was knowingly profiting off illness, death and life-long addiction and engaging in a global cover-up.

In arts and entertainment, MLM is finally breaking through, depicted accurately as a disruptive, tragic, and farcical force in American society. Notable is the hit comedy series *Schitt's Creek*, which includes a brilliant and revealing episode of MLM as a seductive scam.[322] Offering even more insight is an entire series on Showtime, *On Becoming a God in Central Florida,* in which the pathos of MLM provides the dramatic theme.[323]

These developments are important mile-markers on an enduring truth-telling and freedom journey. The end of the journey is not known and doesn't need to be. When the findings of science became more widely known, the tobacco companies joined forces and developed a sophisticated disinformation campaign, led by the PR firm, Hill and Knowlton to create doubt about scientific facts, discredit critics and scholars, and shift blame to the victims themselves. Hill and Knowlton also intensified tobacco lobbying to subvert law enforcement. The campaign succeeded, until it didn't. Per-capita consumption of cigarettes rose until 1961, the highest ever, until truth turned the tide.

MLM has been running a similar dis-information campaign for at least 40 years. During this time, the MLM industry — with some MLM companies turning directly to the tobacco-campaign expertise of Hill and Knowlton — has sought to marginalize consumer watchdogs and critics as "anti-MLM." It has attacked publications that ran investigative articles. It has filed harassing lawsuits to silence individuals and take down critical websites and blogs. It has created false distinctions between "MLM" and "pyramid scheme." MLM has also massively increased its influence in government, contributing to MLM-promoter Donald Trump's presidency and Amway's Betsy DeVos in the presidential Cabinet.

As truth about smoking broke through in America, the cigarette industry launched a campaign to addict and sicken people in other parts of the world. About one in every 3 cigarettes smoked in the world is now smoked in China. Following suit, MLM has already shifted its main efforts to China, which now has greater volume than the USA.

The road to change will likely not be measured in FTC prosecutions but in the level of public awareness. In his classic treatise on corporate crime at the start of the 20th century, *Sin and Society*, Edward Ross argued for piercing the corporate shield and holding executives personally accountable, as Charles Ponzi and Bernard Madoff later were, with criminal prosecution and jail.

Yet, Ross also recognized this would not occur until public awareness expanded to recogniz the new type of crime committed without passion and in the guise of business. He wrote, "As in Hosea's time, the people are destroyed for lack of knowledge."

When the truth of multi-level marketing is no longer unimaginable and unspeakable, but is as clearly recognized as the reality of cigarette smoking, the end of the largest of all cults and its global pyramid scheme will fall like the house of cards it is.

END NOTES

1.   One site similarly focused on the overall MLM phenomenon and receiving significant traffic was MLM-thetruth.com, published for more than 15 years by the late Dr. Jon M. Taylor. There are various others that address individual MLM companies or some particular aspect of the phenomenon. Another with significant traffic and longevity is Pink Truth.com (http://www.pinktruth. com). Published by fraud investigator and forensic accountant, Tracy Coenen, this site is focused mostly on the MLM, Mary Kay, but covers also the fundamentals of all MLMs.

2.   See a report on the Russian documentary at https://pyramidschemealert. org/herbalife-among-mlms-exposed-in-new-russian-documentary/ and the actual film, in the Russian language can be viewed in its entirety at http:// www.1tv.ru/sprojects_edition/si5972/fi34455

3.   Jules Henry, *Culture Against Man*, Random House, 1963

4.   Per capita, Americans now spend $225 each year on lottery tickets. In the top five states for lottery sales, about one-third of the revenue, on average, is used for public services after lottery administration costs and transfers to winners. (*USA Today*, Oct. 26, 2018)

5.   https://www.youtube.com/watch?v=6Rpq-4zYU4o

6.   *The Mind of the South*, by W. J. Cash, 1941, Alfred A. Knopf

7.   A full account of Bill Ackman's ultimately successful campaign against MBIA is the subject of the book, *Confidence Game: How Hedge Fund Manager Bill Ackman Called Wall Street's Bluff* by Christine Richard, Bloomberg Press, 2010

8.   The dossier was prepared by Diane Schulman and Christine Richard of the New York-based research firm, the Indago Group. I assisted the Indago Group's research without knowledge of its ultimate purpose. It largely replicated previous research and analysis that was already in the public domain due to two successful class action lawsuits against the company filed by Boston-based attorney Douglas Brooks as well as a state prosecution and standing court injunction in California. I served as expert in both class action suits against Herbalife.

Additionally, months before Bill Ackman published his "fraud thesis," *Barron's* had looked into Herbalife's "nutrition clubs" in Queens, New York City and Omaha, Nebraska. The most shocking discovery was that the famous anti-poverty program, Grameen Bank, founded by Nobel Peace Prize winner, Mohammed Yunus, was giving out loans to poor Latinos to pay Herbalife setup costs for "clubs." The FTC later determined that among the largest consumer losers in Herbalife were those that invested in the "nutrition clubs." Grameen was in Omaha because of the support of the greatest of all investment gurus, Warren Buffett, who profits from several MLM schemes. See "Where Beauty Is Skin Deep" by Bill Alpert, Barron's, May 12, 2012 (https://www.barrons.com/articles/SB50001424053111904370004577390241476503930)

9. The most notable piece depicting Ackman as all-powerful lobbyist, with Herbalife as vulnerable private company struggling against his unfair manipulations is "After Big Bet, Hedge Fund Pulls the Levers of Power Staking $1 Billion That Herbalife Will Fail, Then Lobbying to Bring It Down" by Michael S. Schmidt, Eric Lipton And Alexandra Stevenson, *New York Times*, March 9, 2014

10. https://www.davispolk.com/professionals/jon-leibowitz/

11. In an article entitled, "Here's Why Herbalife's Shares Are Soaring Today," *Fortune* Magazine reported, "The news sent shares of Herbalife up sharply by 18% in early trading." The article quoted Herbalife management's letter to shareholders, referring to the settlement that required fundamental restructuring of Herbalife's USA business model, "today we announced a settlement with the FTC that does not change our direct selling business model." (http://fortune.com/2016/07/15/herbalife-ftc-settlement/)

12. At the beginning of December 2012, the month in which Bill Ackman announced he had taken a one billion dollar short position against Herbalife, the stock was valued at $33 approximately. Immediately following his forced sell-off as the stock continued to rise, it nearly tripled in value. The price as of early March 2018 was 36 times the company's earnings, double the P/E ratios of Apple Computer.

13. Ross, Edward Alsworth. *Sin and Society: An Analysis of Latter-Day Iniquity* (Kindle Locations 307-308). Digital Text Publishing Company. Kindle Edition.

14. Hoffer, Eric. *The True Believer* (Perennial Classics) (p. 41). HarperCollins e-books. Kindle Edition.

15. *Christian Science* by Mark Twain, 1907. (page 180). (http://www.gutenberg.org/files/3187/3187-h/3187-h.htm)

16. http://lenatoritch.com/project/carl-rehnborg-life-size-portrait-statue/

17. David G. Bromley. In *Religion and the Transformations of Capitalism: Comparative Approaches*, edited by Richard H. Roberts, pages 135–160. Routledge, 1995

18. *Wikipedia* includes a "religion" section in its treatment of Amway. It references a *Rolling Stone* article that reported that Richard DeVos gave more than $5 million to James Kennedy's Coral Ridge Ministries. DeVos was also a founding member and two-time president of the Council for National Policy, a right-wing Christian organization.

19. https://en.wikipedia.org/wiki/Christian_Reformed_Church_in_North_America

20. Van Andel Obituary, *Washington Post*, December 8, 2004 by Adam Bernstein. See also https://creationresearch.org/vacrc-home/

21. Rehnborg Ph.D., Sam. *The Nutrilite Story*, pp. 431-432

22. Rehnborg, *The Nutrilite Story*, 736-737

23. Rehnborg, *The Nutrilite Story*, 1028-1031

24. Rehnborg, *The Nutrilite Story*, 1071-1072

25. Rehnborg, *The Nutrilite Story*, 1209-1212

26. Rehnborg, *The Nutrilite Story*, 1256-1257

27. Rehnborg, *The Nutrilite Story*, 1301-1302

28. "The history of efforts to regulate dietary supplements in the USA", John P. Swann, 23 November 2015, http://onlinelibrary.wiley.com/doi/10.1002/dta.1919/full

29. *The Great American Medicine Show*, David Armstrong and Elizabeth Metzger Armstrong, Prentice Hall, 1991, pp. 237-238

30. Armstrong and Metzger, *The Great American Medicine Show*, pp. 237-238

31. "The history of efforts to regulate dietary supplements in the USA", John P. Swann, 23 November 2015, http://onlinelibrary.wiley.com/doi/10.1002/dta.1919/full

32. The National Institute of Health starkly warns consumers, "Dietary supplements are not required by federal law to be tested for safety and effectiveness before they are marketed." National Institute of Health, "Dietary Supplements" (https://ods.od.nih.gov/factsheets/WYNTK-Consumer/)

33. An investigative article in *The Atlantic* in 2013 examined the widely held beliefs around vitamins and their origins, recounting the numerous studies showing no efficacy and, in fact, showing ill-effects from ingesting

commercially advertised vitamins and supplements. "On October 10, 2011, researchers from the University of Minnesota found that women who took supplemental multivitamins died at rates higher than those who didn't. Two days later, researchers from the Cleveland Clinic found that men who took vitamin E had an increased risk of prostate cancer ... These findings weren't new. Seven previous studies had already shown that vitamins increased the risk of cancer and heart disease and shortened lives." The article also shed light on claims, now almost universally accepted as conventional wisdom, that taking vitamin C prevents, alleviates or cures the common cold. "The Vitamin Myth: Why We Think We Need Supplements" by Paul Offit, *The Atlantic*, July 19, 2013. https://www.theatlantic.com/health/archive/2013/07/the-vitamin-myth-why-we-think-we-need-supplements/277947/

34.   Rehnborg, *The Nutrilite Story*, 1769, 1771-1772

35.   Rehnborg, *The Nutrilite Story*, 1806

36.   Hourly wages at the time were about $.60 per hour, (https://www.bls.gov/opub/uscs/1934-36.pdf) pricing the products at about $2.50, which would be about $40 today.

37.   A few years after withdrawing from the vitamin business, R. Templeton Smith founded Ben Venue Laboratories whose first major product was a hormone extracted from the urine and blood of pregnant mares. The company grew during World War II with antiseptic products used during the war. In 2011-13, beset with lawsuits and quality control problems related to contamination, and following a prosecution by the FDA, the company closed its main plant and laid off more than 1,000 employees.

38.   Rehnborg, *The Nutrilite Story*, 2024

39.   Rehnborg, *The Nutrilite Story*, 2026

40.   Rehnborg, *The Nutrilite Story*, 2081-2082

41.   Rehnborg gained custody through court order two years after the separation, and the son never saw his mother again until he was in his 30s. (Rehnborg Ph.D., Sam. *The Nutrilite Story*, 2418-2420, 2420-2421

42.   Rehnborg, *The Nutrilite Story*, 2119

43.   Rehnborg, *The Nutrilite Story*, 2180-2182

44.   Rehnborg, *The Nutrilite Story*, 2190-2193

45. Rehnborg, *The Nutrilite Story*, 2311-2313

46. Rehnborg, *The Nutrilite Story*, 2308

47. *Vitamania: How Vitamins Revolutionized the Way We Think About Food* (p. 66). Penguin Publishing Group. Kindle Edition.

48. https://en.wikipedia.org/wiki/Watkins_Incorporated#History

49. "Pharmaceutical companies like Roche, Merck, and Pfizer were soon pumping out vitamins, and by 1938, vitamins and multivitamin products had become one of Roche's major sources of income." Price, *Vitamania*, p. 86.

50. Jules Henry, *Culture Against Man*, p. 47

51. Catherine Price's book, *Vitamania*, offers a chronological account of how it came to be that vitamins are almost totally unregulated. Regarding the truth of contents, efficacy and safety, the FDA cryptically explains, "… (supplement) firms (themselves) are responsible for evaluating the safety and labeling of their products … FDA is responsible for taking action against any adulterated or misbranded dietary supplement product *after it reaches the market*." [emphasis added]

52. The near blind belief in the efficacy of vitamins (without evidence) is the theme of Catherine Price's 2015 book, *Vitamania*, in which she writes, "Isn't it strange that we worry about hydrogenated oils, high-fructose corn syrup, artificial sweeteners, and GMOs, but allow synthetic vitamins to be added to nearly anything without question … How can we simultaneously harbor distrust toward drug makers and accept extravagant claims on foods and supplements … at face value? If we were to ask these questions, we might reach an uncomfortable conclusion: that both individually and as a society, we have been seduced by a word." (Kindle Locations 155-157)

53. Price, *Vitamania*, p. 72

54. Price, *Vitamania*, p. 87

55. When Lela Calcote left Rehnborg, she also withdrew her financial support from the company. She was actually Rehnborg's fourth wife. Another, to whom he had married shortly after returning from China had died shortly after their marriage.

56. Rehnborg, *The Nutrilite Story*, 2647-2648

57. Rehnborg, *The Nutrilite Story*, 2348

58. Richard M. Huber, *The American Idea of Success*, McGraw Hill, 1971, p. 258

59. C. Wright Mills, *White Collar*. New York: Oxford University Press, 1953, p. 161

60. Huber, *The American Idea*, p. 260

61. https://www.biography.com/people/dale-carnegie-9238769

62. Huber, *The American Idea*, 291

63. https://archive.nytimes.com/www.nytimes.com/learning/general/onthisday/bday/1124.html

64. Notices of Judgment Under the Federal Food, Drug, and Cosmetic Act, 3381-3383, issued August 1951. The cases reported under Nos. 3381 and 3383 were instituted in the United States district courts by the United States attorneys, acting upon reports submitted by the Federal Security Agency; the Case reported under 3382 was instituted in the District Court of the District of Columbia by Mytinger & Casselberry, Inc. Published by direction of the Federal Security Administrator.

65. "History of the Food & Drug Adm., Date: 10/15-16/86 Place: Rockville, MD Interviewee(s): William W. Goodrich, Last FDA Position: General Counsel of FDA, FDA Service Dates: 1939 – 1971 (http://wayback.archive-it.org/7993/20170114025819/http://www.fda.gov/downloads/AboutFDA/WhatWeDo/History/OralHistories/SelectedOralHistoryTranscripts/UCM372999.pdf) page 110-111

66. "Notices Of Judgment Under The Federal Food, Drug, And Cosmetic Act," Charles W. Crawford, Commissioner Of Food And Drugs, August 7, 1951 (https://casewatch.net/fda/court/nutrilite.pdf)

67. Rehnborg, *The Nutrilite Story*, 2536-2537

68. Rehnborg, *The Nutrilite Story*, 2063-2064, 2681-2682

69. "Doctors' Offices Turn Into Salesrooms," by Abigail Zuger, *New York Times*, March 30, 1999

70. Rehnborg, *The Nutrilite Story*, 2530-2531

71. Rehnborg, *The Nutrilite Story*, 2353-2354

72. Rehnborg, *The Nutrilite Story*, 2537

73. Rehnborg, *The Nutrilite Story*, 2544-2545

74. Rehnborg, *The Nutrilite Story*, 2548-2549

75. Rehnborg, *The Nutrilite Story*, 2553-2554

76. Rehnborg, *The Nutrilite Story*, 2549

77. Rehnborg, *The Nutrilite Story*, 2550

78. https://www.seeing-stars.com/Buried2/ForestLawnGlendale.shtml

79. *The American Way of Death* by Jessica Mitford, 1963, Simon and Schuster, p. 155

80. "The End" by Ben Ehrenreich, *Los Angeles Magazine,* November 2010

81. "Los Angeles is killing us, Finding the Secrets of Mortality at LA's Most Legendary Cemeteries" by Adrian Glick Kudler, *Curbed Los Angeles*, Oct 27, 2016 (https://la.curbed.com/2016/10/27/13396168/los-angeles-cemetery-hollywood-forever-forest-lawn)

82. https://en.wikipedia.org/wiki/Forest_Lawn_Memorial_Park_(Glendale)

83. Waugh, Evelyn. *The Loved One* (p. 154). Little, Brown and Company. Kindle Edition.

84. https://en.wikipedia.org/wiki/After_Many_a_Summer

85. Mitford, *The American Way*, 154

86. Mitford, *The American Way*, 133

87. Mitford, *The American Way*, 141

88. "The End" by Ben Ehrenreich, *Los Angeles Magazine,* November 2010, referring to *The American Way of Death Revisited* by Jessica Mitford

89. https://www.fbi.gov/scams-and-safety/common-fraud-schemes/funeral-and-cemetery-fraud

90. https://www.sec.gov/oiea/investor-alerts-bulletins/investor-alerts-ia_pyramidhtm.html

91. Rehnborg, *The Nutrilite Story*, 2552

92. Rehnborg, *The Nutrilite Story*, 2555-2558

93. Rehnborg, *The Nutrilite Story*, 2547

94. In 2015, the non-profit group, Author's Alliance, deemed *Swindling and Selling* a "caged masterpiece." It noted that today the book is now mostly

"unavailable to scholars, lawyers, students, and the public." In a review of the book, UCLA law professor, Chris Jay Hoofnagle, wrote, "This wonderful book is out of print, and practically unavailable to new generations of lawyers and thinkers who focus on consumer protection... despite Leff's brilliance and masterful discussion, the book has only attracted 27 (scholarly) citations." See https://www.authorsalliance.org/2015/07/20/caged-masterpieces-chris-hoofnagle-reviews-arthur-leffs-swindling-and-selling/. See https://en.wikipedia.org/wiki/Authors_Alliance

95. A similarity between Leff's general examination of "selling and swindling" and this history of "multi-level marketing" as distinguished from actual direct selling is that, in each case, while there is little critical analysis, there is enormous popular interest. Leff noted at least 2,000 cards in the files of the New York Public Library corresponding to works on "sales and salesmanship," yet almost nothing at all in the way of objective analysis. A search of Amazon.com, for "network marketing" brings more than 5,000 entries. All the books that critically examine the subject can be counted on two hands.

96. *Swindling and Selling* by Arthur Allen Leff, The Free Press, a Division of MacMillan Publishing Co., 1976, p. 110

97. Perhaps due to the discomforting closeness between calculated swindling and common practices of selling, behavioral economist, and former president of the American Economic Association, Richard Thaler observed that Arthur Leff "never expected anyone" to read *Swindling and Selling,* and he noted that Leff was "approximately correct" in his prediction. University of Chicago professor Richard Thaler's comments are in a review and discussion of *Swindling and Selling* made as part of the John R. Raben/Sullivan & Cromwell Lecture Series at Yale Law School, delivered October 4, 2010. See https://yalelaw.hosted.panopto.com/Panopto/Pages/Viewer.aspx?id=fcd969eb-2e6c-485c-ad2c-8cad432a2ff4

98. *Ponzi's Scheme, The True Story of a Financial Legend*, Mitchell Zuckoff, Random House, 2005, pp. 26-29

99. See the Wikipedia general discussion of "fractional reserve banking" at https://en.wikipedia.org/wiki/Fractional-reserve_banking

100. Liu, *The Ponzi Factor*, p. 4

101. See *No One Would Listen*, by Harry Markopolos, John Wiley & Sons, 2010, and *The Club No One Wanted To Join – Madoff Victims In Their Own Words*, by

Twenty Nine Madoff Victims (Authors), Alexandra Roth (Compiler, Editor), Erin Arvedlund (Editor), Dougathsan Press of the Massachusetts School of Law, Andover, Massachusetts, 2010

102. See Matt Taibbi's article, "Why Didn't the SEC Catch Madoff? It Might Have Been Policy Not To," *Rolling Stone*, May 31, 2013 (https://www. rollingstone.com/politics/news/why-didnt-the-sec-catch-madoff-it-might-have-been-policy-not-to-20130531)

103. The story of David Thornton's courageous exposure of the Pigeon King Ponzi was later presented in colorful detail in a 7,000-word, illustrated story in *The New York Times Magazine* by author Jon Mooallem, March 6, 2015, entitled, "Birdman" with illustrations by Kristian Hammerstad. (https://www.nytimes. com/2015/03/05/magazine/the-pigeon-king-and-the-ponzi-scheme-that-shook-canada.html)

In 2019, the pigeon fraud incident was made into a theater production, *The Pigeon King*, written and directed by Toronto-based actor and director, Severn Thompson. The play premiered at the Blyth Festival in 2017 and returned the next year at the National Arts Centre in Ottawa. (https://ottawacitizen.com/ entertainment/local-arts/pigeon-king-one-of-canadas-biggest-scams-gets-the-theatrical-treatment-at-the-nac)

104. "Galbraith Gets Seven-Year Prison Term for Pigeon King Scheme" by Brian Caldwell, *Guelph Mercury Tribune*, Mar 18, 2014 (https://www. guelphmercury.com/news-story/4418470-galbraith-gets-seven-year-prison-term-for-pigeon-king-scheme/)

105. "Pigeon King Wins Parole while Victims Divvy up PKI Scraps" by *Better Farming* Staf, *Better Farming*, December 16, 2015

106. University of California at Davis professor, Nicole Biggart, is among the few academics who have examined "multi-level marketing." In a 1989 book, she speculated that the legacy of Charles Ponzi might have inspired the formation of multi-level distribution companies. She wrote, "The memory of a fraudulent form of financial network must surely have been circulating during the time network DSOs (direct selling organizations) were developed." (Nicole Biggart, *Charismatic Capitalism*. Chicago: The University of Chicago Press, 1989, pp. 44-46)

Unlike Arthur Leff, who examined MLM 13 years earlier, Ms. Biggart's book did not examine the pyramid pay plan or the loss rates or whether participants actually engaged in profitable retailing (direct selling). She did not investigate deception in recruiting or address the element of *inherent* fraud of an "endless chain" proposition. Biggart characterized the extreme behavior of participants as evidence of a new form of capitalism, which she called "charismatic."

Biggart relied on "assistance from the Direct Selling Association (DSA)," which "helped (her) understand the political environment of the industry." In her preface, Biggart states that an official of the DSA "read the entire manuscript" before publication. She expressed special gratitude to the MLM, Mary Kay. Currently Ms. Biggart heads the "Chevron Chair in Energy Efficiency, which directs the UC Davis Energy Efficiency Center." The position was created with a $2 million donation from Chevron Corp. See https://www.businesswire.com/news/home/20100601006733/en/UC-Davis-Names-Chevron-Chair-Energy-Efficiency

107.   As explained in a CNN article, Clarence Barron, founder of the *Wall Street Journal* and *Barron's* magazine, revealed that Charles Ponzi's alleged source of income, postage coupon trades, was a hoax "(Barron) figured that Ponzi would have to be moving 160 million coupons around to raise the cash he needed to support the business. Since there were only 27,000 postal reply coupons circulating in the world, Ponzi's story didn't check out." See http://www.cnn.com/2008/LIVING/wayoflife/12/23/mf.ponzi.scheme/

108.   The "MLM" business is totally based upon "person-to-person" solicitations that rely on existing trust and even love between promoter and mark. However, Madison Avenue soon picked up the trend for mass merchandising. The famous 1971 commercial "Buy the World a Coke," featuring the pop song, "I'd Like to Teach the World to Sing (In Perfect Harmony)," shows a culturally and ethnically diverse group of young people on a mountainside joyfully singing that promoting Coca-Cola helps to spread love and unity, person to person. In 2015, the ad was dramatized in the final segment of the television series, *Mad Men*, about the dehumanizing culture of Madison Avenue, appropriately titled, "Person to Person."

109.   A brief and fact-filled overview of the chain letter history is, "You Must Forward This Story to Five Friends, the Curious History of Chain Letters" by Paul Collin, *Slate*, October 12, 2010, http://www.slate.com/articles/arts/culturebox/2010/10/you_must_forward_this_story_to_five_friends.html

110.   https://news.google.com/newspapers?id=PGYp AAAAIBAJ&sjid=qOMDAAAAIBAJ&pg=6811,2593762&hl=en

111. Daniel VanArdsdale's archive of the money-chain letter is free online at: http://www.silcom.com/~barnowl/ and the Snopes.com reference to the archive is at: https://www.snopes.com/fact-check/chain-linked/

112. https://news.google.com/newspapers?id=qUwbAAAAIBAJ& sjid=lUsEAAAAIBAJ&pg=2227,2786298&hl=en

113. Declaration of Dr. Peter J. Vandernat Ph.D., Pursuant to 28 USC Section 1746 on the FTC prosecution of SkyBiz.com, May 2001

114. Rehnborg, *The Nutrilite Story*, 3390-3393

115. *Mytinger & Casselberry, Inc., Lee S. Mytinger and William S. Casselberry, Petitioners, v. Federal Trade Commission, Respondent,* United States Court of Appeals District of Columbia Circuit, Argued October 13, 1961, Decided March 1, 1962. (https://www.leagle.com/decision/1962835301f2d5341680#)

116. The full text of the FTC Complaint and the final order is preserved at https://www.ftc.gov/sites/default/files/documents/commission_decision_volumes/volume-93/ftc_volume_decision_93_january_-_june_1979pages_618-738.pdf

117. In his ruling, Judge Timony wrote, "By an order dated April 12, 1976, I was substituted as administrative law judge because of the heavy workload of the former administrative law judge. (approximately 13 months after the FTC Complaint was filed)"

118. James P. Timony was appointed an Administrative Law Judge in 1976 and retired in 2003.

119. "Against Administrative Judges," by Kent Barnett, UC Davis Law Review, Vol. 49, No. 5, June 2016, p. 1652 (https://lawreview.law.ucdavis.edu/issues/49/5/Articles/49-5_Barnett.pdf)

120. The arguable judicial status of Administrative Law Judges was discussed by Judge Timony himself in his article, "Disciplinary Proceedings Against Federal Administrative Law Judges" published in the Western New England Law Review in 1984. He defended the status, noting, "Critics argue that administrative law judges lack judicial status on the premise that their decisions lack finality and that there are no sanctions for disobedience of their orders." (http://digitalcommons.law.wne.edu/cgi/viewcontent.cgi?article=1482&context=lawreview)

121. https://www.wiggin.com/wp-content/uploads/2019/09/fall-2002-consumer-protection-update.pdf

122.   http://www.apks.com/en/about/firm

123. $200 million in revenue with 360,000 recruits yields monthly purchases of $46 or $12 a week. A 25% markup would produce a $3 gross profit on average. Yet, even that small average did not represent the amount, on average, sold to the general public. The ruling stated, "Much of this amount (average monthly purchases) is consumed by the distributors themselves rather than resold."

124.   The Commission only found Amway's *specific* claims of income to be deceptive where real numbers are used, and it reversed Judge Timony on this part of this ruling. To avoid future prosecutions under this FTC income claim ruling in the Amway case, MLMs have designed famously devious "income disclosures" and other disclaimers associated with income references, offered right along with extraordinary testimonials and generalized claims of "unlimited" income and "wealth beyond your imagination" within reach of all who "don't quit."

125.   https://www.motherjones.com/politics/2014/01/devos-michigan-labor-politics-gop/

126.   https://en.wikipedia.org/wiki/Jay_Van_Andel

127.   An insightful discussion of the new state consumer protection laws, written at the time of enactment, is "Consumer Protection by the State Attorneys General: A Time for Renewal" by John H. Kazanjian in Notre Dame Law Review, Volume 49, Issue 2, Article 9 (1973). He wrote that "pyramid-franchising distributorships" were among the "most pervasive consumer problems throughout the country. The company usually misrepresents the earning potential of the distributors by advising them that they can make large amounts of money by signing up other people as distributors." See https://scholarship.law.nd.edu/cgi/viewcontent.cgi?article=2809&context=ndlr

128.   From direct interview by the author with Bruce Craig

129.   1982 Wisconsin AG suit is preserved at https://pyramidschemealert.org/wp-content/uploads/2018/08/Wisconsin-AG-suit.pdf

130.   http://docs.legis.wisconsin.gov/code/admin_code/atcp/090/122.pdf

131.   Based on direct interviews with former Assistant Attorney General (retired) Bruce Craig, and various public statements he had made about that case.

132.   The 1982 Wisconsin suit stated that Wisconsin had a population of 1,652,261 households.

133.   The Wisconsin suit stated, "If one-fifth (4,000) of the 20,000 Wisconsin Amway Distributors reached the projected $1,230 monthly income (a figure regularly used by Amway recruiters in 1980) ... they would collectively generate a monthly ... retail value of ... $661,017,600 a year (*over $2 billion in current dollars*). This would require the annual purchase of $400 worth (*over $10,000 in current dollars*) of Amway products by each of the 1,652,261 households in Wisconsin." This data and calculations were based only on Amway's current base of participants and did not factor the thousands that had been previously enrolled and already quit the scheme.

134.   "Direct Distributors continually seek large numbers of recruits in order to generate purchases on which a bonus payment will accrue to them as the original recruiting Direct Distributor. There are approximately 20,000 Distributors in Wisconsin, of which 192 are Direct Distributors. In truth and fact, the average annual adjusted gross income for each of the approximately 20,000 Wisconsin Away distributorships was $267 ... The average annual net income (after the deduction of business expenses) for all Wisconsin Direct Distributorships was, in fact, a net loss of $918."

135.   The relevant parts of Behnke's tax return used in the Wisconsin prosecution are preserved at https://pyramidschemealert.org/wp-content/uploads/2018/08/Behnke.Tax-Info.Wisconsin.Amway_.Case_.pdf

136.   The earlier version of SA4400 have been preserved at https://pyramidschemealert.org/wp-content/uploads/2018/08/SA4400.RetailSales.pdf

137.   The exposure of reality, reducing the official story to laughable absurdity, continued with John Oliver's hugely popular HBO show, *Last Week Tonight*, Nov. 7, 2016, which reported data taken from the large MLM, Nu Skin's own "disclosure." Oliver stated, "Nu Skin says around 18 percent of active distributors earned a commission check, which is worse than it sounds because active distributors represent around only 36 percent of total distributors. If you do the math, which they conveniently didn't, that would mean 93 percent of all Nu Skin distributors receive zero commission in a given month. So even if you have never heard of Nu Skin before, it may be paying you just as much as it does 93% of all its distributors." See https://www.youtube.com/watch?v=s6MwGeOm8iI

138.   Among psychologists this is known as the 'illusion of truth' effect." See "How Liars Create the Illusion of Truth" by Tom Stafford, *BBC*, October 26, 2016 (https://www.bbc.com/future/article/20161026-how-liars-create-the-illusion-of-truth)

139. "Trump and Authoritarian Propaganda" by Steve Denning, Senior Contributor, *Forbes*, Nov 6, 2016, See https://www.forbes.com/sites/stevedenning /2016/11/06/trump-and-authoritarian-propaganda/#13556d6f3e0a

140. *Animal Farm, a Fairy Story* by George Orwell, published August 1945, Secker and Warburg, London

141. See "Procter & Gamble Wins Satanic Civil Suit" by Sean Alfano. *Associated Press*, March 20, 2007 (https://www.cbsnews.com/news/procter-gamble-wins-satanic-civil-suit/2/) In response, Amway sued P&G and its law firm. See a brief history of Amway's responses to whistle-blower websites, "Amway and the Internet, a History" (https://www.thetruthaboutamway. com/amway-and-the-internet-a-history-part-i/)

142. *Spellbound, My Journey Through a Tangled Web of Success* by Robert Morgan Styler, Sandy Creek Publishing, 1998

143. Before being prosecuted, the total number of consumers that lost money in Equinox would have been in the hundreds of thousands. It operated for over 8 years without government interference, churning, as all MLMs do, 50-80% of te recruits per year. In its later years, it reported over 100,000 currently enrolled. See https://www.inc.com/magazine/20001015/20767.html

144. From personal telephone interview with Robert Styler

145. *Betting on Zero* was featured in the 2016 Tribeca Film Festival in New York, which I attended. I had assisted director Ted Braun with perspective and background on MLM and was interviewed in the film. While standing in line to enter the theater, attendees were handed flyers by Herbalife promoters or paid workers that falsely accused the film of being secretly backed by William Ackman, thereby impugning the film's credibility and the integrity of the director. I, and others, were referred to in the flyer as "actors."

146. The actual financial backer of *Betting on Zero* was John Fichthorn, co-founder of Dialectic Capital Management, who had no financial connection to Bill Ackman and was not invested in or speculating on Herbalife stock at the time of the film. Fichthorn financed *Betting on Zero* through Biltmore Films, a company he co-founded along with Burke Koonce to finance and produce business and financial films. A PR firm for Herbalife, Podesta and Partners, purchased a large block of tickets at one major film festival where the film was shown, to prevent audiences from attending. When the film was shown in New York at Tribeca festival, flyers were handed out to attendees by unidentified

workers that claimed Ackman was financially involved and that the persons in the film were actually "actors."

147. *Fake it Til You Make It!* by Phil Kerns (Victory Press 1982) and *Amway: The Cult of Free Enterprise*, Stephen Butterfield, Southend Press, 1985

148. *Merchants of Deception: An Insider's Chilling Look at the Worldwide, Multi Billion Dollar Conspiracy of Lies that Is Amway and its Motivational Organizations*, 2009, by Eric Scheibeler (https://www.amazon.com/Merchants-Deception-Conspiracy-Motivational-Organizations/dp/1439247153)

149. *Amway Motivational Organizations: Behind the Smoke and Mirrors*, 1999, by Ruth Carter (https://www.amazon.com/Amway-Motivational-Organizations-Behind-Mirrors/dp/0967107024)

150. Rehnborg, *The Nutrilite Story*, 3305-3306

151. Rhyne had been a college friend of Nixon, a political supporter and campaign organizer and member of Nixon administration. During Watergate, he represented Nixon's long-time personal secretary, Rose Mary Woods, accused of erasing a crucial 18-minute section of Nixon's infamous White House audiotape recordings. Rhyne's defense was that Woods erased the tape, accidentally, while turning in her chair and simultaneously pressing buttons on the tape machine. The difficult physical maneuver was later called the "Rose Mary Stretch." *The New York Times* reported at the time, "A panel of six recording specialists has told Federal District Judge John J. Sirica that the erasure was probably caused by an intentional starting and stopping of Miss Woods's tape machine while the Nixon-Haldeman conversation was being replayed.

152. Huff, Darrell, *How to Lie with Statistics*, W. W. Norton & Company, 1954

153. The origin of the "median" income figure is a DSA-sponsored 2002 "National Salesforce Survey" conducted by Research International. The DSA cited this study in comments it made to the FTC arguing to exempt MLM from disclosure rules (which the FTC complied with). Quoting from the study, the DSA claimed "the average direct salesperson is a female, about 45 years of age, married with children, working less than 10 hours per week on her direct selling business ... A direct seller's median annual gross income from direct selling is about $2,400 per year. This number rises to $25,390 when considering direct sellers who work 30 or more hours per week. Fifty- nine percent of direct salespeople make less than $10,000 per year from direct selling." The DSA statement to the FTC can be viewed at https://www.ftc.gov/system/files/documents/public_comments/2006/07/522418-12055.pdf

154. https://www.ftc.gov/system/files/documents/public_comments/2006/07/522418-12055.pdf

155. "Keynote Remarks of FTC Chairwoman Ramirez DSA Business & Policy Conference, Washington, DC, October 25, 2016.", https://www.ftc.gov/system/files/documents/public_statements/993473/ramirez_-_dsa_speech_10-25-16.pdf

156. The 2017 data on numbers of "direct sellers" in the USA, the breakdown of proportions of them that are full or part time or "discount buyers" and the total "retail" sales are published on the Direct Selling Association's website as "Direct Selling in the United States: 2017 Facts and Data" See: https://www.dsa.org/docs/default-source/research/dsa_2017_factsanddata_2018.pdf. Because DSA data has a strange history of disappearing from the internet after being critically examined, this report is also preserved at https://pyramidschemealert.org/wp-content/uploads/2019/01/dsa_2017_factsanddata_2018.pdf

157. There are many examples to choose from. Consider *Forbes* in the April 1, 2013 article, "Can You Really Make Money In Direct Sales?" by regular contributor, Nancy Collamer, which has received 529,785 views: "How much can you make working for a legitimate direct sales company? Unfortunately, it's a lot less than many zealous direct sales recruiters would have you believe. The median annual income for direct sales consultants in 2011 was $2,400, according to Amy Robinson, spokesperson for the Direct Selling Association. While that figure may seem shockingly low, it's important to realize that 89% of direct sellers run their businesses part-time; most work under 10 hours a week … Reps often get into the business just to buy items for themselves and have no intention of selling or recruiting, Robinson said. That helps brings down the average earnings figure." (https://www.forbes.com/sites/nextavenue/2013/04/01/can-you-really-make-money-in-direct-sales/#725284d669c7)

158. "Direct Sales as a Recession Fallback" by Eilene Zimmerman, *New York Times*, March 14, 2009 (https://www.nytimes.com/2009/03/15/jobs/15sales.html)

159. Dictionary.com defines *sine qua non* as "an indispensable condition, element, or factor; something essential". However, as Dr. Jon Taylor and others have noted, the lack of retail sales is less an inherent feature of a MLM pyramid scheme than it is a *result* of its actual defining characteristics. The "unlimited" expansion of "salespeople" makes profitable retailing on any scale implausible from the start.

160. Webster v. Omnitrition, 79 F.3d 776 (9th Cir. 1996). One of the attorneys for the plaintiff in this landmark case was Boston-based, Douglas Brooks who later brought successful class action lawsuits against other MLMs, including Herbalife and Nu Skin.

161. The disclosure, called a "Sales Aid", SA4400, is preserved at https://pyramidschemealert.org/wp-content/uploads/2018/08/SA4400.RetailSales.pdf

The Amway disclosure explained that when participants purchased products that they "use themselves" the purchases counted toward receiving "bonuses," promised rewards for *buying*, indicating purchases were a price to pay for recruiting-based rewards.

The income disclosure" of Amway is made worse for consumers when it is understood that it only included the "active" Amway "distributors." The majority, 54%, called "inactive" by Amway, had paid fees to join and were legally "distributors." Of the 46% that did make a "sale," called "actives," more than a quarter of them purchased or sold less than $50 a month.

162. https://www.businessinsider.com/david-einhorn-herbalife-2012-5

163. The question was posed by hedge fund manager David Einhorn and quoted throughout the business press:

(Q – David Einhorn): I got a couple of questions for you. First is, how much of the sales that you'd make in terms of final sales are sold outside the network and how much are consumed within the distributor base?

(A): So, we don't have an exact percentage, David, because we don't have visibility to that level of detail.

164. https://www.wsj.com/video/the-big-interview-questioning-the-amway-way/FE12F29C-D022-42B8-8ACD-16A114E0DA96.html (16:20 - 17:00)

165. "In his 1651 text James Primrose noted: 'It can scarce be said, whether to the Bezaar *stone, or to the* Unicornes horn the common people attributes greater vertues, for those are thought to be the prime Antidotes of all'. Primrose draws the reader's attention to the many examples of counterfeit horns, for example whalebones or elephant's teeth, which suggests that there was a discernible market for the item. He even described an experiment to identify whether a horn was genuine, noting: 'into a hollow horn they put a spider, which if she passe *over they will have it to be a counterfeit horn; but if she burst and die, it is natural.'"*

Excepted from "Poisons, Potions and Unicorn Horns" by Paul Middleton, published in *Early Modern Medicine: A Blog about Bodies and Medicine,* Founding Editor and Contributor, Dr. Jennifer Evans, Senior lecturer in History at the University of Hertfordshire. The reference is to the text of 17th Century English physician and researcher, J. Primerose, entitled *Popular Errours. Or the Errours of the People in Physick* (London, 1651), pp. 359-60.

166.   https://www.goodreads.com/quotes/21810-it-is-difficult-to-get-a-man-to-understand-something

167.   This definition, which serves as the FTC's working definition of "multi-level marketing" was cited in the FTC's "Revised Proposed Business Opportunity Rule (RPBOR)" It was taken from an academic paper authored by Peter J. Vander Nat, a (now-retired) Senior Economist and pyramid scheme specialist at the FTC, and William W. Keep, a university professor of marketing, entitled, "Marketing Fraud: An Approach to Differentiating Multilevel Marketing from Pyramid Schemes," published in the *Journal of Public Policy & Marketing* (Spring 2002), p. 140. The FTC cited the paper as the source in Footnote 34 at bottom of page 15 of RPBOR) See: https://www.govinfo.gov/content/pkg/FR-2011-12-08/pdf/2011-30597.pdf

The academic paper does not assert that any business exists that meets the definition and it does not name any MLM company that exemplifies it. The paper was premised upon the FTC's existing policy that "MLM is legitimate" and occasionally prosecuting some MLMs as pyramid schemes. In those cases, the FTC usually cited the absence of retail sales as a decisive factor. The paper attempted to provide a methodology for making the determination.

168.   In 2016, the FTC, inexplicably, did not charge Herbalife with operating a pyramid scheme, but did charge it for making false income claims, continuously paying rewards to recruiters from quota-purchases of recruits rather than from retail sales and causing massive consumer losses, classic red flags of a pyramid scheme. Herbalife claimed "total victory" that the FTC found it was not a pyramid scheme. Pressed by journalists whether Herbalife's claim was true, the chair of the FTC stated, "(Herbalife was) not determined not to have been a pyramid. That (Herbalife's claim) would be inaccurate." The transcript of the press conference is at https://quackwatch.org/mlm/c/herbalife/ramirez/

169.   After the Omnitrition ruling clarified that "retail" meant retail, as the term is commonly understood, the judicial foundation for the FTC to prosecute non-retail-based, endless chain MLMs was firmly established. It

was clearly stated in one of the largest prosecutions after that ruling: Count 5 of FTC Complaint against the large MLM, Equinox International, filed in the United States District Court, District Of Nevada, August, 1999, stated, *"the Equinox program is an inherently unlawful scheme whose essential element is the payment by participants of money to the company in return for which they receive (1) the right to sell a product, and (2) the right to receive in return for recruiting other participants into the program rewards which are unrelated to the sale of the product to the ultimate users … The result of the structure and operation of the program is that financial gains to Equinox participants are primarily dependent upon the continued, successive recruitment of other participants … This type of scheme is often referred to as a pyramid."*

170.   From the 2008 FTC staff report: "They ask the Commission to assume widespread fraud in the multi-level marketing industry but offer no evidence. Instead, the comments that purported to present evidence that legitimate MLMs were in fact unlawful pyramid schemes provided only anecdotal evidence." See footnote #60. (https://www.ftc.gov/sites/default/files/documents/federal_register_notices/staff-report/101028businessopportunitiesstaffreport.pdf)

171.   The MLM scheme was called Business in Motion, operated by Alan Kippax. The investigative report, entitled, "Easy Money" was on the show, *CBC Marketplace*, hosted by Wendy Mesley, February 2009. CBC took notice of the scheme and lack of oversight by the Canada's Competition Bureau (similar to the FTC in the USA) as a result of activism by consumer advocate, Dave Thornton, who had also been instrumental in stopping the "Pigeon King" Ponzi scheme that ravaged Canadian small farmers. The show is available on YouTube at https://www.youtube.com/watch?v=xc-CyhivbKg. My published notes on my work with the show and undercover attendance at a recruitment meeting are preserved at https://www.pyramidschemealert.org/PSAMain/resources/Understanding%20a%20Pyramid.html

172.   "In accepting Amway's guilty plea, Chief Justice Gregory Evans of the Supreme Court of Ontario called the firm's actions 'a premeditated and deliberate course of conduct . . . with the knowledge that it would provide enormous profits and business advantages over a long period of years.'" See "Rearranging 'Amway Event' For Reagan" by Dale Russakoff and Juan Williams, Washington Post, January 22, 1984. Also, there is Wikipedia's account: Wikipedia's account: "In 1982, Amway co-founders, Richard M. DeVos and Jay Van Andel … were indicted in Canada on several criminal charges, including allegations that they … had defrauded the Canadian

government of more than $28 million from 1965 to 1980 ... Amway and its Canadian subsidiary pleaded guilty to criminal customs fraud charges ... paid a fine of $25 million CAD, the largest fine ever imposed in Canada at the time."

173. *False Profits* by Robert FitzPatrick and Joyce K. Reynolds, 1997, *The Network Marketing Game* by Jon M. Taylor, Illustrations by Cal Grondahl, 1997, *Consumed by Success* by Athena Dean, 1995, and *All That Glitters Is Not God, Breaking Free from the Sweet Deceit of Multi-Level Marketing*, 1998

174. The full 2004 *NBC Dateline* episode can be seen on YouTube (in poor quality), beginning with a scene of thousands at an Amway gathering being told Amway is the "best opportunity in the world" at https://www.youtube.com/watch?v=S5xu6bIFSeE

175. *Merchants of Deception: An Insider's Chilling Look at the Worldwide, Multi Billion Dollar Conspiracy of Lies that Is Amway and its Motivational Organizations*, 2009, by Eric Scheibeler and *Amway Motivational Organizations: Behind the Smoke and Mirrors*, 1999, by Ruth Carter

176. See "Amway Sales Group Facing Government Closure Call" by David Brown, Adam Luck and Tom Bawden, *The Times*, November 24, 2007 preserved at https://pyramidschemealert.org/PSAMain/news/TimesReportonAmwayTrial.html

177. In 2014 the CEO of Amway India, William S. Pinckney, described in the media as an American holding an Australian passport, was arrested, for the second time, on charges of operating a financial fraud. Amway had earlier been charged with operating an illegal scheme in 2006. See https://www.ndtv.com/business/amway-india-ceo-arrested-by-andhra-police-389559 and https://pyramidschemealert.org/PSAMain/news/BangaloreMonthly.html. An exposé on how MLM operates in India that delved into the factor of "saturation" by Ramjee Chandran was published in *Bangalore Monthly Magazine* in July 1998. It is preserved at https://pyramidschemealert.org/PSAMain/news/BangaloreMonthly.html

178. Ms. Bernstein's letter to the FTC on behalf of her client, Amway, is preserved at https://pyramidschemealert.org/wp-content/uploads/2018/10/Bernstein.pdf

179. The same practices that would be criminally prosecuted as fraud under current fraud law are generally reduced in scale of offense when they are called "multi-level marketing" in Canada and "pyramid scheme" in the USA.

Pyramid schemes in the USA are usually "regulated" under Section 5 of the FTC Act, with financial fines and other restrictions placed on guilty parties, but no criminal penalty. Canada operates similarly by placing pyramid schemes under the "Competition Act" which actually defines a "pyramid scheme" and places it under the jurisdiction of the Competition Bureau (like the FTC in the USA). The Competition Act does have criminal as well as civil prosecution powers. MLMs are almost never prosecuted criminally.

Competition Act: 55.1 (1) For the purposes of this section, "scheme of pyramid selling" means a multi-level marketing plan whereby (a) a participant in the plan gives consideration for the right to receive compensation by reason of the recruitment into the plan of another participant in the plan who gives consideration for the same right;

When a scheme is deemed "multi-level marketing" it is referred to the Competition Bureau and adjudicated under The Competition Act rather than under Canada's fraud law. Criminal Code Of Canada :(shortened here for clarity): *206. (1) Everyone is guilty of an indictable offence and liable to imprisonment for a term not exceeding two years who (e) conducts ... any scheme ... by which any person, on payment of any sum of money ... shall become entitled under the scheme ... to receive from the person conducting ... the scheme... a larger sum of money ... than the ... amount paid ... by reason of the fact that other persons have paid ... money ... under the scheme.*

180.   *Congressional Record, Senate,* June 4, 1973, page 17862

181.   A comprehensive review of the legal challenge of pyramid scheme law enforcement written at the time of the Mondale bill was published in *William & Mary Law Journal,* Volume 15, Issue 1, Article 6, 1973, entitled, "Regulation of Pyramid Sales Ventures." The article concluded, "Senator Mondale's proposed prohibition of such schemes would constitute a considerable improvement over existing state and federal approaches toward the menaces posed by pyramid sales schemes."

182.   For example, the reference in "Government: The Old Lady's New Look," *Time Magazine,* April 16, 1965

183.   "Rearranging 'Amway Event' For Reagan" by Dale Russakoff and Juan Williams, *Washington Post,* January 22, 1984

184.   "Rearranging 'Amway Event' For Reagan", *Washington Post,* January 22, 1984 (https://www.washingtonpost.com/archive/politics/1984/01/22/rearranging-amway-event-for-reagan/b3e74482-5ce0-4d20-9f98-ebdc9b4d4918/?utm_term=.9cfed5207112)

185. See "Alexander Haig, Returning Fire" by Elisabeth Bumiller, *Washington Post*, June 24, 1984, a profile of Alexander Haig that sheds light on his willingness to go to work for Amway — including his work for Nixon during Watergate, how he was forced to resign from the Reagan administration, his publishing a book critical of Reagan while Reagan was still in office and his later unsuccessful run for the presidency.

186. There must have been some at the FTC that did understand. FTC Commissioner Paul Dixon wrote: "A plan which holds out the opportunity of making money, by means of recruiting others, with that right to recruit being passed on as an inducement for those others to join, and being passable by them *ad infinitum*, contains an intolerable potential to deceive ... Indeed, a tragic aspect of this case is that the challenged marketing plan was not obliterated in its infancy, before the seed of deception ripened into the poisonous fruit of fraud and oppression."

A very readable treatment of the background, pre-Amway decision is offered by former Asst. AG of Wisconsin (retired), Bruce Craig in *Seeking Alpha*, entitled, "An Investor's Guide to Identifying Pyramid Schemes." See http://seekingalpha.com/article/918831-an-investors-guide-to-identifying-pyramid-schemes

187. I personally and briefly interviewed Joe Brownman by phone about a year before he spoke publicly on *The Dream* podcast. He told me he was reluctant to be interviewed on the record because he felt it was improper for an attorney to criticize a court ruling he had lost and he did not want to disparage his long-time employer, the FTC. See Episode 7: "Lazy, Stupid, Greedy or Dead" (https://www.stitcher.com/podcast/the-dream/e/56941786?autoplay=true)

188. "Glenn Turner's Castle" by Troy Herring, January 12, 2018, *OrangeObserver.com* (https://www.orangeobserver.com/article/glenn-turners-castle)

189. "Amway Rejects Canada Court Order" by John Holusha and Special To The New York Time, *New York Times*, Nov. 30, 1982 (https://www.nytimes.com/1982/11/30/business/amway-rejects-canada-court-order.html)

190. "Rearranging 'Amway Event' For Reagan" by Dale Russakoff and Juan Williams, *Washington Post*, January 22, 1984

191. "Rearranging 'Amway Event' For Reagan" by Dale Russakoff and Juan Williams, *Washington Post*, January 22, 1984

192. "Compensation Plan Conversion: Direct Sales to MLM Compensation Plan: Putting Your Company in the Winner's Circle," by Michael L. Sheffield, *Direct Sales Journal*, May 1, 2011 (https://web.archive.org/web/20110501155548/http://www.sheffieldnet.com/srn_artice4.html)

193. http://www.politico.com/magazine/story/2017/01/betsy-dick-devos-family-amway-michigan-politics-religion-214631

194. http://blogs.edweek.org/edweek/campaign-k-12/2016/12/campaign_contributions_betsy_devos_education_secretary.html?intc=main-mpsmvs

195. https://www.forbes.com/sites/danalexander/2017/01/17/devos-says-its-possible-her-family-has-donated-200m-to-republicans/#6aaaa496ac91

196. "Congress distributes a tax break to Amway" by Molly Ivins, *Fort Worth Star-Telegram*, August 7, 1997

197. *The Buying of Congress*, Charles Lewis, 1998, The Center for Public Integrity

198. http://www.motherjones.com/news/special_reports/mojo_400/12_devos.html

199. https://www.opensecrets.org/parties/contrib.php?cycle=2000&cmte=rpc

200. https://en.wikipedia.org/wiki/Enron

201. https://www.nytimes.com/2000/07/30/us/the-2000-campaign-the-money-perks-for-biggest-donors-and-pleas-for-more-cash.html

202. The same pattern occurred in India with Amway entering with U.S. government support, setting off mania followed by massive losses, leading to prosecutions, which were politically squashed, and then multiple MLMs spawned. This is powerfully chronicled in *Marauders of Hope*, a new book by Indian journalist Aruna Ravikumar. (https://www.amazon.com/Marauders-Hope-Aruna-Ravikumar/dp/1071085859)

203. "U.S. Hopes China Will Ease Direct-Sales Ban," by Liz Sly, Foreign Correspondent, Beijing, April 26, 1998, *Chicago Tribune* (https://www.chicagotribune.com/news/ct-xpm-1998-04-26-9804260472-story.html)

204. U.S. Hopes China Will Ease," *Chicago Tribune*, April 26, 1998

205. U.S. Hopes China Will Ease," *Chicago Tribune*, April 26, 1998

206. "Amway Made China a Billion-Dollar Market. Now It Faces a Crackdown" by Ryan McMorrow and Steven Lee Myers, *New York Times*, January 8, 2018

207. "Amway Made China a Billion-Dollar Market," *New York Times*, January 8, 2018

208. "Amway Made China a Billion-Dollar Market," *New York Times*, January 8, 2018

209. https://www.sec.gov/litigation/admin/2019/33-10703.pdf

210. "U.S. Trade Representative Charlene Barshefsky *went to bat* for the companies after the ban." And "Mary Kay's Chien said that the firm had lost about half of its 8,500-strong sales force and will not match last year's $25 million in sales, but is ready to be running full speed. "Our operations never really ceased. ... The government opened one eye and closed one eye. That's how business is done here." *Los Angeles Times*, July 25, 1998 by Maggie Farley. [emphasis added]

Barshefsky also assisted Avon but, at this time, Avon was not using the "MLM" model, as Mary Kay and Amway were. As MLM exploded in China, Avon became uncompetitive there as it did in the USA. It later adopted the MLM scheme partially. Revenues continued to fall. Eventually Avon considered withdrawing entirely from China after, ironically, being prosecuted for corruption in China. A Dec. 31, 2015 article in *China Daily* reported, that between 2011 and 2014, Avon's China revenue had dropped from about $150 million to only about $50 million. The report noted that Amway's China revenue in 2014 was $4.4 billion. Avon effectively was never a significant voice in getting U.S. government protection and was not a significant beneficiary. It always was and is Amway.

211. (*2016*) FTC vs. Herbalife, No. 2:16-cv-05217; (*2015*) FTC vs. Vemma, No. CV15-01578-PHX-JJT; (*2014*) FTC vs. Fortune High Tech Marketing, No. No.5:13-cv-123-KSF; (*2013*) FTC v. BurnLounge, No. 2:07-cv-03654-GW-FMO; (*2004*) FTC v. Mall Ventures, Inc., No. CV 04-0463 FMA (*2004*); (*2003*) FTC v. NexGen3000.com, No. 03-120 TUC WDB; (*2002*) FTC v. Linda Jean Lightfoot; (*2002*) FTC v. Trek Alliance, Inc., No. CV-02-9270; (*2001*) FTC v. Skybiz.Com, Inc.; (*2001*) FTC v. Streamline Int'l, Inc., 01-6885-CIV-Ferguson; (*2001*) FTC v. Bigsmart.com, No. CIV 01- 0466 PHX ROS; (*2000*) FTC v. Netforce Seminars, Inc., No. 00 2260 PHX FJM; (*1999*) FTC v. 2Xtreme Performance Int'l, LLC, No. Civ. JFM 99CV 3679; (*1999*) FTC v. Equinox Int'l, Corp., No. CV-S-99-0969-JBR-RLH; (*1999*) FTC v. David Martinelli, Jr., 3: 99 CV 1272 (CFD); (*1999*) FTC v. Five Star Auto Club, Inc., No. CIV-99-1693 McMahon; (*1998*) FTC v. Affordable Media, LLC, CV-S-98-00669-LDG; (1998)FTC v. Kalvin P. Schmidt,

No C-3834; (1998) FTC v. FutureNet, Inc., No. CV-98-1113 GHK; (1997) FTC v. Cano, No. 97-7947-IH-(AJWx); (1997) FTC v. JewelWay, No. 97-383 TUC JMR; (1997) FTC v. Rocky Mountain International Silver and Gold, Inc.; (1997) FTC v. World Class Network, Inc., No. SACV-97-162-AHS (Eex); (1996) FTC v. Mentor Network, Inc., No. SACV 96-1104 LHM (Eex); (1996) FTC v. Global Assistance Network for Charities, No. CIV-96-2494 PHX RCB; (1996) FTC v. Fortuna Alliance, LLC, No. C96-799M

212.   https://www.youtube.com/watch?v=G2A3zft2AJc

213.   https://www.bloomberg.com/politics/articles/2015-07-31/hillary-and-bill-clinton-paid-43-million-in-federal-taxes

214.   http://nypost.com/2014/04/17/ex-secretary-of-state-albright-sweats-herbalife-ties/

215.   http://www.dsa.org/advocacy/caucus

216.   See "Multilevel Marketers' Influence Growing in Utah, Utah • Companies Enjoy Support of Lawmakers, Others" by Steven Oberbeck, The Salt Lake Tribune, October 24, 2011, https://archive.sltrib.com/article.php?id=52706578&itype=cmsid

217.   http://archive.sltrib.com/story.php?ref=/sltrib/politics/56298281-90/shurtleff-general-attorney-utah.html.csp

218.   http://www.dailymail.co.uk/wires/ap/article-2693118/2-ex-Utah-attorneys-general-charged-bribery.html?utm_source=August+2014+Update&utm_campaign=Newest+Revelations+on+MLM&utm_medium=email

219.   http://harpers.org/blog/2012/08/pyramid-insurance/?utm_source=August+2014+Update&utm_campaign=Newest+Revelations+on+MLM&utm_medium=email

220.   "Why Are There So Many Ponzi Scheme Cases In Charlotte?" by Tom Bullock, WFAE, Nov. 17, 2014 (https://www.wfae.org/post/why-are-there-so-many-ponzi-scheme-cases-charlotte#stream/0)

221.   In 2013 the NC Attorney General's office did participate in a joint prosecution of the Kentucky-based MLM, Fortune High Tech Marketing, which was shut down by the FTC. The scheme had operated nationally for many years and notoriously threatened or sued whistle-blowers and critics. See "Federal, State Regulators Shut Down Fortune Hi-Tech" by Jayne O'Donnell, USA TODAY, January 28, 2013

222.   https://www.youtube.com/watch?v=uMcQPyA9YAM

223. https://www.nytimes.com/interactive/2020/09/28/us/donald-trump-taxes-apprentice.html?auth=login-email&login=email

224. For more detailed information on the prosecution of Fortune High Tech Marketing, see https://pyramidschemealert.org/fortune-high-tech-rests-in-peace-while-zombie-mlms-stalk-the-public/

225. http://www.pyramidschemealert.org/PSAMain/resources/FTC.Kohm.Letter.pdf

226. The lobbying letter submitted to the FTC, signed by former FTC officials, Timothy J. Muris and Howard Beales is preserved at https://pyramidschemealert.org/wp-content/uploads/2019/02/murisbealesrebuttal.pdf

227. Reporting on the appointment of Howard Beales, CNN Money reported, "Beales' appointment promises to be a controversial one, similar to 'putting the wolf in charge of the henhouse,' Matthew Myers, president of the Campaign for Tobacco Free Kids, told the *Post*." See https://money.cnn.com/2001/05/31/news/ftc_beales/index.htm

228. Ms. Bernstein's letter to the FTC on behalf of her client, Amway, is preserved at https://pyramidschemealert.org/wp-content/uploads/2018/10/Bernstein.pdf

229. Bryan Cave, which has lobbied for and represented Amway, also has counted among its attorneys other FTC attorneys including Frank Gorman, formerly legal advisor to the director of the Federal Trade Commission's Bureau of Consumer Protection. Dana Rosenfeld, who served as the assistant director of the FTC's Bureau of Consumer Protection and was senior legal advisor to Jodie Bernstein, joined Bryan Cave at the same time as Bernstein. Bernstein and Rosenfeld later moved together to the law firm of Kelly Drye where, according to the firm's website, *"Our attorneys have worked with FTC personnel ranging from enforcement staff to Commissioners, and we have strong relationships with officials of state Attorneys General."* The firm offers special expertise in MLM and "dietary supplements."

230. "Get-Rich-Quick Profiteers Love Mitt Romney, and He Loves Them Back," by Stephanie Mencimer, *Mother Jones, May 2012*. See:, https://www.motherjones.com/politics/2012/05/mitt-romney-nu-skin-multilevel-marketing-schemes/

Mother Jones had to spend over a million dollars in legal fees defending itself from a libel lawsuit arising from this article. The magazine won but has done relatively little reporting involving MLM since then.

231. http://www.ranker.com/list/the-largest-mitt-romney-campaign-contributors/keaton

232. The settlement called for Amway to pay $34 million in cash and $21 million worth of products, with the attorneys receiving a portion of the cash payment for their fee.

233. Despite the obvious clues leading to an examination of "MLM", operating as legitimate direct selling, the American news media largely did not investigate the MLM phenomenon during this period. One exception was an excellent piece in *The Sunday Times of London*, February 1, 2009 , "Pyramid Swindlers Unmasked: Ponzi Scams Are Being Laid Bare by the Slump", by Dominic Rushe. I was quoted extensively as source on increasing revelations of pyramid fraud during the Recession. Rushe called pyramid schemes "the poor man's Ponzi." Another was "Fraud Gone Wild, Pyramid, Ponzi Schemes Disguised as Valid Investment Opportunities," by Chris Dettro, *The State Journal-Register* Springfield, IL, Dec 23, 2008. That article noted the ubiquity of income opportunity schemes and challenged the notion that the victims fail to perform due diligence, He quoted me, "Without regulation, it is not reasonable to expect the average person would be able to know enough to avoid such schemes."

234. https://www.cnbc.com/id/100366687

235. 2013 CNBC documentary (http://www.cnbc.com/id/100359541)

236. The statements were made in the 2013 CNBC documentary on multi-level marketing, Herbalife and pyramid schemes, in which correspondent Herb Greenberg interviewed the FTC Director of Consumer Protection, David Vladeck:

HERB GREENBERG: Well, if 90% of the distributors are failing, what does that say? If—

DAVID VLADECK: It doesn't mat—

HERB GREENBERG: What kind of a business is it if 90% of 2.7 million every year — right now we're talking 2.7 million distributors for one company.

DAVID VLADECK: It doesn't mean that — that — that doesn't mean that the company made misrepresentations. And it doesn't mean that the people who — who bought these — franchises or participated in these schemes necessarily feel that they were injured.

237. *Federal Register* / Vol. 71, No. 70 / Wednesday, April 12, 2006 / Proposed Rules, 19059

238. *The Verge* article also addressed the larger issue of how the MLM Industry, aka Pyramid Lobby, has spent enormous amounts to prevent investigation or regulations of any kind, while consumer advocates, who are mostly victims or volunteers, have spent zero. See Matt Stroud's article at https://www.theverge.com/2014/4/8/5590550/alleged-pyramid-schemes-lobbying-ftc. Stroud now writes for the *Associated Press*.

239. "The Pyramid Scheme Problem" by Joe Nocera, *New York Times*, Sept. 15, 2015

240. See https://www.ftc.gov/sites/default/files/documents/federal_register_notices/16-c.f.r.part-437-disclosure-requirements-and-prohibitions-concerning-business-opportunities-final-rule/111122bizoppfrn.pdf

241. https://www.ftc.gov/system/files/documents/public_comments/2006/07/522418-70002.pdf

242. https://www.ftc.gov/system/files/documents/public_comments/2006/07/522418-11711.pdf

243. Among the Wall Street figures taking "long" positions, pushing up stock price and pressuring Ackman to abandon his campaign was famed stock trader, George Soros. As reported by *CNBC*, "George Soros (is) taking a large long position in the nutritional supplements maker … Soros's position in Herbalife is now one of his top three holdings …" See: "Herbalife Stock Spikes as Soros Said to Be Betting Big," July 31, 2013. https://www.cnbc.com/2013/07/31/herbalife-stock-spikes-as-soros-said-to-be-betting-big.html

244. California prosecuted Herbalife at that time under its "endless chain" statute, enacted in 1968. One of the last times the state enforced the law was against a fast growing and publicly traded MLM, Your Travel Biz.com (YTB). The May 2009 settlement required that at least 60% of sales by YTB representatives must come from non-representatives (retail customers). The ruling also stripped YTB of much of its "pay to play" revenue in which participants paid monthly fees for "websites." Your Travel Biz closed down. See https://oag.ca.gov/system/files/attachments/press_releases/n1737_ytbstipulatedjudgment.pdf

245. https://www.mlmwatch.org/04C/Herbalife/1986order.html

246. See: https://www.foxnews.com/world/activists-meet-with-california-ags-staff-to-discuss-herbalifes-alleged-predatory-practices and https://

consumerwatchdog.org/newsrelease/consumer-watchdog-calls-attorney-general-harris-act-against-herbalife

247. https://www.opensecrets.org/orgs/summary.php?id=D000022306

248. "Herbalife Still Making False Claims: Ackman Video" by Michelle Celarier, *New York Post*, December 11, 2014 (https://nypost.com/2014/12/11/herbalife-still-making-false-claims-ackman-video/)

249. http://www.nationallawjournal.com/id=1202768427209/FTC-and-Herbalife-Snub-Big-Law-for-Consulting-Firm-As-Compliance-Monitor?slreturn=20170216234138

250. https://www.opensecrets.org/news/2013/12/herbalife-battle-weapons-include-lobbyists-campaign-dollars/

251. https://www.ftc.gov/system/files/documents/cases/160715herbalifecmpt.pdf

252. https://www.ftc.gov/system/files/documents/cases/160715herbalifecmpt.pdf

253. https://www.ftc.gov/system/files/documents/cases/160715herbalife-stip.pdf

254. https://www.ftc.gov/enforcement/cases-proceedings/refunds/herbalife-refunds

255. https://en.wikipedia.org/wiki/Ruth_Marcus_(journalist)

256. http://www.sourcewatch.org/index.php/Jonathan_D._Leibowitz

257. https://www.davispolk.com/professionals/jon-leibowitz/

258. http://ir.herbalife.com/releases.cfm?Year=&ReleasesType=&PageNum=2

259. http://fortune.com/2016/07/15/herbalife-ftc-settlement/

260. http://fortune.com/2016/07/15/herbalife-ftc-settlement/

261. "Herbalife Hires Biden's Former Chief of Staff" by Haley Sweetland Edwards, *Time Magazine*, July 25, 2014

262. Editorial Observer; "'The Shame' That Lincoln Steffens Found Has Not Left Our Country" by Adam Cohen, *New York Times*, April 11, 2004, See: https://www.nytimes.com/2004/04/11/opinion/editorial-observer-shame-that-lincoln-steffens-found-has-not-left-our-country.html

263.   http://articles.latimes.com/2013/sep/05/business/la-fi-villaraigosa-herbalife-20130906

264.   https://www.dsa.org/forms/committee/CommitteeFormPublic/view?id=7F3000604E6

265.   http://thehill.com/blogs/congress-blog/economy-budget/288332-the-ftc-got-it-right-on-herbalife-settlement

266.   Herbalife hired the law firm of Boies, Schiller and Flexner, whose lead partner, David Boies had famously represented Al Gore in Gore v. Bush. It was widely thought that the Boies firm would file a lawsuit against Ackman. This same firm had recently waged a successful class action lawsuit against, Amway, charging it with operating an illegal pyramid scheme, and winning tens of millions in fees in the settlement. I served as an expert witness in the case. Along with several colleagues we had given the Boies firm an extensive training in "multi-level marketing" methods of fraud and deception. The Boies case against Amway was almost identical to Ackman's thesis on Herbalife — illegal pyramid scheme — as the Amway and Herbalife schemes are essentially identical. Boies leveraged the knowledge it gained in the case *against* Amway to take the other side to *defend* Herbalife.

267.   Among the experienced analysts and activists who conferred with Bill Ackman after his thesis announcement, English writer, David Brear did in fact strongly emphasize that Herbalife's cultic power over people constituted its greatest threat, more so than even operating a pyramid scheme. Brear reportedly had several phone conversations in which he compared Herbalife to Scientology and other historical cults. His blog, *MLM, the American Dream Made Nightmare* has been published continuously since 2012 and has been viewed more than 1.7 million times. See http://mlmtheamericandreammadenightmare.blogspot.fr. Also see this blog applying the cult characteristics to Herbalife: http://mlmtheamericandreammadenightmare.blogspot.com/2013/01/herbalife-has-exhibited-universal.html

268.   *Amway: The Cult of Free Enterprise*, Stephen Butterfield, 1985

269.   Another respected literary source of insight into the cultic identity of multi-level marketing, which Bill Ackman's researchers might have found, is Australian psychologist, Louise Samway's book, *Dangerous Persuaders*:

"Amway is adopting similar techniques to many cults in order to attract recruits, then to keep them involved and committed to the cause. ... The approach of the marketing organization is usually quite evangelical. It asks if there is something missing your life, and offers all sorts of emotional inducements: 'reach your full potential,' 'find the real you,' 'gain greater meaning and more meaningful relationships in your life.' In many ways Amway is more like a fundamentalist religion than a direct marketing business, with money as the god." See *Dangerous Persuaders* by Louise Samways, Penguin Books Australia, 1994, p. 52

270.   The Dec. 26, 2014 segment can be heard at https://www.thisamericanlife.org/543/wake-up-now

271.   http://3.bp.blogspot.com/-6HO6KIhUTRk/Urm4B-2x3eI/AAAAAAAAI-Y/iDDXbFkhLBo/s1600/DSA+1.JPG

272.   "Cleaning Up?" by Richard Behar, *Forbes,* March 25, 1985

273.   "Herbalife suspends 'cult' distributor" by Michelle Celarier, *New York Post,* May 25, 2013

274.   According to Cameron Freeman who ran the Large Group Awareness program, called *LifeStream,* from 1987 to 1998, William Penn Warren's, *Mind Dynamics* was the seed of many the most popular "human potential" programs that were developed in 1970s and 1980s. They included:

• Werner Erhard, founded *est* in 1971, renamed "The Forum" and is now known as *Landmark Education.*

• Jim Quinn founded *Lifestream* in 1973.

• Bob White, Randy Revell, Charlene Afremow, John Hanley founded *Lifespring* in 1974.

• Bob White left *Lifespring,* went to Japan, and started a training organization there called *Life Dynamics.*

• Randy Revell left *Lifespring* and founded the *Context Trainings.*

• Charlene Afremow joined Erhard's organization as a trainer. She later left in a dispute and went back to *Lifespring.*

• Howard Nease founded *Personal Dynamics.*

• Thomas Willhite founded *PSI World Seminars.*

• Stewart Emery worked for *est* and later founded *Actualizations.*

• See https://cameronfreeman.com/personal/confessions-cult-leader-lifestream-seminar-experience/confessions-cult-leader-learned-life-running-personal-development-seminar-company/

275. See "The Human Potential Movement Gone Awry, Outside the Limits of the Human Imagination" by Win McCormack, *New Republic Magazine*, April 12, 2018

276. Huber, *The American Idea of Success*, p. 258

277. Huber, *The American Idea of Success*, p. 260

278. Side 1: https://thecrosspollinator.wordpress.com/2019/04/18/william-penn-patrick-happiness-and-success-through-principle-side-1/

Side 2: https://thecrosspollinator.wordpress.com/2019/04/12/william-penn-patrick-happiness-and-success-through-principle-side-2/

279. Turner's famous story was uploaded to YouTube in 2007, and shows over 16,000 views to date. See https://www.youtube.com/watch?v=6Rpq-4zY U4o&list=PLB18A698E83D4A9F2&index=3&t=0s

280. Quoted in *The Ministry of Truth* by Dorian Lynskey, Knopf Doubleday Publishing Group, 2020, Kindle Edition, p. 175

281. https://www.amwayglobal.com/our-story/founders/

282. "Investigating Cults" by Richard Delgado, *New York Times,* Dec. 27, 1978. See: https://www.nytimes.com/1978/12/27/archives/investigating-cults.html

283. "The Cult Controversy, Spiritual Quest or Mind Control?" by WashingtonPost.com staff, April 26, 1997, See: https://www.washingtonpost.com/wp-srv/national/longterm/cult/cultmain.htm

284. *Cults in Our Midst: The Continuing Fight Against Their Hidden Menace* by Margaret Thaler Singer, 2003 by Jossey-Bass (first published 1995), and *Thought Reform and the Psychology of Totalism: A Study of "Brainwashing" in China by Robert Jay Lifton*, Norton, 1961

285. Conway, Flo. *Snapping: America's Epidemic of Sudden Personality Change* . Stillpoint Press. Kindle Edition.

286. *Take Back Your Life: Recovering from Cults and Abusive Relationships*, Janja Lalich and Madeleine Tobias, Berkeley, Bay Tree Publishing, 2006. The list of cult hallmarks was adapted from a checklist originally developed by Michael Langone. See the full list at https://mncriticalthinking.com/characteristics-associated-with-cultic-groups/

287. "Watch Out for Tell-tale Signs" by Rick Ross, The Guardian, May 27, 2009.

288. https://freedomofmind.com/bite-model/

289. https://freedomofmind.com/multi-level-marketing-groups-defraud-consumers/

290. Ross, Rick. *Cults Inside Out: How People Get In and Can Get Out.* Kindle Edition. Location 3018

291. http://mlmtheamericandreammadenightmare.blogspot.com/

292. http://mlmtheamericandreammadenightmare.blogspot.com/2020/05/ironically-ftc-now-warns-10-corporate.html

293. Writer David Brear offers one of the clearest and easiest to understand list of "universal and defining" characteristics of cults, revealing them as enduring historical phenomena in many cultures and lifting them out of the realms of technical or academic jargon. See http://mlmtheamericandreammadenightmare.blogspot.com/2012/03/universal-identifying-characteristics.html

294. http://mlmtheamericandreammadenightmare.blogspot.com/2012/03/universal-identifying-characteristics.html

295. MLM's unique outward disguise as a traditional American-style sales company of ordinary or health-related goods makes recognition of its true cult nature all the more difficult for those in and outside of it. However, adherents of all cults, even the more exotic or violent ones, express the deluded sentiment that a deceptive and harmful cult movement and its leaders are honorable and beneficial. This is the result of thought-control or "undue-influence" methods used by cults. The combination of the benign disguise with the powerful cult persuasion tools gives MLM far greater capacity to spread and to insulate itself from exposure.

296. Ross, *Sin and Society,* pp. 75-77

297. The final ruling on the Koscot MLM case, stated, "Respondents' marketing plan ... due to its very structure precludes the realization of such rewards to most of those who invest therein, such plan is inherently deceptive. Furthermore, such plan is contrary to established public policy in that it is generally considered to be unfair and unlawful and is by its very nature immoral, unethical, oppressive, unscrupulous, and exploitative. Therefore, such plan was and is inherently unfair ..." The "MLM" that Turner was operating that actually led to the prison term was not Koscot, which had been closed due to FTC prosecution, but yet another he had founded, called Challenge, Inc.

298. http://www.nytimes.com/1987/08/22/business/glenn-turner-sentenced.html

299. https://www.glennwturner.com

300. https://www.sec.gov/litigation/litreleases/lr17832.htm

301. http://www.wral.com/news/local/story/11157466/

302. https://www.youtube.com/watch?v=o19bSi84sS0

303. https://www.justice.gov/archive/usao/nce/press/2005/2005-Apr-29.html

304. http://www.charlotteobserver.com/news/local/crime/article91087617.html

305. As testimony to close connections of the MLM "industry" to Donald Trump and the National Republican Party today, employee of IHI and sister-in-law of convicted scammer, Stanley Van Etten, was mysteriously selected to be a featured speaker at the 2016 Republican National Convention. Michelle Van Etten, was described as owner of a "small business" who employed over 100,000 people. It turned out she is a participant in the MLM, Youngevity, based in Texas. Youngevity previously sold a food supplement containing the stimulant ephedrine before it was banned for lethal health risks. The company has been promoted by conspiracy theorist, Alex Jones. See https://www.theguardian.com/us-news/2016/jul/18/michelle-van-etten-republican-convention-youngevity and her family connection to Stanley Van Etten is referenced at https://bizstanding.com/p/international+heritage+inc-37791480 and

https://bizstanding.com/ng/org-prof-profile/37791480-7369317776582043-2-1-b4dfa and

http://www.joesdata.com/executive/Michelle_Van_Etten_3011909808.html

306. http://www.sequenceinc.com/fraudfiles/2014/09/mlm-lawyer-sued-for-legal-malpractice/

307. http://www.dsa.org/news/individual-press-release/dsa-honors-four-companies-with-industry-awards

308. https://www.sec.gov/litigation/admin/2013/33-9460.pdf

309. https://www.the-dispatch.com/article/NC/20151217/News/605039512/LD

310. https://seekingalpha.com/article/1888271-bill-ackmans-folly-with-herbalife-7-assumptions-that-led-him-astray

311. During the Wall Street campaign, hedge fund manager William Ackman dispatched investigators to China where MLM is illegal. Based on the investigator's report, in March 2014, Ackman charged that Herbalife was violating China's anti-MLM law and called for an SEC probe and prosecution. No action from U.S. regulators was taken. Almost six years later, based on its own investigation, the Dept. of Justice announced a criminal indictment against Herbalife's top Chinese managers. The DOJ charged Herbalife had used $25 million to bribe officials in China to grant it operating licenses despite the law and to suppress publicity on its operations. See: https://www.justice. gov/opa/press-release/file/1217421/download?utm_medium=email&utm_ source=govdelivery

312. The pattern of *criminally* prosecuting MLMs when the government argues, in extremely rare instances, that they sell "investments," and *civilly* when called "business opportunities" was repeated with Kansas-based MLM, Renaissance the Tax People (RTTP). Originally prosecuted in civil court for operating a MLM pyramid, three years later CEO, Michael Cooper was criminally prosecuted by the Dept. of Justice for fraud. RTTP sold a typical MLM "business opportunity" based on endless chain recruiting. A feature of the scheme was the claim that the business provided an income tax shelter. A similar claim is made by most MLMs but was highlighted at RTTP. When Cooper died in 2020 while still in federal prison, *The New York Times* published a story about the scheme by financial writer, David Cay Johnson. Avoiding the political contradictions of MLM, Johnston never referenced RTTP's recruiting plan, which was the basis of the illegal income offer. Kansas investigators called it "multi-level marketing" as the company characterized itself. At the trial, RTTP hired the most notable MLM advocate at the time, Dr. Charles King, to claim it is a "legitimate MLM." Yet, Johnston's article never used the term "multi-level marketing." Instead, Johnston called it "a tax-avoidance business." See https://www.nytimes.com/2020/04/10/us/michael-c-cooper-dead.html

I served as expert witness for the state of Kansas in the civil case against RTTP. See https://www.pyramidschemealert.org/PSAMain/news/taxpeopledown.html

313. *Elmer Gantry*, by Sinclair Lewis, Harcourt Trade Publishers, 1927

314. Leff clarified that if the preacher and followers, for example, both sincerely believe that their joint devotions are true and real — including the followers giving money as part of gaining divine blessings dispensed by

the preacher — there is no swindle. There is no swindle not because divine blessings were delivered. No one could verify that. A swindle occurs only when the promoter knows or does not care that his promises are not fulfilled and his false claims and promises are shaped to bring extreme personal financial gain. This is often manifested in the leader's lavish lifestyle, private violations of the morals preached, and inappropriate or illegal use of donated funds.

315.   The fictional character, Elmer Gantry, has been associated with the most famous preacher of his time, Billy Sunday. The character, Sharon Falconer in the novel appears to be based on real-life evangelist Aimee Semple McPherson, who founded the denomination, International Church of the Foursquare Gospel in 1927.

316.   After being prosecuted for pyramid fraud, some MLMs have claimed they would transform to traditional direct selling companies, without a MLM recruiting component. The changeover either does not happen or fails or is a ruse for continuing MLM, often under new names. MLM companies have no foundation on which to make a successful transition – a stable customer base or sales force, a differentiated product, price advantage, brand equity, market demand.

I have directly observed only one case of an MLM successfully changing its model to legitimate sales. It is North American Power, a Texas-based reseller of gas and electricity serving 12 deregulated states. In January 2015, the company announced it was terminating its MLM sales model. Referral sites were taken down and the recruiting incentive payments ended, though past referrals were compensated. However, NAP was never completely based on MLM. A minority of its revenue was sourced from the MLM program. Therefore, abandoning MLM was feasible. An activist member of NAP, Rogier van Vlissingen agitated for the change with a detailed letter to the company chairman in July 2014, citing potential for prosecution or corruption of the entire business, which may have prompted the change six months later. Van Vlissingen became an insightful analyst and public critic of MLM. He has written extensively on the inherent deception of the MLM model. Some of his essays can be found on the popular investor forum, *Seeking Alpha*. See https://seekingalpha.com/author/rogier-van-vlissingen#regular_articles

317.   See https://www.newsweek.com/john-oliver-last-week-tonight-herbalife-pyramid-scheme-517881 and https://business.time.com/2013/01/09/is-herbalife-a-pyramid-scheme-the-target-of-market-manipulation-or-just-a-good-gripping-yarn/?iid=sr-link2

318. https://blogs.wsj.com/speakeasy/2016/11/07/john-oliver-takes-on-herbalife-and-multilevel-marketing/

319. https://slate.com/business/2018/12/multilevel-marketing-podcast-review-the-dream-facebook.html

320. http://bettingonzeromovie.com/#home-section

321. https://pyramidschemealert.org/wp-content/uploads/2019/07/First-Amended-and-Consolidated-Complaint.pdf

322. https://www.youtube.com/watch?v=LFxswvvn24g

323. https://www.indiewire.com/2019/06/on-becoming-a-god-in-central-florida-showtime-kirsten-dunst-1202150598/

A

B

C

T

Taibbi, Matt
Author who researched how SEC failed to see Madoff fraud · 83

Taylor, Jon M., author, consumer educator about MLM pyramid
schemes · 109, 110, 314, 329 '

The American Way of Death · 49

The Mind of the South · 2

Third Way, political strategy related to Ponzinomics · 211

Thornton, David
Canadian anti-fraud activist · 85, 332

Timony, James P., Administrative Law Judge in Amway FTC Case, 1979 · 129, 131, 132, 134, 137, 138, 148, 177, 324, 325

Trump Network · 298

Trump, Donald · xvii, xix, 156, 229-30, 286, 347

Turner, Glenn · 2, 204-5, 272, 296, 346

Twain, Mark · 12, 156

U

Unicorn, as a metaphor for 'retail-based' MLM · 179-83, 224

V

VanArsdale, Daniel, Chain Letter Historian · 96-98

Vandernat, Peter Dr., FTC pyramid scheme expert · 109, 297

van Vlissingen, Rogier · 349

Villaraigosa, Antonio · 255

Vladeck, David · 238, 240, 246, 252, 340

W

Waugh, Evelyn, author of satirical novel about cemetery sales · 57

Wead, Doug · 234

Z

Zarossi, Louis · 80

Zuckoff, Mitchell · 80

Made in United States
North Haven, CT
21 January 2022

15054255R00205